out of chaos

# out of chaos

Reflections of a university president and his contemporaries on Vietnam-era unrest in Mankato and its relevance today

James F. Nickerson

MINNESOTA STATE UNIVERSITY MANKATO
**FOUNDATION**

*For information:*
Ann Rosenquist Fee, Director of Publications
Minnesota State University, Mankato
232 Alumni Foundation Center
Mankato, Minnesota 56001
ann.rosenquist-fee@mnsu.edu
507-389-2523

Designed and printed by Minnesota State Mankato Printing Services.
ISBN 097291341-6

*Executive editor:* James F. Nickerson
*Audio recording services:* Jim Gullickson, Paul Musikov
*Copy editor:* Marta Cleaveland
*Managing editors:* Suzanne Bunkers, Ann Rosenquist Fee
*Project manager:* Kathy Musikov
*Research services:* Rose Blumenshein
*Typing services:* Minnesota State University, Mankato Office Support Services

Cover design by Kris Higginbotham.
Cover images from the 1972 *Katonian* courtesy of Minnesota State University, Mankato Archives.

*To the memory of my wife, Nita.*

# Contents

On October 2, 2003, President Richard Davenport and friends of the University dedicated the Nickerson Conference Room in the Centennial Student Union. *Photo by Gregg Andersen.*

# Foreword

*by Minnesota State University, Mankato President Richard Davenport*

James Nickerson served as president during one of the most challenging times of the past century. He came from a background where the college and university president was an academic first and foremost. Yet the turmoil of the Vietnam War required him to step outside this traditional role.

Dr. Nickerson developed a new type of leadership that the era seemed to require, one that exemplified free speech and thinking and demanded constant critical analysis as well as active democracy. He instinctively knew that little learning would take place unless he allowed more freedom in the classroom for open discussion of the issues that were troubling the nation and the students themselves. It was a matter of colleges and universities surviving a challenge that had the potential to devastate the very foundation of higher education.

President Nickerson felt the pulse of the nation and understood he would have to be a different kind of leader in order for Mankato State College to survive. He achieved this, and also achieved exemplary leadership among college and university presidents throughout the nation.

What happened in Mankato during this period was unique in that we had an active anti-war movement, one of the largest in the country, yet with little property damage, few injuries and no deaths. There were ample opportunities for things to get out of hand, but they never did. Why? Because of Dr. Nickerson's leadership as well as the actions of people like Abbas Kessel, Charles Alexander and numerous others whose stories appear here in their own words or in the recollections of others. They used their power and their persuasion in the wisest of ways.

Dr. Nickerson and his team had created at Mankato State College an atmosphere and structure of student empowerment and also of responsibility, of consequences. The student demonstrators were expected to think, to reason, to decide – not just be led blindly into chaos. And time after time, when the moment of decision came, they chose nonviolence. That is what made the Mankato outcome unique.

Professor Emeritus H. Roger Smith says it well: "Dr. Nickerson's efforts through his staff and faculty and the forward-looking programs they guided had set the stage for these demonstrations. The empowerment he had given the students on the MSC campus gave them a responsibility for thoughtful and nonviolent acts against the College or the community."

During the era at hand, Mankato State College was on the brink of becoming a university. Today, Minnesota State University, Mankato is preparing to take another major step, that of offering doctorate degrees in addition to our 150 undergraduate programs of study, 16 pre-professional programs, and 82 graduate programs. (We pursue this with appreciation for Dr. Nickerson, who first tried to get doctoral programs approved by the Legislature during his tenure here.) The University has six colleges, 1,300 faculty and staff, and nearly 14,000 students – the highest in a decade – including 1,600 graduate and professional students and over 600 international students from 71 countries. Alumni number 100,000 worldwide.

There is no question that much of our present success is due to the groundwork laid by Dr. Nickerson and his team. That culture of responsibility, collaboration and empowerment is as strong and distinctive today as it was during the time so richly recounted in the pages that follow.

President James F. Nickerson from the May 10, 1972 *Daily Reporter.*

# Introduction

*by President Emeritus James F. Nickerson*

In general, most of us are unskilled in the art of demonstration and protest. There is an etiquette of contact whether parade, sit-in or march, which is made more difficult by the fact that our work ethic presses us to punish or demand penance for any transgression often without regard to intended or unintended consequences to the individual or his environment.

Keeping the peace and protection for the safety and well being of citizens is our role, whether we're city officials or educators, but not at the expense of suppressing even strident or tasteless opposition. We will be judged by the final results of our compromise and reconciliation.

We are all familiar with the phenomenon of being caught up in the fever of a demonstration. Some observers are alienated by the crudeness of the message or the rudeness of the bearer, perhaps by one's own antagonism to the particular message. It is important to realize that the very bringing of the message via public demonstration underscores the importance of the problem or its need to be addressed. Face-to-face and eye contact are key. If contact is lost between principal parties through anger or thoughtlessness, or if comment is directed toward the demonstrator rather than the issue, the point of the demonstration is lost. Similarly, careless or thoughtless comment directed toward the intended receiver can be equally damaging.

We need to remember that the other party to the demonstration may be our friend, perhaps our own child; that the aggressive or confrontational approach does not solve the problem that can only be solved by compromise and adjustment. This is the ultimate purpose of all government – to compromise and reconcile our competing differences enough so we can work together.

Few of us have taken time to consider the meaning of public demonstrations. For most of us, we just remember the fun of a parade, the high school band, the Fourth of July parades and other public get-togethers.

But more recently, we are seeing a few protest parades, political rallies, church revivals. But we haven't thought much about the public demonstration as part of the media or that it is carrying a message for us.

I am aware that a number of people were disappointed in many of the decisions made by the Mankato State College administration back in the 1960s and 1970s. Apparently we were being perceived as too soft. At least we were not holding the demonstrators up to the letter of the law or regulation. There were rationale and reason behind these decisions. In a number of cases where the demonstrator was insistent and rude and had thrust themself upon the listener in a manner considered threatening in trying to "reach" the listener, it appeared beyond acceptable behavior. Some responded in kind. Some parents felt so threatened by their own children, they could not understand what had happened to them. This is one reason why so many classrooms were open to any visitors as students listened and discussed, often with unscheduled speakers, war and war-related matters.

Our children needed to speak, and we elders needed to listen. Neither we nor our children were free of responsibility. But the letter of the law was of little help at this point. Nor was there defense for the violence that came later. Occupying or taking over a building, street, highway or bridge is symbolic of power and control and gets headlines, but it is misdirected and causes anger and often retaliation, ill will and slows the process essential for meeting face to face to make adjustments and accommodations. Our energy was better spent in conferring at appropriate levels with an adequate behavior that showed consideration.

Parades, bands, flag-wavers, protest marches and political rallies are here to stay. Let's enjoy them or at least hear what the opposition has to say. Violence and anger have no place in the demonstration. Both block any orderly progression toward accommodation of the difficulty.

Students and others who were incensed by the seeming indifference of their parents and the community to what they perceived as a betrayal of the people of the United States by its leadership, the continuation of the tragic war and loss of life, resorted to violence as a means to get their attention. But violence does not solve the problem. We must search further for peaceful solutions of our differences.

As partner to the decisions and actions taken by the city of Mankato and the College during the time described in this book, I salute and praise the leadership and enterprise of Mankato residents as they met the challenges of the dangerous and volatile days of the Vietnam period. We may meet comparable crises in our future, but we have demonstrated as a community that while impatience, intolerance and fear may dull or slow our responses, that will not be the case for long. Congratulations to Greater Mankato and Mankato State College, now Minnesota State University, Mankato, and to all who were touched by the events of the Vietnam era.

May 1972 rally on the campus mall. Photo from the 1972 *Katonian*.

# Acknowledgements

To the people who contributed to this book, I am proud to present your work. This is your book, your writing, your judgment of what you felt was important. I wish each of you could have sat in on each roundtable discussion about the College, the community and the people who made a difference here during the Vietnam era. Every conversation carried us into depths of new information and understanding. These pages are a unique collection of insights and judgments of you and your friends during a difficult but stimulating period in our lives.

To the core organizing group – Dave Boyce, Paul Hadley, Mark Halverson, John Hodowanic, Charlie Mundale, H. Roger Smith and Don Strasser – I am indebted.

To each of you who have been a part of this project, thank you.

And to the community of Mankato, I salute and praise your leadership and enterprise as you met the challenges of the dangerous and volatile days of the Vietnam era. Without your tolerance and patience, our history of those days would read quite differently.

May 1972 march at the bridge. Photo from the 1972 *Katonian.*

# Chronology

*The following chronology situates anti-war activities at Mankato State College within the context of major events during the Vietnam Conflict, 1964-1975. Compiled by Suzanne Bunkers, May 2006.*

# 1964

*2 May:* The first major student demonstrations against the Vietnam War took place in New York City, San Francisco, Boston, Seattle, and Madison, Wisconsin.

*1 August:* The U.S. destroyer Maddox, the U.S. aircraft carrier Ticonderoga, and three North Vietnamese torpedo boats engaged in battle in the Gulf of Tonkin.

*7 August:* The U.S. Congress approved the Gulf of Tonkin Resolution, authorizing President Lyndon Johnson to "take all necessary measures to repel any armed attack against forces of the United States and to prevent further aggression." The Resolution allowed war against North Vietnam without a formal Declaration of War from Congress.

*26 August:* President Johnson was nominated at the Democratic National Convention. During his campaign he declared, "We are not about to send American boys nine or ten thousand miles away from home to do what Asian boys ought to be doing for themselves."

*October-December:* At UC Berkeley, led by student Mario Savio, the Free Speech Movement arose out of debates, demonstrations, sit-ins, and other activities.

*1 November:* Vietcong mortars shelled Bien Hoa Air Base near Saigon. Four Americans were killed, 76 wounded. Five B-57 bombers were destroyed, and 15 were damaged.

*3 November:* Lyndon B. Johnson defeated Barry Goldwater by a huge margin to win the Presidency of the United States.

# 1965

*18 January:* Malcolm X denounced United States involvement in Vietnam: "It shows the real ignorance of those who control the American power structure... it shows her ignorance, her blindness, her lack of foresight and hindsight; and her complete defeat in South Vietnam is only a matter of time."

*2 March:* American bombing raids of North Vietnam, labeled "Operation Rolling Thunder," began. The first American combat troops, the 9th Marine Expeditionary Brigade, arrived in Vietnam to defend the US airfield at Danang. American forces clashed with North Vietnamese units in the Ia Drang Valley, with heavy casualties on both sides.

*24-25 March:* Students for a Democratic Society (SDS) organized the first teach-in on the University of Michigan. The event was attended by about 2,500 and consists of debates, lectures, and events aimed at protesting the war in Vietnam.

*7 April:* The U.S. government offered North Vietnam economic aid in exchange for peace, but the offer was rejected. Shortly thereafter, President

Johnson increased America's combat strength in Vietnam to more than 60,000 troops.

*17 April:* Students for a Democratic Society (SDS) and the Student Nonviolent Coordinating Committee (SNCC) and other activists organized approximately 25,000 people in an anti-war march on Washington, D.C.

*28 July:* In a nationally televised address, President Johnson informed Americans that 50,000 additional U.S. troops were being deployed to South Vietnam.

*15-16 October:* Anti-war rallies occurred in 40 American cities and in international cities including London and Rome.

*30 October:* 25,000 marched in Washington in support of U.S. involvement in Vietnam.

*27 November:* 35,000 anti-war protesters circled the White House, then marched to the Washington Monument for a rally.

*17 August:* The U.S. Army launched "Operation Starlite," the first major battle of the Vietnam War, in which the U.S. forces were victorious. Ground forces, artillery, ships and air support killed nearly 700 Vietcong soldiers. U.S. forces sustained 45 dead and more than 200 wounded.

*17 November:* North Vietnamese forces moving east toward Plei Mei ambushed an American battalion. When the fighting ended, 60 percent of the Americans were casualties, and almost one of every three soldiers in the battalion had been killed.

*27 November:* Between 15,000 and 25,000 anti-war demonstrators rallied at the White House during an SDS-organized March on Washington for Peace in Vietnam.

# 1966

*8 January:* U.S. forces launched Operation Crimp, the goal of which was to capture the Vietcong's Saigon headquarters.

*5 February:* The White House rebuffed a group of about 100 war veterans and former servicemen who had come to the capital to return medals and honorable discharge and separation papers as a protest against the Vietnam War.

*March-May:* The practice of protesting U.S. policy in Vietnam by holding "teach-ins" at colleges and universities became widespread, following the first "teach-in" with seminars, rallies, and speeches, held at the University of Michigan-Ann Arbor in March 1966. American B-52s bombed North Vietnam for the first time.

*26 March:* At the Second International Day of Protest against the Vietnam war, held in New York City, a large contingent of Veterans For Peace led an antiwar march of 30,000 people down 5th Ave. Demonstrations also took place in Chicago, Boston, Philadelphia, San Francisco and other major cities around the country. Many of these protest marches were led by contingents bearing signs reading "Veterans and Reservists For Peace."

*4 June:* A three-page anti-war advertisement, signed by 6400 teachers and professors, appeared in *The New York Times.*

Veterans from World Wars I and II, along with veterans from the Korean war, staged a protest rally in New York City. Discharge and separation papers were burned in protest of U.S. involvement in Vietnam.

*May-June:* North Vietnamese forces crossed the Demilitarized Zone (DMZ) and encountered a U.S. Marine battalion. The largest battle of the war to date broke out near Dong Ha. After three weeks, the U.S. forces and South Vietnamese Army troops drove the NVA back over the DMZ.

*4 July:* The national convention of the Congress of Racial Equality (CORE) adopted two resolutions: one calling for withdrawal of US troops; the other attacking the draft as placing a "heavy discriminatory burden on minority groups and the poor."

*15 October:* Huey P. Newton, Bobby Seale and David Hilliard developed a skeletal outline for The Black Panther Party.

*27 December:* American forces in Vietnam numbered over 385,000 men, plus an additional 60,000 sailors stationed offshore. More than 5008 combat deaths and 30,093 wounded were recorded.

# 1967

*14 January:* In San Francisco's Golden Gate Park, the first "Human Be-In" (aka "A Gathering of the Tribes") served as a prelude to the San Francisco

"Summer of Love," which made the Haight-Ashbury district the center of an American counterculture.

*8-10 February:* American religious groups staged a nationwide "Fast for Peace."

*25 March:* Dr. Martin Luther King, Jr. led 5,000 people down State Street in Chicago to protest the war in Viet Nam. This was the first anti-war march in which Dr. King participated.

*7-15 April:* Six Vietnam veterans founded Vietnam Veterans Against the War (VVAW) to fight for veterans' rights and voice the growing opposition among returning servicemen and women to the still-raging war in Indochina. VVAW grew rapidly to a membership of over 30,000 throughout the United States as well as active duty G.I.s stationed in Vietnam.

*15 April:* Spring Mobilization to End the War (MOBE). 400,000 marched in an Anti-Vietnam War protest from Central Park in New York to the United Nations building. Massive protest rallies and marches against the war in Vietnam occurred, including crowds estimated at 100,000 in New York City and 50,000 in San Francisco. "March Against Death" was the theme of these demonstrations.

*24 April:* American attacks on North Vietnam's airfields began, inflicting heavy damage.

*28 April:* Boxing champion Muhammad Ali (Cassius Clay) refused induction into the armed forces, citing religious reasons. Ali received a five-year prison sentence (reversed by the Supreme Court in June). The World Boxing Association revoked his title and license.

*May:* In air battles over Hanoi and Haiphong, American air forces shot down 26 North Vietnamese jets, decreasing the North's pilot strength by half. American military forces intercepted North Vietnamese Army units moving in from Cambodia, resulting in nine days of continuous battles.

*13 May:* In New York City, 70,000 marched in support of the war.

*4 July:* In Philadelphia, Vietnam Veterans Against the War participated in an antiwar demonstration across the street from Independence Hall.

*17 October:* University of Wisconsin students demonstrated, demanding that corporate recruiters for Dow Chemical, the producers of napalm, not be allowed on campus. Madison police beat and tear-gassed demonstrators.

*21-23 October:* The "March on the Pentagon" drew more than 55,000 protesters. In London, protesters tried to storm the U.S. embassy.

*30 November:* Senator Eugene McCarthy officially entered the race for the Democratic presidential nomination, running on an antiwar platform.

*4 December:* Four days of anti-war protests began in New York City.

*31 December:* U.S. troop levels in Vietnam reached 463,000 with 16,000 combat deaths to date.

# 1968

*21 January:* North Vietnamese Army attacked the American air base at Khe Sanh, deploying 20,000 troops. The 5000 U.S. Marines stationed there soon found themselves encircled and under siege . . . The battle at Khe Sanh lasted 77 days.

*24 January:* The U.S. Supreme Court ruled that a criminal prohibition against burning a draft card did not violate the First Amendment's guarantee of free speech.

*30 January:* The North Vietnamese Army and NLF/PALF troops launched the Tet Offensive. (Tet Nguyen Dan, called 'Tet', is the Vietnamese holiday celebrating the lunar New Year.) Within days, American forces turned back the onslaught and recaptured most areas. 37,000 Vietcong troops were killed, and 2,500 U.S. troops were killed during the Tet offensive. The American losses were a serious blow to public support.

*February:* The Battle for Hue continued for 26 days as U.S. and South Vietnamese forces tried to recapture the city.

*1 February:* Richard Nixon entered the race for the Republican nomination for President of the United States.

*8 February:* Alabama Governor George Wallace entered the U.S. presidential race as an Independent.

*16 March:* Senator Robert Kennedy announced his candidacy for the Democratic nomination, criticizing President Lyndon Johnson for his handling of the war.

*16 March:* Soldiers of Charlie Company, 11th Brigade, U. S. Army, entered the village of My Lai and killed approximately 300-400 civilians. The event became known as the My Lai Massacre.

*22 March:* North Vietnamese forces attacked Khe Sanh, and U.S. forces responded with heavy bombing.

*31 March :* Lyndon Johnson withdrew from the Democratic primary race.

*4 April:* Reverend Dr. Martin Luther King, Jr., was assassinated. Dr King had been outspoken against U.S. involvement in Vietnam and in his quest for civil rights for African-Americans. His assassination led to racial unrest in more than 100 American cities.

*23 April:* At Columbia University in New York City, students occupied several campus buildings. They were routed by city police a week later with 150 injuries, 700 arrests. A month-long student strike followed.

*27 April:* Vice-president Hubert H. Humphrey announced his candidacy for the Democratic presidential nomination.

*27 April:* An antiwar march in Chicago drew from 3,000 to 8,000 people.

*3 May:* General student and worker uprisings occurred in Paris and other cities in France to demand greater academic and social freedom and to protest against the war in Vietnam.

*6 June:* Robert F. Kennedy was assassinated in Los Angeles just after winning the California Democratic presidential primary election.

*23-24 August:* At Fort Hood, 100 Black G.I.s held a meeting to discuss deployment to Chicago for the Democratic Convention for Riot Control duties.

*23-28 August:* In Chicago, the Democratic National Convention was the scene of numerous protests and demonstrations by anti-war activists. Hubert H. Humphrey won the party's nomination on the first ballot.

*2 September:* In Honolulu, 106 reservists sued the U.S. Army to block their activation, claiming it was illegal because "Congress has not declared war and the President has not declared a national emergency."

*27 October:* In London, 50,000 people protested against the war.

*31 October:* President Johnson announced he would halt all bombing of North

Vietnam on 19 November 1968. The B-52 bombing halt was maintained until 15 April 1972. The U.S. bombing "sorties" were shifted to Laos from 1 November 1968 on through 1972; over 25,000 sorties were flown, with the most occurring in 1971.

*5 November:*  Richard M. Nixon, the Republican candidate for President of the United States, defeated the Democratic candidate, Hubert Humphrey, and the conservative independent candidate, George Wallace. Nixon received 43.4 percent of the popular vote, compared to Humphrey's 42.7 percent and Wallace's 13.5 percent.

*6 November:*  Students at San Francisco State University went on strike, shutting down the campus for six months and ending the strike only after the University agreed to create the first ethnic studies department at an American university.

*29 November:*  At Fort Jackson, 68 basic trainees sent a letter to President Johnson demanding an end to the war.

*7 December:*  In Philadelphia, at the University of Pennsylvania, a G.I. teach-in, organized by the Fort Dix Free Speech Movement, was held.

*31 December:*  536,100 American soldiers were serving in Vietnam. 30,000 Americans had been killed in Vietnam. An average of 1,000 per month died during that year, and the war had left an estimated 4 million South Vietnamese civilians homeless. "Draftees" accounted for 38% of all American troops in Vietnam. Over 12% of the draftees were college graduates.

# 1969

*20 January:*  Richard M. Nixon took office as President of the United States. He promised to achieve "Peace with Honor" by negotiating a settlement that would allow the half million U.S. troops in Vietnam to be withdrawn, while still allowing South Vietnam to survive.

*25 January:*  Paris peace talks opened with the U.S., South Vietnam, North Vietnam and the Viet Cong in attendance.

*February:*  Operation Dewey Canyon (I). An entire regiment of the 3rd Marines penetrated several miles into the neutral country of Laos, conducting combat maneuvers along Highway 922 and beyond, while suffering dozens of casualties who were refused evacuation in order to prevent press discovery.

*13 February:* At Fort Jackson, a Pray-in for Peace was held.

*23 February:* A coordinated offensive by the NLF/PALF started. A total of 110 targets in South Vietnam, including the City of Saigon, were attacked. Two days later, 36 U.S. Marines, camped near the border with North Vietnam, were killed in a raid conducted by the North Vietnamese Army.

*26 February:* At Fort Jackson, G.I.s United Against the War in Vietnam petitioned to hold meetings on-base.

*4 March:* President Nixon threatened to resume bombing North Vietnam in retaliation for Viet Cong offenses in the South.

*15 March:* U.S. troops went on the offensive inside the Demilitarized Zone for the first time since 1968.

*17 March:* President Nixon authorized Operation Menu, which involved secret bombing of Cambodia by B-52s, targeting North Vietnamese supply bases near the border of Vietnam.

*18 March:* At Son Phu, South Vietnam, a G.I. antiwar demonstration took place.

*9 April:* 300 students at Harvard University seized the administration building and locked themselves in to protest the war. They were later forcibly removed from the building.

*30 April:* U.S. troop levels were at 543,400. This was the highest level reached at any time during the war. A total of 33,641 Americans had been killed by this date, more than had been killed during the entire Korean War.

*10-20 May:* Battle of "Hamburger Hill"—After the U.S. had captured the hill, the troops were ordered to abandon it by their commander. The North Vietnamese army moved in and recaptured the hill, unopposed.

*14 May:* President Nixon proposed an "8-point peace plan" that would include mutual withdrawal of all non-Vietnamese forces to designated bases over a 12-month period, after which remaining troops would be totally withdrawn.

*19 May:* Joe Miles and 17 other G.I.s filed a lawsuit in Federal Court against the Secretary of the Army and the Fort Bragg Commander (Lt. Gen. John Tolson), seeking an injunction which would prohibit the defendants from interfering with the Constitutional liberties of G.I.s at Fort Bragg.

*8 June:* President Nixon met with Nguyen Van Thieu, President of South Vietnam and announced a policy of "Vietnamization" of the war and a reduction of US troops in Vietnam.

*18-22:* Students for a Democratic Society held its national convention in Chicago.

*26 June: Time* magazine reported that some U.S. troops in South Vietnam were reacting unfavorably to Nixon's decision to withdraw 25,000 men from Vietnam. The report cited the reaction of Specialist 4/c Arthur Jaramillo, a Sergeant in the 25th Division, who said, "You can have this war and shove it. Why don't they pull us all out?"

*27 June: Life* magazine displayed portrait photos of all 242 Americans killed in Vietnam during the previous week, including the 46 killed at "Hamburger Hill." The photos had a stunning impact on Americans nationwide.

*4 July:* In Champaign-Urbana, Illinois, a G.I.-Civilian antiwar march took place. At Case Western Reserve University, a National Antiwar Conference was held on 4-5 July.

*8 July:* Phased U.S. troop withdrawal began and continued from July 1969 through November 1972.

*15-17 August:* The Woodstock music festival – the "Festival of Life" – convened in upstate New York.

*3 September:* Ho Chi Minh, the leader of the North Vietnam government, died.

*5 September:* The U.S. Army initiated murder charges against Lt. William Calley concerning the massacre of Vietnamese civilians at My Lai.

*16 September:* President Nixon ordered the withdrawal of 35,000 soldiers from Vietnam and a reduction in draft calls.

*22 September:* In Colorado Springs, an Anti-Nixon G.I.-civilian demonstration took place.

*10 October:* In Fayetteville, 100 G.I.s from Fort Bragg's "G.I.s United" led 700 civilians in the city's first antiwar march. At Fort Sam Houston, G.I.s submitted a request to distribute the Bill of Rights on base.

*12 October:* 4,000 anti-war demonstrators, Black Panthers, and other activists clashed with 1,000 military police at Fort Dix, New Jersey. The MPs used tear gas to disperse the crowd.

*15 October:* A "Vietnam Moratorium" peace demonstration was held across the United States. During the moratorium, approximately one million Americans participated in anti-war demonstrations, protest rallies and peace vigils. 50 members of the U.S. Congress also participated. *Life* magazine called these Moratorium demonstrations "a display without historical parallel, the largest expression of public dissent ever seen in this country." In Vietnam G.I.s wore black arm bands to express their solidarity with the Moratorium.

*3 November:* President Nixon stated that he planned to withdraw all U.S. troops from Vietnam, based on a secret timetable.

*9 November:* 1,365 G.I.s signed an antiwar petition printed in *The New York Times,* urging civilians to take part in November Moratorium demonstrations.

*13-14:* In Washington D.C., the National Conference on G.I. Rights was held.

*15 November:* The 2nd Moratorium Against the War in Vietnam took place. A "Mobilization" peace demonstration drew an estimated 250,000 in Washington, D.C., for the largest anti-war protest in U.S. history.

*19 November:* Congress gave the president the authority to institute the "draft lottery" system aimed at inducting 19-year-olds before older men. Nixon signed the bill into law on 26 November 1969. Under the new law, the period of prime eligibility was reduced from seven years to one year. Maximum eligibility would begin on a man's 19th birthday and end on his 20th birthday.

*24 November:* In Pleiku, South Vietnam, 200 G.I.s of the 71st Evacuation Hospital held a Thanksgiving Day Fast to protest the war.

*1 December:* The first draft lottery since WWII was held at Selective Service Headquarters in Washington, DC. Those men whose birthdays fell on days with low numbers would likely be drafted.

*2 December:* The U.S. House approved a resolution endorsing Nixon's efforts to achieve "peace with justice."

*15 December:* President Nixon ordered an additional 50,000 soldiers out of Vietnam.

*24 December:* In Saigon, South Vietnam, 50 active duty G.I.s held an antiwar rally, calling on their fellow soldiers to hold a "cease fire" during the upcoming Vietnamese Tet holiday season. Their rally was broken up by MPs.

*31 December:* 474,400 American troops were serving in Vietnam.

# 1970

*15 January:* 80 G.I.s from Fort Bliss picketed a speaking engagement by General William Westmoreland.

*2 February:* B-52 bombers struck the Ho Chi Minh trail in retaliation for the increasing number of Viet Cong raids in the south part of Vietnam.

*21 February:* Henry Kissinger began secret peace talks with North Vietnam's Le Duc Tho, talks which continued for two years.

*14 March:* In Washington, D.C., a G.I. Rally for Peace and Justice took place outside the White House. In Vancouver, the American Deserters Committee organized a G.I.-Civilian antiwar demonstration.

*20 March:* Cambodian troops under Gen. Lon Nol attacked Khmer Rouge and North Vietnamese forces inside Cambodia.

*20 April:* President Nixon announced the withdrawal of another 150,000 troops over the next 12 months, eventually lowering U.S. troop numbers to 284,000.

*23 April:* President Nixon called for far-reaching draft reform and issued an Executive Order that ended all occupational deferments and most paternity deferments, with "extreme hardship" as the only exception.

*30 April:* President Nixon announced the U.S. and South Vietnamese incursion into Cambodia "...not for the purpose of expanding the war into Cambodia but for the purpose of ending the war in Vietnam and winning the just peace we desire." The announcement generated widespread protests across the United States.

*2 May:* American college campuses across the country erupted in protest over the invasion of Cambodia. An antiwar petition, sponsored by the Reservists Committee to Stop the War and signed by more than 1000 Reservists and National Guardsmen, was published in *The New Republic* magazine.

*4 May:* On the campus of Kent State, in the midst of a student demonstration, the Ohio National Guard fired at students, hitting thirteen and killing four of them. Demonstrations erupted at hundreds of college and universities across the U.S.

*5 May:* *The New York Times* quoted President Richard Nixon's official statement in response to the shootings at Kent State: "This should remind us all once again that when dissent turns to violence it invites tragedy. It is my hope that this tragic and unfortunate incident will strengthen the determination of all the nation's campuses, administrators, faculty and students alike to stand firmly for the right which exists in this country of peaceful dissent and just as strong against the resort to violence as a means of such expression."

*9 May:* A peaceful anti-war rally held at the Ellipse in Washington, DC, was attended by about 80,000 people, including ten members of Congress.

*14 May:* Students at Jackson State College in Mississippi who were protesting violence and discrimination against African-American students and the killings at Kent State were fired on by police. Two students were killed and twelve wounded.

*15 May:* Crosby, Stills, Nash & Young released Neil Young's anti-war anthem "Ohio" about four unarmed students being slain by the Ohio National Guard on the Kent State University campus while protesting the U.S. invasion of Cambodia. According to Neil Young's biographer, Jimmy McDonough, "In ten lines, Young captured the fear, frustration and anger felt by the youth across the country and set it to a lumbering D-modal death march that hammered home the dread."

After the events at Kent State and Jackson State, there was a wave of demonstrations on hundreds of college campuses. An average of 100 demonstrations or student strikes took place per day in the United States. More than 500 colleges had to temporarily close their doors.

*16 May:* Armed Forces Day. Festivals, picnics, and rallies took place at military bases across the U.S. At the Great Lakes Naval Training Center, more than 500 demonstrators rallied and heard speeches. The Armed Forces Day displays there were cancelled due to what Rear Admiral H. S. Ronkin called the threat of "dissident elements."

*13 June:* President Nixon established "The President's Commission on Campus Unrest." The Commission held 13 days of public hearings in Jackson, Mississippi; Kent State, Ohio; Washington, D.C., and Los Angeles, California.

No convictions or arrests of military or law enforcement officers resulted.

*24 June:* The U.S. Senate repealed the 1964 Gulf of Tonkin Resolution.

*30 June:* U.S. troops withdrew from Cambodia. More than 350 Americans had died during the incursion.

*11 August:* South Vietnamese troops took over the defense of border positions from U.S. troops.

*24 August:* B-52 bombing raids occurred along the Demilitarized Zone.

*24 August:* A homemade bomb exploded outside the Army Math Research Center on the campus of the University of Wisconsin at Madison, killing a graduate student and injuring five others.

*4-7 September:* During the Labor Day weekend of 1970, Operation RAW ("Rapid American Withdrawal") was a march from Morristown, NJ, to Valley Forge State Park by over 150 Vietnam Veterans Against the War (VVAW) members. Mock search and destroy missions were conducted by the veterans and "guerrilla theater" actors during the march.

*26 September:* The Concerned Officers Movement held a press conference in Washington D.C., protesting US involvement in Southeast Asia. They released a statement, signed by more than 80 active-duty officers: "We the undersigned are members of the Concerned Officers Movement, a group of active duty officers in the Armed Forces who want to publicly express their opposition to the war in Indochina. We believe that we have the constitutional right to make our convictions known. We believe that in doing so we are acting in accordance with our obligations as officers, to defend the Constitution."

# Events at Mankato State College (MSC) in 1970

*April 1970*

- Mankato Citizens for Peace took out a full-page anti-war ad in the *Mankato Free Press*.

- MSC Student Senate acted on demands to remove military recruiters from the campus.

*May 1970*

- MSC students held a torchlight parade after an anti-war speech by the Rev. John Frey, a Presbyterian minister from Chicago. The march jammed the Front and Main intersection and left traffic at standstill for one and a half hours. Organizers called for two days of boycotting classes. An attempt to burn a Navy recruiter van was aborted, with a few rocks thrown through Post Office windows. Political science Professor Abbas Kessel cautioned demonstrators against counterproductive actions.

- Students went on strike to protest the May 4 Kent State University slayings in Ohio, the renewed bombing of North Vietnam, and the invasion of Cambodia.

- Students burned effigies of President Nixon and Vice President Agnew at a demonstration in front of the Post Office. Professor Abbas Kessel urged nonviolent protest.

- Eleven hundred protesters gathered in downtown Mankato for a parade and rally. Mankato Mayor Clifford Adams, Professor Abbas Kessel, and student leader Tom Clinton were among the speakers. (The previous night, two veterans burned Vietnamese-style huts built on the MSC upper campus mall. No one was injured.)

- A MCS upper campus speak-out condemned the May 14-15 killing of two black students at Jackson State College in Mississippi. Two thousand individuals attended a teach-in on the upper campus mall. Speakers included College President James Nickerson as well as students and faculty. Calling for action, not words, twenty students staged a sit-in on the steps of the downtown Mankato Post Office. A memorial service for the war dead was held in front of Old Main, the administration building.

- A silent march of 700 students closed the week of demonstrations.

# June 1970

- The MSC campus was not closed, but students were given alternative ways of finishing spring quarter.

*From the MSC Katonian 1970-1971 (page 49):*

"A moratorium is a period of permissive or obligatory delay. This dictionary definition sums up the focus of the movement held October 15 [1969] across the nation as a show of protest to the Nixon administration that large and growing numbers of Americans want out of the Vietnam war now. The moratorium was aimed at suspending business-as-usual in order to allow protest, debate and thought about the war.

"M-Day at Mankato State began with the distribution of black arm bands and flyers to area citizens on Front Street. Throughout the day, concerned and interested faculty and students rapped about the war at teach-ins in the Centennial Student Union and Old Main . . . Peace vigils were held all day in the Newman Center and Campus Lutheran chapels. A peace service, held in the Union ballroom, was directed toward peace and the agony of war. According to one campus minister, the purpose of the vigil and the peace service was to show that the matter of peace is not only a political affair, but a Christian concern as well. . . .

"On November 13, two days before the Washington and San Francisco mass marches, Mankato State students who supported the moratorium marched from Highland campus to Front Street and on to the Post Office where a rally was held. The Post Office was selected as a rallying point because it is the only federal building in the city and it houses recruiters from the armed forces. The rally was also held as a send off for 80 students who were leaving to participate with an estimated 250,000 others in the march in Washington D.C."

*1971 Katonian article, "Will you join in building a wave that will bring this country back to us?" (36-39):*

Story tells of the "End the War" rally held to gain support for a nationwide strike against the war on November 6, 1970:

"On October 16-17, seventy-five state coordinators of the Vietnam Veterans Against the War (VVAW) from Minnesota, Iowa, Wisconsin, Nebraska, and the Dakotas participated in the workshop at the Centennial Student Union" (36). John Kerry (national spokesman for VVAW) spoke, as did Warren Spannaus (attorney general of Minnesota), Rudy Perpich (lieutenant governor of Minnesota), Vance Hartke (U.S. senator from Indiana), Donald Fraser (U.S. congressman from Minnesota), Al Hubbard (VVAW executive committeeman).

# 1971

*1 January:* The U.S. Congress outlawed the presence of U.S. troops in Laos or Cambodia.

*4 January:* President Nixon announced that "the end is in sight."

*13 January:* President Nixon signed a bill repealing the Gulf of Tonkin resolution.

*19 January:* U.S. fighter-bombers launched heavy air strikes against NVA supply camps in Laos and Cambodia.

*January 1971:* A Gallup poll showed that 60% of Americans with a college education favored withdrawal of US troops from Vietnam, 75% of those with a high-school education favored withdrawal, and 80% of those with only a grade-school education favored withdrawal.

*31 January-2 February:* A Vietnam Veterans Against the War (VVAW) sponsored event, the "Winter Soldier Investigation" was held in Detroit around the time of the trial of Lieutenant William Calley, a trial involving the massacre, by American soldiers, of civilian inhabitants of the village of My Lai. The veterans at the Investigation were attempting to give testimony to the fact that My Lai was not the only time or place where such treatment of the Vietnamese people took place. The WSI was conducted to gather testimony from soldiers about war crimes being committed in Southeast Asia as a result of American war policies. Intended as a public event, it was boycotted by much of the mainstream media, although the *Detroit Free Press* covered it daily and immediately began investigating what was being said.

*8 February:* Operation Dewey Canyon II: the second U.S. invasion of Laos. However, after word leaked out to the press, it was renamed Operation Lam Son 719, and the U.S. role was that of support in a South Vietnamese led invasion. By March 18th, three battalions of South Vietnamese troops were airlifted out of Laos in a rout denied by both Saigon and Washington.

*February:* Graham Nash recorded "Oh! Camil" ("The Winter Soldier"). After attending the Winter Soldier Investigation Nash, numb from hearing the horrors of war, wrote this song about a member of VVAW and how war impacts veterans and the general public.

*29 March:* U.S. Army Lieutenant Calley was convicted for the My Lai Massacre.

*1 April:* A two-year extension of the draft passed the U.S. House (239-99) in a roll-call vote. The Senate also passed the bill on 24 June, following a long debate.

*19-23 April:* Operation Dewey Canyon III. This peaceful anti-war protest organized by VVAW took its name from two short military invasions of Laos by US and South Vietnamese forces. Dubbed Operation Dewey Canyon III, it took place in Washington, D.C, and was referred to by the participants as "a limited incursion into the country of Congress." The level of media publicity and Vietnam veteran participation at the Dewey Canyon III week of protest events far exceeded the Winter Soldier Investigation and any previous VVAW protest event.

*24 April:* Over 200,000 people gathered for a mass antiwar demonstration in Washington, D.C.

*29 April:* Total American deaths in Vietnam surpassed 45,000.

*3-5 May:* A mass arrest of 12,000 protesters occurred in Washington, D.C.

*17 May:* At Chanute Air Force Base, a group called Concerned Black Airmen held an on-base service dedicated to the memory of Malcolm X.

*13 June:* The New York Times began publishing excerpts from *The History of U.S. Decision Making Process on Vietnam Policy*, better known as the "Pentagon Papers," a secret Defense Department archive outlining decisions about Vietnam taken by previous White House administrations. The Nixon administration appealed to the Supreme Court to halt the publication.

22 June: The U.S. Senate passed a non-binding resolution urging the withdrawal of all American troops from Vietnam by the end of the year.

*28 June:* The source of the Pentagon Papers leak, Daniel Ellsberg, surrendered to police.

*30 June:* The U.S. Supreme Court ruled 6-3 in favor of *The New York Times* and *Washington Post* publication of the Pentagon Papers.

*June:* At a secret meeting in Paris, the North Vietnamese government presented a nine-point peace proposal to Henry Kissinger. The North Vietnamese plan called for the withdrawal of all United States military personnel in Southeast Asia, withdrawal of all United States support of the Thieu government in South Vietnam, the forming of a single Vietnamese government of 'national concord' and a cease-fire following agreement on political and withdrawal issues.

*3 October:* President Thieu of South Vietnam was re-elected.

*7-8 August:* In Idaho, G.I.s and civilians from the Mountain Home Project marched against genocide in a 40-mile trek across the desert to Boise.

*9 October:* Members of the U.S. 1st Air Cavalry Division refused an assignment to go out on patrol by expressing "a desire not to go." Also during October, sailors aboard the carrier USS Coral Sea circulated a petition opposing the war in Vietnam and demanding that the ship stay home. 1,200 sailors, one fourth of the crew, signed the petition. At a mass rally, more than a thousand antiwar protesters gathered to support them. Three junior officers resigned and condemned the war, and 35 sailors deserted the ship.

*31 October:* The first of nearly 3,000 POWs held by the Viet Cong were released.

*6 November:* In Long Binh, South Vietnam, 60 G.I.s held a meeting to discuss strategies to end the war and get back to the U.S.

*10 November:* Aboard the USS Coral Sea, three junior officers publicly resigned their commissions to protest the Vietnam war.

*December:* Fifteen VVAW activists barricaded and occupied the Statue of Liberty for two days. Simultaneous protests took place at the historic Betsy Ross house in Philadelphia (for 45 minutes) and Travis Air Force base in California (for 12 hours). Other VVAW members in California also occupied the Saigon Government conciliate in San Francisco.

*17 December:* U.S. troop levels in Vietnam stood at 156,800.

*26-30 December:* The U.S. bombed military installations in North Vietnam, citing violations of the agreements surrounding the 1968 bombing halt.

# 1972

*8 January:* At Travis Air Force Base, 100 active duty airmen and women supported by 100 dependents and community people participated in a 24-hour vigil in protest over the escalation of the air war in Vietnam.

*25 January:* President Nixon announced a proposed peace plan for Vietnam and revealed Henry Kissinger's secret peace negotiations with the North Vietnamese. However, Hanoi rejected Nixon's peace overture.

*10 March:* The U.S. 101st Airborne Division was withdrawn from Vietnam.

*23 March:* The United States suspended the peace talks in Paris, citing North Vietnamese refusal to seriously discuss concrete issues . . . The Peace Talks in Paris resumed on 27 April, but were suspended again in May and resumed on 13 July.

*30 March:* The North Vietnamese launched a major offensive across the DMZ, the biggest since Tet 1968. During this "Eastertide Offensive," 200,000 North Vietnamese soldiers under the command of General Vo Nguyen Giap waged an all-out attempt to conquer South Vietnam.

*2 April:* President Nixon authorized the U.S. 7th Fleet to target NVA troops massed around the Demilitarized Zone with air strikes and naval gunfire.

*4 April:* President Nixon authorized a massive bombing campaign targeting all NVA troops invading South Vietnam along with B-52 air strikes against North Vietnam.

*8-12 April:* In reaction to President Nixon's May 8th announcement regarding the mining of Haiphong and other harbors in North Vietnam, violent anti-war clashes occurred across the U.S.

*10 April:* Heavy B-52 bombardments ranging 145 miles into North Vietnam began.

*12 April:* NVA Eastertide attack on Kontum began in central South Vietnam, with the intention of cutting South Vietnam in two.

*15 April:* Hanoi and Haiphong harbor were bombed by the U.S., and protests against the bombings erupted in the U.S. At Wright Patterson Air Force Base, active duty airmen, veterans and civilians demonstrated at the base gates for the 14th straight week.

*26 April:* President Nixon announced the withdrawal of 20,000 more troops.

*8 May:* President Nixon ordered the mining of all North Vietnamese ports without first consulting Congress.

*15 May:* The headquarters for the U.S. Army in Vietnam was decommissioned.

*17 June:* The Watergate Hotel break-in and attempted bugging of the Democratic Party Headquarters occurred in Washington, D.C.

*4 July:* Peace Rally in Washington, D.C., drew thousands of supporters.

*11 July:* A North Vietnamese Army attack on An Loc was defeated by South Vietnamese troops, with the assistance of American B-52 air strikes. South Vietnamese troops started a major counter-offensive campaign against the North Vietnamese Army in Binh Dinh Province.

*18 August:* 1,200 U.S. veterans and supporters participated in a cross-country caravan that ended at the Republican National Convention in Miami to "protest the coronation of King Richard."

*23 August:* The last U.S. ground combat troops left Vietnam.

*16 September:* Quang Tri City was recaptured by South Vietnamese troops.

*29 September:* U.S. military raids against airfields in North Vietnam destroyed ten per cent of the North Vietnamese Air Force.

*8 October:* The U.S. government agreed to allow North Vietnamese troops already in South Vietnam to remain. In return, the North Vietnamese government dropped its demand that South Vietnamese President Thieu step down so the South Vietnamese government could be dissolved.

*22 October:* In Saigon, Henry Kissinger visited President Thieu to discuss the peace proposal.

*26 October:* Radio Hanoi revealed the terms of the peace proposal and accused the U.S. of trying to sabotage the settlement. Henry Kissinger announced, "Peace is at hand."

*7 November:* Richard M. Nixon defeated George McGovern to win the U.S. presidential election in the biggest landslide to date in U.S. history.

*14 November:* President Nixon promised President Thieu secretly "to take swift and severe retaliatory action" if North Vietnam violated the proposed peace treaty.

*30 November:* American troop withdrawal from Vietnam was completed, although 16,000 Army advisors and administrators remained to assist South Vietnam's military forces.

*18 December:*  After peace talks broke down again, President Nixon responded with "Operation Linebacker II', a massive bombing campaign known as 'The Christmas Bombings."

# Events at Mankato State College (MSC) in 1972

## April 1972

-   A campus-wide strike was planned. Professor Carolyn Shrewsbury presented a strike resolution. A mass rally was held at noon, along with small teach-ins.

-   Strike action included voter registration, letter writing to congressmen and a speak-out.  More than 500 students participated.

-   An all-night vigil at the Post Office was held. Plans were made for a May 4 parade, mini-courses and forums.

## May 1972

-   Anti-war protesters joined in at the end of Loyalty Day parade downtown.

-   A march from the MSC upper campus to the downtown Post Office took place.  A torchlight parade of 70 students laid the groundwork for commemoration of the Kent State killings.

    A march to the Post Office of fewer than 100 students occurred as some individuals tried to remove their draft records.

-   A MSC upper-campus rally condemned President Nixon's mining of Haiphong Harbor in North Vietnam. Following the rally, 2,500 students marched downtown to Front and Main, with some breaking off to block Highway 169 ramps. At about 5:30 p.m., the blockaders were dispersed by police and sheriff's deputies.

-   Faculty and students proposed alternatives to classes in view of anti-war activities. Pete Seeger, the folksinger and war protester, gave a concert at MSC. A peace march took place at Sibley Park. Eighty students left Mankato on buses to lobby congressmen in Washington.

- A "Prayer for Peace Rally" drew 4,000 students and townspeople to a peace discussion.

- President Nickerson offered MSC students the options of continuation of classes, withdrawal without credit, negotiation of incompletes, independent studies, half-credits and problem courses, but the President kept MSC open.

- Two hundred students occupied Old Main in a 30-minute incident, resulting in minor damages and injuries. Police in riot gear cleared the building.

- The Peace Coalition made plans. Activities included canvassing the community, petitions, videotaping people's comments on the war.

- Seventy-five to 100 students held a negotiated weekend sit-in at Old Main.

- A candlelight march for peace was attended by 500 people.

- Many MSC classes incorporated anti-war activities into assignments.

# July 1972

*4 July:* MSC students attended the 4 July 1972 Peace Rally in Washington, D.C.

# November 1972

*3 November:* A Vietnam War Teach-In sponsored by the MSC Student Mobilization Committee (SMC) was held in the front-door lobby of the Centennial Student Union. Participants included the SMC, Vietnam Veterans Against the War (VVAW), the Minority Groups Study Center, and MSC faculty members.

*4 November:* MSC students were bused to Minneapolis for an anti-war march & rally.

*1971 Katonian article, "Teach-in Focuses on Asian Conflict" (page 41):*

"The Vietnam war was the main topic of a teach-in which convened in the front-door lobby of the Centennial Student Union on November 3 [1972]... The primary function of the teach-in, according to Vicki Bolton, Student Mobilization Committee chairman, was to expose new information on specialized areas of the war. Several speakers, including both students and faculty, expressed their points of view and answered questions from the audience.

"Mike Fagin, director of the Minority Group Study Center, talked about racism involved in the war. Art Levin, journalism department chairman, spoke of the effects of mass media regarding the war; and Dr. Lewis [Mickey] Croce, associate professor of history, revealed some historical aspects of the war. Other MSC faculty members also involved in explaining various points of the Asian conflict were Dr. James Goff and Mike Scullin.

"First-hand information from veteran psych-medic John Anderson contributed further to the scope of the teach-in. A final viewpoint to be emphasized was that of the Vietnam Veterans Against the War as expressed by Bob Idso, Mike McEvoy, and Bob Corbett.

"Conducted just three days prior to an anti-war movement march in Minneapolis and St. Paul, the teach-in was also intended to attract students to sign up and be bussed to the rally. The march brought students together from all over Minnesota and surrounding areas to protest American involvement in Vietnam."

*The 1971-72 Katonian (pages 10-21) includes this information about the formation of "A Task Force for Change":*

"In the summer preceding the '72 school year the Chancellor of the State College Board reflected that many changes and a great deal of significant progress had been made within the state college system. Yet through further examination he and the board had further determined the need for other changes in that system...'Students need a kind of education that permits them to deal with rapid change rather than one that provides a set body of knowledge,' observed Chancellor [G. Theodore] Mitau...'There can be no innovation without critical self-examining. It is only be reassessing our priorities, closing down the less important in order to open up the more important, that we will be able to respond to realities and to continue quality education'" (11).

"President Nickerson, just prior to the start of fall quarter in his annual address to the faculty, called for 'the creation of a representative task force to coordinate our explorations and evaluations of the new...' (11). Harold Fitterer was named chairman of the task force."

*April 18, 1973: The Task Force for Change issued its 44-page report (see pp. 208-209 in Katonian)*

# 1973

*8 January:* Peace negotiations between Henry Kissinger and Le Duc Tho resumed in Paris.

*9 January:* All remaining differences were resolved between Kissinger and Le Duc Tho.

*23 January:* President Nixon announced that an agreement had been reached that would "end the war and bring peace with honor to Vietnam and Southeast Asia."

*27 January:* Official end of the Vietnam Conflict. The Paris Peace Accords were signed by the U.S., North Vietnam, South Vietnam and the Viet Cong. Vietnam remained divided. South Vietnam was considered to be one country with two governments, one led by President Thieu, the other led by Viet Cong, pending future reconciliation.

*27 January through 29 March:* 587 military and civilian prisoners were released by the North Vietnamese; during that same period, 23,500 US troops were withdrawn from South Vietnam.

*29 March:* 67 more U.S. POWs were freed in Hanoi. The same day, the US withdrew its remaining 2,500 troops from South Vietnam. President Nixon declared that "the day we have all worked and prayed for has finally come."

During 15 years of military involvement, over two million Americans served in Vietnam with 500,000 seeing actual combat. 47,244 were killed in action, including 8000 airmen. There were 10,446 non-combat deaths. 153,329 were seriously wounded, including 10,000 amputees. Over 2400 American POW and MIAs were unaccounted for as of 1973.

*19 June:* The United States Congress passed the Case-Church Amendment, which forbade any further US military activity in Southeast Asia, beginning on 15 August 1973.

*16 July:* The U.S. Senate Armed Forces Committee began hearings into the secret bombing of Cambodia during 1969-70. As a result of the hearings, Congress ordered that all bombing in Cambodia cease effective at midnight, August 1973.

*14 August:* The United States stopped its bombing in Cambodia.

*31 August:* The "Gainesville 8" were found not guilty on charges of conspiracy to disrupt the 1972 Republican National Convention in Miami Beach, Florida. Seven members of Vietnam Veterans Against the War (VVAW) and 1 non-member were acquitted on charges of plotting violent disruption of the 1972 Republican National Convention. The federal jury in Gainesville, Florida, acquitted all eight after fewer than four hours of deliberation.

*7 November:* The U.S. Congress passed the War Powers Resolution, which required that the President obtain the support of Congress within 90 days of sending American troops abroad.

# 1974

*9 May:* The U.S. Congress began impeachment proceedings against President Nixon.

*27-30 July:* The U.S. House Judiciary Committee voted three articles of impeachment against President Nixon in connection with the Watergate burglary and the subsequent cover-up.

*9 August:* Richard M. Nixon resigned the Presidency, and Gerald R. Ford was sworn in as the 38th U.S. President.

*16 September:* President Ford announced a conditional clemency program for Vietnam-era military deserters and draft evaders. The program continued through March 31, 1975, and required fugitives to take an oath of allegiance and also perform up to two years of community service. Out of an estimated 124,000 men eligible, approximately 22,500 took advantage of the offer.

*October:* The Politburo in North Vietnam decided to launch an invasion of South Vietnam in 1975.

# 1975

*21 January:* President Ford stated that the U.S. was unwilling to re-enter the war.

*19 March:* Quang Tri City fell to NVA.

*24 March:* Tam Ky was over-run by NVA.

*25 March:* Hue fell after a three day siege. Millions of refugees and South Vietnamese troops fled south.

*26 March:* Chu Lai was evacuated.

*28 March:* Da Nang was shelled as 35,000 NVA prepared to attack.

*29 March:* U.S. Marines and Air Force helicopters began a massive airlift. In 18 hours, over 1,000 American civilians and almost 7,000 South Vietnamese refugees were flown out of Saigon.

*30 March:* Da Nang fell as 100,000 South Vietnamese soldiers surrendered after being abandoned by their commanding officers.

*31 March:* NVA began the "Ho Chi Minh Campaign," the final push toward Saigon.

*21 April:* President Thieu resigned as the president of South Vietnam.

*30 April:* The last Americans departed from Saigon, concluding the United States' presence in Vietnam. North Vietnamese troops entered Saigon and met with little resistance. South Vietnamese President Duong Van Minh delivered an unconditional surrender to the Communists. The war was over.

An estimated total of 2,122,244 people were killed during the war in Vietnam. Of these, 58,169 were Americans. Of those Americans, 11,465 were teenagers. An estimated 3,650,946 additional people were wounded, of whom 304,000 were Americans. 153,329 Americans were categorized as 'seriously' wounded. That total includes 10,000 amputees.

An estimated 444,000 North Vietnamese and 220,557 South Vietnamese military personnel and 587,000 civilians were killed.

6,727,084 tons of bombs were dropped. This is about two-and-a-half times the total tonnage dropped on Germany during World War II. The dollar cost of the United States involvement in the war in Vietnam is estimated at $140 billion.

The statistics cited above are taken from "War and Protest: the U.S. in Vietnam" URL:   http://www.bbc.co.uk/dna/h2g2/alabaster/A715024

# Sources

"American Future: Trying to Make Sense of a World in Turmoil"
http://americanfuture.net/?cat=9

"The Events: a Chronology of U.S. Involvement in the Vietnam War"
http://oakton.edu/user/~wittman/chronol.htm
http://www.historycentral.com/vietnam/events.html

"Fighting 15th" Vietnam War Timeline
http://www.landscaper.net/timelin.htm

"The History Place: The Vietnam War"
http://ww.historyplace.com/unitedstates/vietnam/index.html

Kessel Institute for the Study of Peace and Change, Minnesota State University, Mankato MN   http://www.mnsu.edu/kessel/index.html

Rhodes, Henry A.  "The News Media's Coverage of the Vietnam War."
http://www.yale.edu/ynhti/curriculum/units/1983/4/83.04.03.x.html

"Sir! No Sir!": a Chronology of G.I. Resistance."
http://www.sirnosir.com/timeline/chronology_protests.html

Strasser, Don.  Timeline: "Anti-war activities at MSC, 1970-72."  Mankato, MN, 2005.

"UC Berkeley Anti-Vietnam War Protests in the San Francisco Bay Area & Beyond"
http://www.lib.berkeley.edu/MRC/pacificaviet/#1960

"Vietnam War: the Bitter End, 1969-1975"
http://www.vietnamwar.com/timeline69-75.htm

"Vietnam War Timeline"
http://www.english.uiuc.edu/maps/vietnam/timeline.htm

"Vietnam War Timeline"  http://www.vietnam-war.info/timeline/

"Vietnam: Yesterday and Today: Chronology of U.S.-Vietnam Relations:
http://www.oakton.edu/user/~wittman/chronol.htm

"War and Protest: the U.S. in Vietnam"
http://www.bbc.co.uk/dna/h2g2/alabaster/A715024

*[The URLs listed above were most recently accessed on 24 May 2006.]*

Old Main. From the 1972 *Katonian*.

# Reflections

*President Emeritus James F. Nickerson's memories, analyses and insights regarding campus unrest in response to the Vietnam War and its relevance today*

Forty years ago, we were at war with Vietnam, a war that lasted 10 years with the loss of more than 58,000 American lives and the lives of countless Vietnamese. It was an unpopular and poorly explained war, one being waged halfway around the world. It was a war with heavy casualties and a not-too-evenly-applied military draft, resulting in the migration of many American students of draft age to Canada.

College students at the time included quite a few dissidents and newly hatched critics. They had something to say, and we needed to listen. Ultimately we did so, after much deliberation and with great hope for a peaceful and satisfying outcome. Through actions and official policy, we achieved this and more. What happened – and didn't happen – in Mankato represented an institution of higher learning, a community, and people of different generations and political persuasions working together responsibly and thoughtfully, to relatively peaceful ends.

Those of us in positions of authority found our roles difficult. To suppress and punish yielded little. For much of the established community, if our leaders tried to listen or bend regulations to find ways to discuss issues on more equal footings or explore new methods and new approaches to longstanding problems, such actions were seen as weakness, indecisiveness and even irresponsibility.

We were surprised by and unprepared to deal with what a number of social critics now view as a social revolution reaching from the schools, colleges, main streets and city officials to Congress and the White House--in the forms of demonstrations, sit-ins and occasional violence and death. These actions involved community leaders, residents, students, shoppers, storekeepers, drivers and pedestrians. Highways were blocked, and bridges were closed. Here in Mankato, more than 1,000 people of student age were not attending Minnesota State College. These people were in Mankato visiting friends, bunking illegally in dorms or apartments, or joining informal communes that were forming in the area.   That was where the action was.

This period was marked by a general disregard for established authority, a rejection of the wisdom of experience and of elders. Opinion, judgment or actions of anyone over 30 were suspect and even categorically rejected by many. Dress, diet, living conditions, drug use, a new sexual freedom and non-hygenic living became means of protest, endangering the lives of many.

At the same time, American colleges themselves were undergoing major changes. It was a period of rapid growth, but enrollments were fluctuating widely from year to year, causing serious budgeting problems. New fields of study and new staff were being added, many as adjunct faculty who had no job security.

Since 1955, a new spirit had been infusing the greater Mankato community--a spirit of enterprise and excitement. After 80 years of clinging to the east ridge of the Minnesota River Valley, the College had purchased land on the hilltop for a new campus. This was the beginning of major planning for a new institution--the orderly development of a more versatile regional institution for the Upper Midwest, an institution that would one day be called a "university" and that would offer appropriate programs. These ambitions were supported by the Minnesota State College Board and the state legislature as well as by the central and western regions of Minnesota.

In the mid-1950s, construction began on the first MSC upper-campus buildings, the A and B wings of Crawford Center. Three buildings were available by the beginning of the 1959 academic year.  A split campus existed until 1979, when two lower campus buildings were abandoned and sold. The campus move signaled a major step in the development of the university.  In the midst of this change, and its surrounding community, Mankato State College met the trials of the Vietnam War era.

War conditions, as reported by returning service members were disturbing. The war seemed to have lost its focus, almost as if the United States government did not want to fight to win. Those who criticized the war effort were often accused of being disloyal to the troops.

Campus unrest did not appear in Mankato until the fall of 1968. A student had written an essay, entitled "Herbie and I,"[1] published in a college magazine–an essay critical of the Catholic community in Mankato and an essay that most senior readers considered to be in bad taste. The state printing contract for all student publications had been won by a local printer who was a leader in the Catholic community; the printer refused to print the essay, even though it had been cleared by all appropriate review groups within the College. The issues were freedom of speech and the student press, the sanctity of contract, and the status of students as they carried out normal responsibilities. After several weeks of acrimony, the matter was settled by allowing the printer to insert a foreword to the article, stating his objections and disclaiming any responsibility.

Later that year, Scoop Jackson, a U.S. senator from the state of Washington as well as a noted hawk who supported the military, spoke at a Mankato State College convocation. As Sen. Jackson was being introduced, 30 or 40 students seated in the front row rose on cue and pelted the senator and the platform party with marshmallows, then quietly exited the auditorium in five minutes or less. As president and emcee for the senator, I could do little more than chuckle and congratulate the demonstrators for their creative idea and quiet exit from the auditorium. Then we went on with the program, and Sen. Jackson seemed to enjoy the incident and gained a few headlines from it.

The most infamous event to take place during this period was the blocking of Highway 169 and the bridge from Mankato to North Mankato in May 1972. For me, it began about 3 p.m. with an urgent phone call to my office. An angry voice said, "Your damn kids are down here, maybe a couple thousand blocking 169 and the bridge. Cars and trucks are backed up for well over two miles. Can you get them off the highway?"

I replied, "Maybe. I doubt it, but I will do whatever I can."

"Fifteen minutes is all you got, then we'll move on them. We'll hit them with mace and clubs."

He hung up.

My colleagues and I quickly reviewed maps of the area, checked our gear and sped downtown to see what could be done. When we pulled onto Highway 169, we were ushered to the head of the line of official cars. There must have been five sheriff's cars and perhaps 40 state troopers' cars in the line, along with nearly 50 uniformed officers standing by.

A quick briefing by the sheriff of Nicollet County indicated the demonstrators had taken over the highway an hour before, and traffic was backed up at least a mile in each direction. The Sheriff's Office was ready to take action if I failed in talking with the leaders--action including mace, physical removal if necessary, arrest, and whatever might follow.

I should explain why the sheriff of Nicollet County was the peace officer instead of Charles Alexander, the chief of police of Mankato. Back in the 1960s and 1970s, southbound Highway 169 switched from the west bank of the Minnesota River over to Mankato on the east bank, crossing Main Street Bridge. Thus, as the highway passed through the two cities of Mankato and North Mankato, it fell into two jurisdictions.

I preferred to tackle this negotiation alone without police escort. I moved about within the crowd, spotting students whom I knew. I was hoping to find the leadership that I knew existed to move the demonstrators off the highway and away from imminent danger. An interesting thing occurred. Even though there were a dozen or more demonstrators whom I recognized as student leaders, none seemed to know anything about the intent of this group, nor did they feel they could turn the group away from the highway, even for the group's own safety. They were not hostile, just not cooperative, and there was nothing they felt they could do. After a few minutes, I made a brief speech indicating what would happen if the demonstrators should have to be forcibly removed from the highway. It was evident that they would not move.

For me, I must admit this was one of the most lonely and isolated moments of my life. With friends who wouldn't or couldn't talk to me or who were not ready to assume their usual responsibility of leadership, I reluctantly gave up and returned to the cluster of officers, knowing what I was sure would happen as force was applied to remove the crowd.

A disagreement, however, arose among the police, who were about to remove the demonstrators from the highway. The sheriff's group was not ready to release the demonstrators. The police chief's group, considering the probable injury and continuing struggle, favored release. The College offered to bring in buses to clear the site. This situation represented one example of issues that might arise in each encounter until we can resolve in our minds how to handle angered demonstrators who cannot find alternative actions to take.

This is not to suggest the inconvenience and danger to all those involved in the issue was unimportant, but we must realize that neither violence nor anger nor retribution can resolve the problem. It can be resolved only through discussion, negotiation and compromise. The negotiation for dissolving the highway blockade was quite successful with no major injuries beyond a need for first aid, no hospitalizations, and no arrests.

Following this highway incident, two separate attempts to take over Old Main and to occupy the president's office took place. The first attempt was the idea of a spontaneous group that had broken away from the main march that was heading downtown, later to fill Second Street. The splinter group heading for Old Main was small, a dozen or less. The building was empty, since most occupants were downtown, watching the developments surrounding the main march.

The splinter group, which appeared to be planning a hostile takeover, was re-routed by a small group, comprised of campus security and Mankato police, that had followed the protesters when they broke from the march. The plan was almost too limited for a successful takeover. There was some use of tear gas in routing the group from Old Main.

The later, successful takeover of Old Main was a negotiated demonstration. One demand of the more extreme of the activists was to close down the institution. This action seemed too drastic, even to most demonstrators. The student leadership came to the president's office, and we discussed alternatives that might carry their message and be less disruptive.

The demonstrators wanted to show student power, and the president's office presented the target. The leaders of the demonstrators wished for no violence or damage, and we insisted that the building should be able to carry on its full functions. Faculty, students and other users were to have access to all parts of the building. The president's office would be open around the clock, and staff would be available for discussions and so forth.

Two faculty and two students remained on duty with the president and his staff for the 62-hour occupation. My wife, Nita, and I slept in our camper in back of Old Main and were otherwise available full time to talk with demonstrators.

There was one breakdown in the arrangement. The cafeteria had to be placed off-limits because of early morning food service demands. Late one night, the demonstrators did break into the cafeteria for refreshments but evacuated when threatened with eviction and arrest by the Mankato police.

About 4 a.m. one morning, security forces awakened me to report that the cafeteria had been taken over. I went to see the mess, not knowing what to expect. Then I addressed the demonstrators, stating that they had broken our agreement and that I had no choice but to hand authority over to the Mankato police.

I gave the demonstrators one minute to leave if they preferred. To my surprise, within that one minute they scattered like cockroaches when a light is turned on. They went out the doors, out the windows--overturning chairs and tables, leaving only the messy cafeteria. The demonstration, which had served its purpose, was abandoned after 62 hours with minimal damage in the form of a few cigarette burns in the carpets and the cost of the food they had eaten.

Only a week or so earlier, on May 4, 1970, the Ohio National Guard had been called in to quell a campus riot at Kent State University. The Guard, which was armed, fired a volley, and four students were killed. The reaction on the

Mankato campus, by students and authorities, was immediate: we opposed bringing the Minnesota National Guard to Mankato.

Mankato Police Chief Charles Alexander, however, explored the protocol necessary for requesting the Guard, if necessary. It was determined that he would make the initial request, which would be evaluated by the Adjutant General's Office (that of Colonel Paul Meyer of Mankato). Col. Meyer reported this protocol to me in my office. We were opposed to bringing in the Guard except as a last resort. Details were discussed with the governor's office by phone. No further action was taken, and the Guard was not called.

In a matter of days following the incident at Kent State in Ohio and the May 14, 1970, killings of students by police at Jackson State in Mississippi, the Mankato student body authorized a memorial to be erected on the Mankato State College upper campus.

Contrary to the belief of many, the Vietnam War period proved to be a time of breakthrough for the combined community of Mankato State College and the city of Mankato. Out of chaos came a new order, a new vision.

It was a time of development and growth, a period of vitality and energy within what is remembered by most of us as a period of storm and stress and disappointment. The war was the defining feature but by no means the exclusive factor. In the life of the College alone, a new campus on the hilltop had been authorized by the Legislature and, by 1965, nearly a half-dozen academic buildings and two major residence hall complexes were occupied or ready for use.

The new plans and facilities attracted a changing student body. Within three years, registrations from the Twin Cities and southern suburbs increased to 3,500, or roughly one-third of the student body. Students' program choices began to move toward business-related subjects and preprofessional programs, a nursing program, with less concentration in teacher education. Students were being treated as adults with full rights as citizens, as opposed to the in loco parentis (in the place of a parent) of the recent past. They had created an active student government with increased responsibilities and budget control.

We also had a new president and new executive team of vice presidents and deans, and we were recruiting new faculty, many of them younger and with strong support and backing from the community, the State College Board and the Legislature. We also had a concentrated drive from within the community to bring the College to university status and seek a name change accordingly.

For the city of Mankato, this time meant growth, experiment and a number of self-studies done jointly with the College. A sense of a routine existence was transformed into heightened interest and anticipation of community and school life, which, apparently, exerted both positive and negative influences on behavior on young residents, positive in terms of heightened interest in the world and negative in terms of people becoming actively critical of the slowness of change from the status quo.

Physically, a new enclosed mall and, later, a civic center and a 5,000-seat auditorium were built downtown as a result of the studies of the time. Parking and an attractive corporate park were soon to follow. Now, almost 40 years later, downtown is almost unrecognizable.

The United States withdrew from Vietnam in 1974 with neither a declaration of victory nor admission of defeat.

Today, we are at war in Iraq and Afghanistan, a struggle that continues as a bloody fight carried out through assassination, harassment of attempts at self-government and almost daily suicide bombings with no end in sight. The cost of the war is reaching into hundreds of billions of dollars and is putting a strain on our domestic economy.

To many observers, there are ominous clouds forming today, suggesting the possibility of civil unrest and disruption not unlike we experienced in the 1960s and 1970s. There are those who fear a return of the disruption of community and family life, especially on or near college campuses. The testimony of the interviews and reflections on the following pages shows a pattern of approach to such unrest by officials and individuals.

Unlike a number of other cities with colleges, Mankato relied on an unconventional approach during the Vietnam era. Rather than harsh treatment, strict supervision and isolation, the interesting thing about the Mankato approach was neither to control nor to suppress, although, in effect, it was able to do so when needed.

The attitude of officials, monitors and others in contact with the demonstrators was that of support and assistance, to be sure that the exercise was successful. After all, demonstration was a legal enterprise and deserved support as such. It should be noted as well that the anti-war sentiment did prevail over many the doubts of some officials and monitors.

The demonstrators were neither dangerous nor threatening; they were students who constituted no danger to the officials. With these conditions and attitudes, it was easy for officials to assume the role of assisting the demonstrators. This attitude of semi-partnership and assistance presented itself in most of the demonstrations of the period. Apparently, this lack of hostility diffused the leadership itself. This was quite in contrast to what was happening with other college town demonstrations. The net result of this tolerance and assistance by Mankato was minimal violence and disturbance.

Today, as unrest escalates with the war in Iraq, we are hopeful that the greater Mankato community will meet any challenges with the same wisdom and tolerance that helped the community weather the Vietnam War period. The clues for how to do so lie within the following contributions.

[1] Todd S. J. Lawson, "Herbie and I." *Plaintiff: the Literary-General Magazine.* Edited by Todd S. J. Lawson. Vol. 5, No. 1 (Fall 1968): 33-42. Published at Mankato State College. The magazine's title page contains this disclaimer: "The opinions expressed in this magazine are not necessarily those of the Mankato State College administration, faculty or student body."

May 1972 sit-in. Photo from the 1972 *Katonian*.

# Contributions

*Reflections on the era of campus unrest submitted by former students, members of the Mankato State College faculty, staff and administration, and members of the Mankato community*

**Kent Alm, '70**
**Former Acting President**

*Relations with Governing Boards*

I'd like to offer some thoughts about relations with governing boards. I feel quite comfortable in so doing as I was the chancellor (called commissioner then) of the North Dakota Board of Higher Education for several years.

The chancellor is the chief operating officer of the governing board. That means the presidents of the various institutions report to him. He/she likes that arrangement. The presidents seldom do. Chancellors, most frequently, are chosen from candidates who have been presidents of colleges or universities, or at least have had significant administrative experience in institutions of higher learning. This is a significant requirement. Chancellors with that background usually understand the issues facing campus administrators and try to be helpful and understanding.

None of the above was extant during the "reign" of G. Theodore Mitau, the chancellor during the Nickerson years at Mankato State. Mitau had no significant administrative experience whatsoever. His profession was as a professor of political science at a small private college. Little, if anything, in his background, therefore, prepared him for the chancellorship. In fairness to him, I'm sure he was an outstanding teacher. I had an occasion to listen to his description of Germany during the Hitler years, and it was almost spellbinding. But, unfortunately, the Peter Principle seems to apply here. He simply was out of his element as chancellor.

It is my opinion that Mitau thought he sat on a throne. That he would give orders and his minions would carry them out. We were his minions. He set out to minimize the institutions and maximize the board office. A case in point: The presidents, historically, had presented their own annual budgets to the Minnesota Legislature. The budgets had been approved by the board, but the presidents made the presentations. Mitau changed that.

Hereafter, Vice Chancellor Norman Dybdal would present the budgets. The presidents were to be there to answer questions if the chancellor called upon them. Mitau's own performance before the Legislature was, to be charitable, colorful.

Mitau embarked on what he called his "Listen and Learn" program. He had said he would go to each campus and meet with faculty and students. In these meetings, he had said he would listen and learn from the campuses. That, of course, was not what happened. It was the campuses who were to listen and learn from the chancellor.

I think it's reasonable to say that the presidents of the state colleges tried to do what the chancellor wanted and found it appropriate not to challenge him. All, that is, except President Nickerson. He challenged the chancellor time and time again. Nickerson was always on solid ground. The chancellor, however, developed an antagonism toward Nickerson. He could not tolerate one of his minions challenging him. That antagonism existed until the end of the Nickerson years. It should be pointed out that, ultimately, all of the presidents had had enough of Mitau. I understand they sent one of their number to tell Mitau they had had enough and that he should resign. He did. That series of events attests clearly to the correctness of the Nickerson position as well as to his courage.

I could expand on this topic. There were many, many things Mitau did and/or said that were inappropriate or unproductive or both. It should be clear, however, that I did not admire the man and found him to be a disruptive factor in our ability to manage the College.

In the following pages, I shall endeavor to recall and put to print various events, occurrences, and situations that transpired at Mankato State during the years of the presidency of Dr. James Nickerson. I had the honor of serving as vice president for academic affairs during all but the first of those years.

The comments I shall make are, of course, representative of the way I looked at those events then and now, clouded, admittedly, by the passing of more than 30 years.

The College was in a frenzied enrollment increase when I arrived in 1967. It was a new experience for the institution and for the community. What had been a sleepy little small town college of a few thousand students was transformed, in a very short time, into an institution of nearly 16,000 students. Everyone in the community was not thrilled with the expansion. The larger number of students created different kinds of problems. These problems generally stemmed from overcrowding of everything, including housing, transportation, community services, entertainment, etc.

The College itself was organized as a small teacher-preparing institution. In fact, it is my opinion that it was operated more like a public secondary school than like an institution of higher learning. To recognize this condition and to make the necessary changes required for a post-secondary institution was a major challenge for the College during the Nickerson years.

*The Changing Student Body*

The College had traditionally served as a regional institution. That is, it drew the vast majority of its students from the region surrounding Mankato. But things began to change as enrollment skyrocketed. A significant number of students came from outside the region, especially from the Twin Cities. The student body, historically, was made up primarily of Caucasians. Now large numbers of minority students were enrolling, including a significant number of black students. The College and the community had to learn to adjust to this change. The transition didn't always come easily. The black students demanded certain things. They wanted a Black Studies program and a Black Cultural House. They organized themselves with a spokesman. The College was not accustomed to students demanding anything. Tensions resulted.

Institutions across the country were experiencing student demonstrations, especially related to Vietnam. Mankato did not escape this trend. There were student demonstrations, sit-ins, street marches and bomb threats. This was upsetting to the community. Many could not understand why the president "allowed" these things to occur. The fact is there wasn't much he could do about it. The truth is, however, that Dr. Nickerson managed these situations far better than presidents at other institutional or community property. Non-students from elsewhere created some of the problems.

I remember particularly one event that could have turned ugly. Students decided to "occupy" the administration building (Old Main). Dr. Nickerson, instead of calling on law enforcement for help, decided to sit-in with the demonstrators. He and his wife, Nita, sat on the floor in Old Main all night with the students. The demonstration ended with no serious damage other than a few cigarette burns in the new carpeting.

On another occasion, the demonstrators marched through downtown Mankato. Again, Dr. Nickerson marched with them. Other than inconveniencing some of the residents who were driving their cars, nothing of significance occurred. Yet, the president was criticized for his actions (or inactions). This was all a part of the community learning about the circumstances that accompany large numbers of students.

*College Organization*

When Dr. Nickerson arrived in 1966, the administration included the president and several deans. Dr. Nickerson appointed the first vice presidents in the history of the College. They included vice president for academic affairs, vice president for administration and vice president for student services. These were traditional offices found on most campuses.

As was previously noted, the College was organized more like a high school. The faculty had very little authority or "clout." The Faculty Senate was given a far greater role. The administration brought many issues to the Senate that heretofore had been decided by administration, especially the president. As would be expected, the Faulty Senate began to "feel its oats" and, at one time, even passed a resolution of censure against the administration. That would have been an unlikely event a few years earlier. It was a sign of the institution growing up.

A Council of Deans also was created. Heretofore, the right hand didn't always know what the left hand was doing. The council met with the vice president for academic affairs weekly. They shared information, concerns and ideas concerning the management of the College. President Nickerson was always informed of these meetings. He gave us a lot of latitude to do our jobs, but he insisted on being kept in the loop.

It was the opinion of the administration that a strong athletic program was an integral part of the institution-building. So the College applied for and received membership in the North Central Conference. Mankato State competed successfully in all sports, especially wrestling, baseball, track and swimming. It took a while to get the major sports (football and basketball) up to speed.

The burgeoning student body necessitated an expansion of the student health program. A student health center was created with a renovation of Gage Hall, and a full-time director, Dr. Harry Brauer, was employed

## College Programs

I'll mention only a few programs that, in my mind, were really significant.

The first was Wilson Campus School. It was organized as a school for training student teachers. No research activities or other educational experimentation occurred there. That had to change. Dr. Don Glines was employed with the mission of infusing the school with a large dose of educational innovation. He did so. Wilson achieved national recognition, and the waiting list of students wishing to attend was long. To achieve that change, Wilson had to be taken out from under the supervision of the dean of education and placed under the associate vice president for academic affairs. The dean was not supportive of the change.

Another interesting program was the hiring of an artist in residence and placing him in a very public place in the student union. Dr. Arnoldus Gruter, a Canadian artist, originally from Amsterdam, filled the position and performed remarkably for several years. The Art Department had its feathers ruffled over his appointment. It was not consulted, and, in retrospect, should have been.

I would be remiss if I didn't mention the establishment of the Aviation Program. Admittedly, it was my efforts that brought it about. We got a loan from Mankato Citizens Telephone Co. to buy two Piper trainers, and hired Rod Grove to run the program. It was successful and remains so today. Minnesota Department of Administration officials were unimpressed, but they got over it.

The Urban Studies Program was one of the College's truly outstanding efforts. It enjoyed a fine reputation in the region and in the state.

The Computer Science Program under Dr. Donald Henderson's leadership was the best among the state colleges by far. Enrollment growth in that program was exceptional. Unfortunately, the Chancellor, G. Theodore Mitau, pulled Henderson up to St. Paul for an extended time to engage in Mitau's plan at centralizing. That plan was generally a failure.

## The Exodus

For reasons nobody knows for certain, but everybody has an opinion about, enrollment at the College began a sharp decline in the early 1970s. Enrollment declined 25 percent. Since we were "formula funded" based on student credit hours, we had to reduce the budget and thus the faculty accordingly. We reduced the faculty by 150 positions over three years. The challenge was to do so in such a way as to improve the institution at the same time. We accomplished this reduction in faculty with faculty input and approval. This method served the institution well, since not a single faculty member complained to the Minnesota State College Board or to the courts. The details are less important than the outcome.

*Conclusion*

The years under the presidency of James Nickerson were among the best and most exciting of my 40 years in education. Jim was one of the best in the country. In the years following my term at Mankato, I was privileged to work with hundreds of college and university presidents nationwide, and Jim was as good as any of them. Aside from being my mentor, he remains my close friend.

*Kent Alm lives in Dent, Minnesota.*

### J. W. (John) Anderson, '74

It was September of 1970. I had just been discharged from the Army and was leaving Fort Dix, NJ. Uncle Sam had just let me out early to go to college in Minnesota. As I got to the post gate, something came over me. I had just spent almost three years of my life in Uncle's army and I felt confused, used, pissed off and, at the same time, relieved.

I knew when I was drafted that my life after high school was going nowhere, yet I did not want to be in the military. I was young, naive, and impressionable. Even the word "Vietnam" scared the hell out of me. But now it was over. Or was it? The Army had gotten what it wanted out of me. I'd served my country, yet I had this hollow feeling inside.

Both my parents were WWII veterans and were proud of that fact. Shouldn't I be proud too? After all I had served my country, but to what end? Why were we in Vietnam? Why were boys my age dying in droves? Why was the Vietnamese population being killed in a genocidal fashion? Why were people in the streets protesting my government's actions? Why were students being slaughtered on their college campuses? What had happened to this great country I grew up in? Well, maybe that's the way life was, or maybe I should not trust a government that had lied to me. And now that I was a "veteran" I saw no honor in having served my country, with no one seeming to care about veterans. Not the government and certainly not government agencies like the Veterans Administration. I was alienated not only from the government but also, it appeared, from society in general. So, I took my sorry ass off to Mankato, Minnesota to attend Mankato State College. While a pittance, the VA would provide a slight subsidy to attend college.

I had been in Mankato prior to my military service. I had attended Bethany Lutheran College for a short period, as a failed means to avoid the draft. However, after weighing a number of factors I chose to go back to Mankato, this time to attend the "big" college...Mankato State. While I knew I had no choice but to grow up quickly in the Army, little did I realize, on my way to Minnesota, that I would grow differently at MSC. I would grow emotionally, intellectually, spiritually, and politically. What's more, I would learn empathy and compassion.

By the time I got to Minnesota to attend Mankato State, I was really anxious. Here I was a 22-year-old freshman. I don't think I'd ever felt this alone. At least in Uncle's army I had buddies I could count on. Now what do I do? I thought. When classes started I felt even more alone. What was I doing here with all these kids who didn't have a clue about what was going on beyond their academic borders? So, for the first few quarters, I became a loner, went to classes, and got high every chance I could. But no matter what I did, I could not get away from the Vietnam War. It was all around me; on the news, in the movies, on campus, in the music; especially in the music.

In the spring of 1971, I felt that there had to be other vets who had the same values I had. After all there were a lot of vets on campus. In the student union one day I ran into a Vietnam vet who invited me to a Vets Club "smoker." I got to the meeting and I could have sworn I was at a fraternity meeting. Guys talking about what they were going to do at the fraternity charity festival. No talk about the war or its effects outside of ridiculing the students who were protesting it. Come on, throw me a bone, what is this: VFW, the younger? Just then I spotted another vet who looked just as bewildered as I must have appeared. He told me about a "Teach-In" that would be happening later in the week. The focus was on the campus antiwar movement and it was being sponsored by the Student Mobilization Committee (SMC).

It was at the SMC Teach-In that I first heard of Vietnam Veterans Against the War (VVAW). There was an open mike in the lobby of the MSC Student Union, and as I listened to fellow veterans, I realized I was not alone in my thoughts and beliefs. I got up and talked about the mangled bodies that we came across daily in medical air-evacuation duties and how fellow G.I.s went literally crazy as part and parcel of their role in the war.

I was approached by a few veterans who had spoken earlier about their roles in the war and how they had become antiwar vets. They had just started a local chapter of VVAW. Always the hesitant one, I hemmed and hawed about getting involved. I did agree to go to an antiwar march in the Twin Cities that weekend.

At the antiwar march in Minneapolis, the Vietnam veterans were to march in the front. There were hundreds of us. I couldn't believe it. I was able to talk to a number of VVAW members from across the state. Finally I realized that I was not alone in my thinking. I found what I was looking for. It was here that we organized for Dewey Canyon III, a limited incursion into the foreign land of Washington, DC and the halls of Congress, in April of 1971. It was here that I joined VVAW.

Dewey Canyon III, as it came to be known, was named after Dewey Canyon I and II, which were two separate invasions of Laos. The first was in January and February of 1969 by elements of the 3rd Marine Division and the subsequent invasion during the first seven days of the 1970 South Vietnamese invasion of Laos.

Dewey Canyon III was amazing. Organized by the national office of Vietnam Veterans Against the War, the actions of over 1,000 Vietnam vets from across the country would capture the imagination of the American people as the VVAW emblem became a mighty fixture on national network news.

Headlines of the nation's papers reported the marches of the vets on Congress, the Pentagon, and the White House, and the occupation of the Supreme Court steps. The nation cried with the vets locked out of Arlington National Cemetery and held its breath as over 1,500 Vietnam veterans returned their medals from that war, an event unparalleled in history. These powerful events, led by VVAW, served as a catalyst that propelled the events of that spring of 1971 into the most massive protests yet seen against the war in Southeast Asia.

The irony of the week's activities was the U.S. government's fencing off of the Capitol from its veterans. This demonstrated that the government did not know or care what they had created by sending its boys off to an undeclared and undefined war. All the government knew was that the contingent of veterans camped on the mall was the first time in history returning servicemen had voiced opposition to a war that was still raging.

Upon returning to MSC, our campus VVAW organized and was recognized as a "legal" student organization, membership grew and a number of us ran for and won seats in the Student Senate. We were gaining local political clout and were getting our message out about the "real" war in Vietnam. We were invited to address high school and college classes all over southern Minnesota, and students and teachers alike were listening.

Things did settle down in the fall of 1971, but this was a temporary lull. In the spring of 1972, Nixon did it again. This time with the bombing of North Vietnam and mining of Haiphong Harbor. This unleashed pent up student emotions. There were antiwar rallies, parades and protesting in front of the only federal building in town – the Post Office. Of course, the events that still are burned into my memory include the rally and march to downtown, when the crowd then diverted to Highway 169 to close off traffic north and south as a means to get the message out. Traffic was completely closed down and not until the Nicollet County Sheriff came at us with night sticks and pepper fog did we disperse.

Looking back, this was not the smartest anti-war tactic but it was non-violent until the authorities turned it into a police riot, so to speak. Once back on campus though it was like being in a protected land. There were food and beverages served and we were able to bandage up the "wounded." Later that evening (probably to keep us off the streets) there was a live band provided outside Centennial Student Union (CSU).

Also during this same month there was another take-over of Old Main. This time, rather than a police action, the college administration, through Dean Scott, I believe, negotiated terms in which students would leave peaceably. This is where my recollection gets a bit fuzzy, but I believe the trade-off for leaving Old Main after a tense weekend was that a student peace office would be established and appropriated funds and a certain amount of students would be bused to Washington D.C. for a nationwide anti-war rally and to lobby the Minnesota congressional delegation about ending the war.

Between 1972 and 1975 our local VVAW organization became the leader of the antiwar movement on campus. We encountered some victories and some failures, learned about "pepper fog," found out the Nicollet County Sheriff liked to swing his night stick, and had R.A. Dash visit our homes. However, through it all the message did get through to the student community and the local community as well.

The Mankato VVAW office also focused on other issues of concern to veterans, such as bad discharges, SPN codes, jobs, amnesty and military recruiting on campus. The Mankato VVAW office organized a regional VVAW meeting that was accompanied by a peace conference sponsored by VVAW and the Mankato State Student Union Board. Members of the VVAW national office attended and both John Kerry and Al Hubbard of the national office addressed the conference, as well as US Senator Vance Hartke from Indiana.

I believe I came of age at Mankato State after that fateful week in April, 1971. As mentioned previously a number of the VVAW contingent won seats on the student senate and expressed our views on not only the war but students having control of their institutions. A peace office was established and appropriated funds. A Student Bookstore was established during this same timeline and eventually was chosen a "National Model" by the *College and University Press Newsletter*. Moreover, I was fortunate enough to be elected to the Union Board of Directors and continued the fight to keep military recruiting off campus and question why students did not have more input into Student Union decisions.

While I was considered an "activist" student at MSC, I did allow time for classes and eventually earned a bachelor of science degree in 1974 and a master of arts degree in 1976. And as I turned my attention to family and career potential, I withdrew from my participation in student activities and VVAW, outside of the occasional political or arts and entertainment column for *The Reporter*. After all, I had to finish graduate school, Nixon was gone, the war was finally winding down and with a family to care for, I had to move on. Of course this didn't mean that values embedded in me from MSC were gone. I was just in hiatus, probably for longer than I will openly admit. Nor did this mean I no longer had the occasional unannounced visit from the FBI. VVAW was still considered a threat to J. Edgar and labeled a subversive organization, and of course I needed watching.

It is now over thirty-five years since I first enrolled in school at Mankato State College and also learned about Vietnam veteran's Against the War (VVAW). Do I still consider myself a member of VVAW? Yes, I am a card carrying member of VVAW. I have considered myself a member since that fateful day in 1971. There are a still a number of VVAW members from our college years who get together to discuss the most recent war and its impact on our lives, families, and the world.

The impact of Vietnam and my anti-war days at MSC will be with me for the rest of my life. I believe I can be proud of the fact that VVAW played a large role in ending U.S. involvement in Vietnam. Unfortunately, this same military madness still hovers over Washington, D.C., and apparently politicians and power brokers in that city have learned nothing from the past. Again, the government has found the need to lie about its military exploits. I have not and will not buy what the current administration is selling and as an anti-war veteran, I look upon this and any war as Dwight D. Eisenhower when he stated "I hate war as only a soldier who has lived it can, only as one who has seen its brutality, its futility, its stupidity."

So what values do I still carry from my days at MSC? Simply put, I do believe that I grew emotionally and intellectually as well as learning compassion and empathy for those less fortunate than myself and hopefully, over the years, I did something about it. Moreover, I still have the values acquired 35 years ago when I first joined VVAW and that VVAW means a voice for veterans who are not enamored of war and military achievements. It means striving to redirect government resources so that the 30-plus percent of homeless Vietnam veterans can find homes, jobs, and health care. It means a world without war for our children and grandchildren. And it means peace, and unfortunately given the current Pax Americana policy of corporate exploitation and military power, there is still plenty of work to do.

*Men who were fighting for all of our lives*
*Are now fighting for children, for homes and for wives*
*Fighting for the memory of all who fell before*
*But the soldiers of peace just can't kill anymore*
  - Graham Nash

*J. W. Anderson lives in St. Paul Park, Minnesota.*

### Eddice Barber
### Professor Emerita of English

During the Vietnam War days, I was a member of the United Campus Ministry Board. I do not remember the name of the woman who was the campus minister, but I remember she was involved in a protest against the war. Once, she seemed to be leading a group, and I went to see what was going on; I think we didn't say or do much.

I remember the bomb threats in classroom buildings and the evacuations. After no bombs were ever found, the administrators decided we could continue our classes during the threats, but students could leave if they wished. In a general education class of probably 30 or more students, only two decided to leave when I announced there was a threat. Others just said, "Let's go on with the class."

In a senior literature class for English majors, the students decided on their own and then told me that if any bomb threats came, I was to go with them to an apartment of one of the students near the campus and continue the class. "We want to learn what we can before graduation," they said.

One of my colleagues who did not have tenure decided it was more important to oppose the war than to meet his classes. One of his classes was scheduled next door to one of mine; I knew he was not present and the class did not meet, but I said nothing. He was not re-employed. He appeared before the Department Personnel Committee and said he just thought it was more important to oppose the war than to meet his classes.

*Eddice Barber lives in Mankato, Minnesota.*

### Dave Boyce '72

I was born during the Great Depression, but never realized that one existed till I was taught so in high school and later. We always had enough to eat, a warm and loving home, and were like most folks in the neighborhood. The town of Mankato, at 11,000 population, was a great place to live. We had a city bus line only three blocks from home that took us to within six blocks of the high school. Later, we walked both ways to save the fare and spend it on malts and burgers. That was two miles to, two miles from.

All during grade school and into junior high, we were taught about the wonderful country we lived in and, in particular, that we had "saved the world for democracy" in World War I. During our late grade school years, World War II began in Europe and China; then in junior high, we were in it. Pearl Harbor occurred, and we joined in the idea of buying bonds (stamps for us kids) and rationing gasoline, sugar, meats, fats, shoes and other commodities. As Boy Scouts, we became "civil defense messengers." The world was that way till the war ended. Items became once again available for purchase; even cars, tires and gasoline.

I was a year too young for WW II and a year too married for Korea, so I avoided the military of the time. Work took me through a year of manual labor before landing a white-collar job and shortly moving into my father-in-law's music store, Backlund's. After two years working with him, he offered to sell the business to me on a contract-for-deed basis, and we were off and running. A good friend, who was older than I, said, "You've got it made for life." So it seemed.

Things changed, sometimes for the better, sometimes not. As Mankato grew, we did in the store as well. The influx of college-aged people and the "re-introduction" of music caused us to look more and more to them for support. We introduced numbers of them to time payments, trying to escape the charge accounts of the time. This strategy sold more high-priced items to young people who were often coerced into over buying both their needs and pocketbooks. This caused problems for us a well. The banks had us co-sign the note, so if things got too far behind, we were forced to pay off the loan and then attempt to repossess the item, if we could locate the buyer. At about the same time, the growth of the market brought added outlets to the city – some of them were the folks who wholesaled to us under another name. Change was the order of the day.

The influx of new merchants brought in chains and malls that used "downtowns" that were not downtown. Many of the old merchants decided to call it quits; others moved from the downtown area to these suburban shopping areas. This split the attraction of a Central Business District and invited the merchants who could avail themselves of mass buying at a hefty discount. We, in turn, found our sales to families slipping; we became more and more dependant on the younger people. Stereos, guitars, amps, etc., took the spotlight. As a result, we made "friends" with the student-age person. It behooved us to do so. We had two adult-age persons on the floor; the rest of our personnel were from the students. They worked part time at tasks from sales, to service, to delivery, to bookkeeping, to lessons, to sweeping out the old store.

All of this contact with younger people brought us into conversations that dealt with the U.S. presence in Vietnam. Coming from the experiences of WW II and Korea, most folks my age and older didn't spend a lot of time questioning it until we had our heads provoked by talking to younger people. Some of them were Vietnam veterans, like our bookkeeper and our repairman. Both supported the action in Vietnam. Other Vietnam veterans were students. Many of them were opposed to action and what had happened to them. Some were into substances that helped them forget what they had been asked to do and what had happened to them.

We stayed in touch with both police and ministers. Our customers could generally locate a "runaway" and have them contact family, with the provision that we would not name names. It worked well, although some parents deeply resented our not naming the contact so they could return their child home. They didn't realize that the phone call they received wouldn't be there for the next parents if we did. We lost some business that way, but gained others. It established a good relationship with those veterans and others who opposed the war.

At the time of the disruptions in Mankato, we were involved as a family; our sons were both eligible for the draft. We urged them to become conscientious objectors. We got into counseling other youth faced with the draft, going C.O. or moving to Canada.

I recall walking home from a Monday-evening opening at the store about 9 p.m. and meeting a large group coming down Highland Avenue. They were headed for the downtown, still considered the home of the "establishment" (what establishment?). The events that followed brought actions that have been better described by others. The early part of it, I watched as it moved along Front Street past the store. Eventually, though, a friend from the campus stopped by and asked me to accompany him as the young people marched across the Front Street Bridge to North Mankato to block traffic there and on the Veterans Bridge in order to speak to the people in the vehicles. This had brought threats of injury; we worked with the Mankato Police to try to prevent that.

The young people succeeded in "shutting down" the city. Our place of business needed $300 income per day to "break." Every other store had a like problem. We looked at the receipts for the day, found $26 there – a long way from breaking even. This brought action from the city merchants to enter into conversation with young people, and we shortly experienced a series of town meetings that persons from all sides of the issue attended to speak their thoughts and concerns. While there was still disagreement, people heard and considered other points of view and came to know one another.

This time was a good experience, a time that has helped shape the rest of my life.

*Dave Boyce lives in Mankato, Minnesota.*

## John Brady '76

*From Child Soldier to Adult*

I returned from a war I did not understand but knew I survived without visible wounds. A child of twenty years, I wandered for two years in and among the stupor of late nights, exploring life on the academic campus that was yet to become meaningful. I wondered why others were protesting a war that I did not understand but one from which I carried tastes and smells. Oh yes, I also carried the prejudice against a people whose country I somehow knew I had helped damage for no good reason.

My wanderings brought me to Mankato State College for what was to be an attempt at my third year seeking an education for my future. The year prior, I had heard of a large peaceful demonstration on the campus and in the streets of Mankato. I found myself in a college whose president was supportive of the type of civil disobedience that draws attention to failed foreign policy issues. One day, I would come to know him and understand, to some degree, the fabric from which this peaceful leader was fashioned.

I knew nothing of this debate but would some day come to understand the importance of learning from the mistakes of those who go before us. College experience became a part of my history, as I emerged into what was to be a journey through the community which was shaped in part by James Nickerson and the bold others who coordinated one of the largest peaceful demonstrations in opposition to the Vietnam War.

The day would come when I would have the privilege to sit and listen as this great leader would share with me his perspective into why we must express our beliefs and try to help others understand the murky truth which haunts us. I marveled at how a true community leader must be strong and steadfast as the issues of hate and ignorance become an overwhelming part of our public persona. Now, many years later, as I gain insight into his world, I can truly appreciate the contributions of those who dare to question.

My perspective has matured, and I can now see clearly what was invisible to me as a young veteran without a true grasp of his experience. I have come full circle from not knowing to gaining a glimpse into the truth. I see now, that after many more failed foreign policy decisions, we still stumble as lives in other lands are disrupted in the name of what some call freedom. I still wonder what it is all about.

Mankato State College President James Nickerson, now an informed and insightful elder, helps us come to terms with our past and wrestle with the present. To this man, we all owe a great deal.

*John Brady is the mayor of Mankato.*


## Robert M. Browne, '56
### Former Acting Assistant Vice President for Administrative Affairs

During the period of student demonstrations, I was acting as assistant vice president for administrative affairs under Dr. Robert Hopper, vice president.

My major responsibility to the state of Minnesota and to Jim Nickerson as president of the College was to safeguard the employees and physical property. Former police chief of Mankato, Mr. Frank Korth had a key role in this safeguarding.

During the peaceful student demonstrations, a splinter group comprised of mostly blacks, had taken over Old Main on the lower campus. Frank Korth and I were patrolling the upper campus when we received a hysterical plea from the employees of the campus radio station on the fourth floor of Old Main. We responded immediately and removed these employees from the building. While in the building I decided to check the executive offices on the main floor. We found them empty and secure. The cafeteria and business office had been broken into, and some furnishing had been damaged. The intruders were milling about in the hallway near the main entrance and had armed themselves with broken pool cues, rocks, pieces of concrete and pieces of chain as weapons. They were calling out threats to Chief Korth and me. It was at this time that I requested Chief Korth to summon the police.

Blue Earth County Sheriff LaRoy Wiebold arrived on the scene and joined us, and the three of us left the building through the main entrance. On the way out, one of the intruders threw a fairly large piece of concrete, striking Sheriff Wiebold on the shoulder. The police then arrived and drove the intruders from the building.

There were many other problems with this same student group, but this was the major incident during the war demonstrations.

*Robert Browne lives in Mankato, Minnesota.*

*Harold D. Burch*
*Professor Emeritus of Curriculum and Instruction*

Today, a trip down Second Street in Mankato at midday on any Wednesday reveals a peaceful demonstration against the war in Iraq. The group that gathers in the little park across from the Post Office on Wednesdays is more comfortable with prayers for peace than with hurling taunts or bombs at the noonday traffic.

My family and I moved to Mankato in September 1969. The student protests had started in Mankato as well as in other parts of the world.

The previous academic year, 1968-1969, as well as the summer of 1969, I was fulfilling a residency at the University of Kansas in Lawrence.

We were not new to the efforts of those who protested the Vietnam War. From 1966 to 1968, I was teaching at Kellogg Community College in Battle Creek, Michigan, when young people from the Job Corp Center in a nearby town marched toward Battle Creek. Authorities finally stopped the march against President Johnson, his policies and the federal offices and facilities in Michigan. A number of such events greatly increased for me the importance of civil and human rights.

In Lawrence, we lived in an apartment on a hill a couple miles south of the campus. Living directly above us that year was another graduate student and his wife. Their little girl was about the age of our oldest daughter, and they were best of friends. In addition to being a student, Tom was a stringer for *Time* magazine. Some of his reporting resulted in rocks being thrown through his family's living room window. Later, a student was killed, and sit-ins led to tear gas being used in several campus buildings.

There was tear gas at Mankato State, too. And there were bomb threats. I never took part in the marches, but I empathized with those who did. The day of the march to the bridge, I was in the Twin Cities area visiting schools. On the way back, I stopped at Erickson's gas station in St. Peter, a favorite faculty spot for refueling state vehicles. Lois Mussett stopped (she must have been headed for a night class) and said Highway 169 was blocked and we should take Highway 22 back to campus.

During spring quarter, 1970, the campus began to close down several weeks early. Students were given the option of no more attendance and still end the quarter with passing grades. The majority of students in the College of Education elected to remain in their assigned schools and complete the full period of student teaching.

There were many other memories, but time has erased many of them. But it now occurs to me that the struggles of so many for civil rights and human rights and peace were a major influence for me as I endeavored to write a dissertation based on the notion that "love in action" could be a viable force in the pursuit of education.

*Harold Burch lives in Mankato, Minnesota.*


**Inella Burns**

*The following account is an excerpt from* A Family Chronicle *by Bert E. Burns, former chair of the Department of Geography. Burns died in 1997, but his family graciously offered his personal journal entries about the campus protests.*

*May 9, 1972 Tuesday*

Nixon revealed last night his decision to move the Viet Cong baselines to keep materials of war out. He consulted no one in Congress—just went ahead. So we've had quite a day. The new Law Enforcement Center was bombed during the night and badly damaged. Old Main was evacuated from 10:00 to 12:00 p.m. I came home with my slides and maps again for safekeeping.

This afternoon 2,000 or more students, some picked up at high school, milled about and finally closed the highways. The confrontation came at the Century Club. The Highway Patrol decided upon 5:20 p.m. as the zero hour for clearing, though the marchers had agreed to leave at 6:00. So they came in with the tear gas, the night sticks, the hard hats and all and got it cleared in half an hour or so. Several injuries, two still in the hospital but "nothing serious."

The faculty Senate is sending two people to Washington to present the situation to the Minnesota Congressmen. There may be caravans of students going also. There is where they may make an impact – not here.

Mankato is thoroughly uptight. "They" assume the bombing was done by the students, though it is doubtful. Traffic was slowed or stopped far to the west and solidly to St. Peter – a three-hour delay, of course. Some said there were lines back to Truman, which I doubt. Luckily, no one was hurt. It's so futile, so frustrating. People fume over that but do nothing about the miserable war. Except for the kids, nothing happens. If they try "representative government" there is no apparent change – the President doesn't have to consult Congress, it seems. If they try violence, they are condemned and rightly so, but they do get some attention.

President Nickerson is right in there – cool, energetic, trying to represent all groups fairly. He earns his money, believe me. Everyone is afraid of tomorrow.

*May 10, 1972 Wednesday*

Things went reasonably well today in Mankato. Someone blew up a National Guard truck during the night, unfortunately. Another bomb scare in Old Main this afternoon – I told Marie, our secretary, to stay home the rest of the day and came home myself to work on my slides of England for my evening mini-course. Most of the class was there, but the sound of a crowd kept drifting in and we left early.

I went to the mid-day rally. An interesting thing to observe. One group of student protesters got all excited and took over the "podium" for ten minutes or so and turned off most of the assemblage with their obscene talk and brassy demands of the president. He answered them firmly and clearly and kept his dignity.

The Gustavus kids arrived with their president who pledged a check to pay for busses to Washington. That's where the decisions must be made. The country seems to support Nixon heavily. At last! We're going to win the war! That we are the aggressors doesn't seem to enter their heads. They're too busy being mad at the college kids.

Ours had their student march. There were some clever leaders among them asking to keep their heads cool. But a splinter group broke off and headed for the highways. Traffic was rerouted and no harm done – just lots of inconvenience. H. Roger Smith was active and vocal and spoke strongly but sensibly, urging them to talk to service clubs, church groups, etc. and in words they would understand and accept. But that didn't get on the T.V. cut – only the early inciting part. H. Roger was on the radio and will be a most unpopular man amongst the townsfolk. But without him, there may have been real trouble. He sort of became the leader in a leader-less mob which could go any direction. He, Bert Davenport, and George Stoops were faculty marshals, as well as Abbas Kessel.

The University of Minnesota went berserk and the National Guard is out. There will be tragedy in this again, one fears. Why must the public require violence before it will accede to change! Every derned revolution has been that way.

*May 12, 1972 Friday (3:20 a.m.)*

Can't sleep so may as well tie in yesterday's happenings. Morning rain suggested smaller crowds. Department chairmen meeting to discuss a system of grading for those who may now wish to drop out. Seems cumbersome and complex to me, but I was out-voted. Home to learn that the strikers took over and cleared out Old Main shortly after I left. "Security" called for help and the police were called. Guess there were stones thrown and windows broken but no damage to the interior. I had removed maps and weather instruments from the corridors Wednesday night, but I don't know if we had even closed the doors to the classrooms or the cartography lab. Called Marie and she said she thought they had only cleared the building. Bert Davenport said the grad students locked some doors and went on with their work. The police cleared the mob out, so all lights are on and the doors are locked and I hope we open for business tomorrow.

Saw Nickerson at the Inn Towne tonight and he said he rather thought the Old Main incident was the climax. There was an evening meeting of townsfolk and students on the mall tonight. Don't know if anything concrete came or not.

Bert Davenport said only a few went to Old Main. Perhaps that was fortunate because the veterans' groups are said to be organized with guns and weapons for the next student invasion. (Surely not!!!) Davenport helped keep the major share up on the mall. Good thing there are people like him on the staff to mingle with and give some direction to that mixed-up bunch. Any number of the stay-at-home staff are bitterly critical of such people. They think they're leading the kids on and inciting them – don't realize how they are helping to keep the action calmed down and directed.

Bert and H. Roger got them away from Front and Main Wednesday night – where trouble with the townsfolk was imminent – by planting a keg or two of beer up on the Newman Center parking lot. Those were the crowd noises he heard during mini-course class.

*May 12, 1972 Friday*

Still Friday! It has been a long day! Didn't sleep well for one reason or another. A 9:00 a.m. faculty meeting sorted things out a little. Nickerson reviewed the situation and Charlie Mundale explained the grading system to be adopted so students can't leave early with their credit fully earned. A bedlam of questions, naturally, but we can manage. One or two objected and Charlie "s'plained" to them just how serious the situation is, how near tragedy we are as students and townsfolk polarize, and how necessary it is to try to keep the middle moderate out of the rough-house camp. A killing or two here at Mankato could set off the entire nation just as did Kent State. As is, most are reasonable – probably not more than 300 are the uncontrollables. But the others would join on in an instant if there were a cause.

Charlie didn't say that – he used a runaway western stagecoach term and "us" trying to capture the lead horse to ride him to quiet – and not knowing if we can do it! He got a rousing prolonged burst of applause that showed the faculty to be strongly behind him.

Thus I spent the day running down photo negatives for a mural for a Mankato, Kansas celebration and a department meeting in the early afternoon. And didn't those wretched kids take over Old Main at 2 o'clock in the middle of it. They're up there now for the night. Courteous and all – told the ladies not to be frightened – they're just staying for the weekend, dogs and all. Hope it stays that way. This is the middle non-civil disobedience group, but those damned little splinters can always break out.

*May 25, 1972*

The big threatened rally based around the appearance of one of the Chicago Seven and two others of similar ilk and which had the town all but cowering – drew 250. They marched down to Kato Engineering to talk about war contracts, which is, of course, reasonable to do.

Incidentally, Nixon seems to be doing well in Moscow and now that the public clamor (student clamor, for the most part) is dying down – which he depends upon, knowing human nature as he does – things are going reasonably well in Vietnam, we're told. The Southern regulars are getting their butts whomped, that's what! But we pound and pound with our bombing and no one quite hears the paddles as they swat.

*Inella Burns lives in Mankato, Minnesota.*

### Verona "Ronnie" Devine Burton
### Professor Emerita of Biology

Back in the 1960s, there were some students with an attitude toward college to which I had never been exposed before. During WW II, I remember young men being drafted in the middle of their college lives. I thought this was a mistake. After the war, I campaigned for the draft to be postponed until after graduation. The idea was adopted.

During the 1960s, I remember being in the college auditorium with some other faculty proctoring some final exams. I saw a student open the exam book, turn to the last page, pick up the answer sheet and run down the page marking an answer for each question. As long as he was in college, he was safe from the draft.

I remember seeing an ad in a Philadelphia newspaper seeking to hire college-appearing young people for organizing campus demonstrations.

I remember bomb threats, evacuations and demonstrations. It was a difficult time to teach. Until then, most students had their classes as a top priority and campus life was a friendly, safe experience.

*Verona Burton lives in Mankato, Minnesota.*


**G. Merf Cansler**
***Professor Emeritus of Psychology***

I agreed to share my reflections about those troublesome and anxious times on the Mankato State College campus during the Vietnam War because I thought a compendium of different perceptions of the events could serve as an impetus for future research. I thought it would be a simple task. However, after writing, editing and rewriting several times, I am beginning all over again. It has been a gut-wrenching and emotional experience. Long-buried memories of past experiences which had penetrated the depth of my psyche surfaced to a conscious level. This seemingly simple project forced me to question why, as a professor, I had unduly emphasized rational problem-solving approaches to living while not acknowledging and accepting the centrality of emotion in our beliefs, myths, symbols, rituals, ceremonies and traditions of our society. Inadvertently, my perceptual rigidity led me to focus on the negative aspects of emotion, hostility and anger, but not on the creative aspects of emotions.

The anxiety and anguish the Vietnam War caused penetrated into every nook and cranny of this nation – on campuses and in our homes. The deep emotion expressed in the bumper sticker and chant, "Hell no, I will not go," emotionally affected our two sons who graduated from colleges and universities in 1967 and 1969. As a veteran of three years in the Army Air Corps during World War II, I tried to be helpful and supportive of any decisions they would make to resolve their internal conflicts. (I could write a book about one son's struggles with Selective Service boards and the unstinting assistance of Pastor Donald Bond, Professor Clarence Perisho, American Friends Society, U.S. Senator Walter Mondale and Vice President Hubert Humphrey and their efforts to help him achieve conscientious objector status and assignment for alternative service. Another book could be written about the harassment and accusations hurled at our second son for being a "draft dodger" because of a football injury. It would be most humorous. Medical doctors in Minnesota finally convinced military authorities in Texas, after a zillion dollars in telephone calls, that his injury was real, not feigned. This personal vignette does not encompass the scope and depth of the shared emotions we experienced, only the subtlety and delicacy of them.)

I make no claim of expertise in mob psychology, but I believe my observations of people functioning in mobs may serve as a base for evaluating mob behavior in Mankato in the early 1970s. Some of the mobs I have observed are:

- The angry clash between labor union members and "scabs" at a steel plant in Kansas City, 1940. Cars were over-turned, burned, and people were bludgeoned with clubs and seriously injured. (I don't recall whether anyone was killed, but I vividly remember that my teenage cousin and I did not pick up or fill out employment forms. Instead, we ran away like scared rabbits!)
- Thousands of aircraft employees panicked during an 11 p.m. shift change when they discovered a blackout of San Diego, 1942. People were crushed, and some were seriously injured as they rushed to the overpass of the parking lots. (As an observer on the periphery, I wondered how they would find their cars in the dark and what they would do if they found them — sit there or turn on the lights and be bombed by imaginary Japanese airplanes. Also, I wondered why plant managers did not notify employees of the blackout, hold them, keep the mammoth doors closed and avoid exposing that large aircraft factory to the enemy?)
- Panty raids of 5,000 students at University of Missouri, Stephens College and Christian College in Columbia, Missouri, 1950. There were personal injuries and considerable property damage.
- Mobs marching and protesting in Mankato, Minnesota, early 1970.

The mobs I observed in the 1940s were transient, whereas the mobs here in the 1970s continued for several days but did not erupt like a Mount Vesuvius.

I assume other contributors to this compendium have mentioned and may have discussed various events that occurred in the 1970s. I shall mention some of the major events without describing them or attributing emotions to them. We are aware that even descriptive words like a television camera cannot accurately and completely capture the moods or tone of an event at a given moment. Because of its restricted focus, the television camera, for example, cannot and does not accurately include much of the geographic setting and certainly not the psychological climate or atmosphere of the event being filmed.

A reader may judge whether any of the following events evoke or arouse intense emotions of anger, fear, joy or sadness: the bombing of the Law Center; the bombing at the National Guard Building; the blocking of traffic at strategic intersections of the city; masses of students marching downtown; masses of students gathered downtown and on the campus mall; bomb threats on campus; disrupting and closing classes; occupation and takeover of Old Main; holding the president and his wife captive in Old Main.

These are only words on a page devoid of feelings. On the other hand, imagine yourself being directly involved in one of these events. Would you be able to avoid responding emotionally? Probably not.

This brief background or information, valuable as it is, does not provide a basis for understanding why these mob activities did not result in serious personal injuries, much property damage and deaths.

I attribute the containment and prevention of volatile and destructive behavior to the collegial and collaborative leadership style of Dr. James Nickerson. He was not an authoritarian nor a crafty and duplicitous Machiavellian. His style was open and authentic. It seems to me, he demonstrated a sense of detachment with concern for objectivity and a sharp focus on problem solving. He addressed students and faculty on conflict resolution and had a psychologist and sociologist present lectures related to conflict. I thought his frequent faculty and staff meetings kept them informed, reassured and their anxiety diminished. I have little information about the frequency of meetings with Police Chief Charles Alexander, Fire Chief Ray Erlandson, City Manager William Bassett, and William "Corky" Finney, a black student liaison with the police department and the Black Student Union. (Finney recently retired as police chief of St. Paul).

I think it was remarkable that through the collaborative efforts of these community leaders, anger, fear, anxiety and confusion were not allowed to escalate into hostility of blaming, belittling and berating others. Of course, there were faculty, staff and townspeople who did not know about or appreciate the president's collaborative style of leadership. They saw him as the "hippie" president who aided and abetted students to "raise hell." They thought he should get tough and "expel that whole damn bunch of hippies."

Professors Abbas Kessel and H. Roger Smith played significant roles in preventing the outburst of hostility from becoming rage. Pastor Donald Bond opened the doors of the First Congregational Church for discussions that greatly reduced tensions.

Pete Seeger, a folksinger, spoke to a mass of students on the mall, sang a song or two and then invited them to attend the concert in the Otto Arena. They followed in reverent, hushed silence. That silence, calmness and serenity is beyond my ability to describe. (I wish another person who attended that meeting on the mall and walked to the arena would corroborate my memory of this silence. In the vernacular of some youth today: "It was awesome.")

Of all of the events listed, none seemed to have more potential for ending in serious injury and death than the planned rescue of the president and his wife from Old Main where students were thought to be holding them captive after the takeover of that administration building. A group of inordinately angry citizens with clubs was planning to attack those "hippies" and "niggers" and to free the hostages. I don't know the size of the group nor what prevented the attack from occurring. I did not know then nor now whether the public's perception that President Nickerson and his wife were captives was correct or whether the president was there attempting to ameliorate and dampen the anxiety and hostility of the students. I can only deduce that collaborative efforts prevented an incident from occurring like the one in Montgomery, Alabama in 1965 – on a lesser scale, of course. (Anger and rage ignore state lines.)

In conclusion and for the record, I continued with my classes, taking attendance and expecting students to meet course requirements during this stressful period. I did not cancel classes for students to attend mob meetings on the mall. In fact, I discouraged attendance at such meetings, explaining that they did not expand knowledge of the subject matter we were studying, and, furthermore, that the high decibel level and the incendiary nature of the speeches exacerbate feelings of anxiety and hostility rather than enhance feelings of calmness and serenity. The drop-out rate was minimal and course completion superb. (I write that with a sense of pride because we had cooperatively detached ourselves, but not without concern, and had transcended the cacophony of the social-psychological climate that would have heightened our anxiety, not reduced it. President Nickerson had done that same thing but on larger scale, with his collegial and collaborative leadership.)

*G. Merf Cansler lives in Mankato, Minnesota.*


### Benjamin Carey

I was the district foreman and in charge of maintaining the upkeep of the state highways in Maintenance District 7A. This included Mankato and North Mankato.

My memory tells me that Gov. Wendell Anderson made a statement that when the students at the University of Minnesota in the Twin Cities acted up in that area, he had said he didn't blame them – in other words, the blocking of roads or whatever else they had done up there earlier that year in protest of the Vietnam situation. This may have triggered the protests down here in Mankato.

The students took over Old Main on Fifth Street in Mankato and blocked many of our state highways for three to four days during daylight hours. People were very upset this entire period. The State Patrol was in charge of trying to keep these highways open. As I recall, the local police or Blue Earth County and Nicollet County did not get included in the situation, because it was the state highways on which the students would lie right down to block all traffic.

They were down on the intersection of Front and Main streets blocking Township Highway 14 late one afternoon, when a motorcycle ran over one or two people.

Another area that was a big problem was on Township Highway 60 by the present YMCA down the ramp on to Mankato's South Front Street. The students were up above on the Township Highway 169 northbound. My highway crew was waiting to go down the ramp, but there was a group of students lying on the down ramp. While they were in line waiting, a group of men got out of a bus from the Windom area that was behind the state vehicle. They made the statement that "no bunch of rascals is stopping us from getting to the Twins baseball game." They dragged the students by the legs and also by the hair, boys and girls both, and waved on the bus and state truck and others to South Front Street.

In that same area, my personal friend Richard Kozitza had a Derby Gas Station where the present Burger King restaurant now stands. He was out of business for three or more days when the Red Cross came in and used the station for caring for injuries the students were receiving from encounters with motorists. One day, a student came in and said, "Mother, I need a bandage on my finger." When Mr. Kozitza heard that, he said, "I'll bandage it for you." He then ousted the Red Cross operation when he knew the son of a worker was one of the protesters.

Also in this period of students blocking roads, the law enforcement center was badly damaged by an explosion of some kind.

*Benjamin Carey lives in Mankato, Minnesota.*

### Florence Cobb
### *Professor Emerita of Physical Education*

Can you imagine arriving by plane from the Twin Cities and landing in Mankato on the upper campus of Mankato State College? That was 1968, and James Nickerson was president.

My husband, Robert Cobb, had been hired to replace the chairman of the Health Science Department at the College. He assured me in moving to Mankato we were filling a needed presence. In a relatively short time, we were in place – teaching, networking, parenting and getting to know the college and community.

This was a time of national unrest – protesting the war – racial conflict and academic dilemma. My family was involved as parents, educators and community servers. I sensed and experienced the support of the James Nickerson administration at Mankato State College. He stepped forward to provide an expressive arena for students, activating college staff and community leaders to support expressive space and dialogue for students.

He identified the new Mankato State College racial demographics with the increase of African-American students dealing with social change, academic expectation and accomplishment. Nationally recognized leaders came to campus to speak and network with students and staff. The Minority Group Studies Center was established. An African-American and a Native American house were located on campus, thus providing a needed secure gathering place for each group to confront social and political agendas. Many of these students were first-generation college attendants who were motivated by the Civil Rights movement. Dr. Nickerson was approachable, not afraid of dialogue with students. He smoked a pipe. He stood tall. He was a good listener, and he played music!

His administration promoted the establishment of the "Chair of Ideas." This provided the college and community with a selected person, placed on campus, on an intense platform addressing current issues and solutions. This chair was filled by verbal dialogues until James Tanner, Nita Nickerson and I (all three recently exposed to the craft of tai chi) convinced the administration to select tai chi master and dancer Al Huong.

Al brought connective energy and harmony to the campus, teaching tai chi, dance and choreography to students, staff and community groups. Long will I remember the massive farewell party we hosted for him in the student union ballroom.

Nita (as we called her), the wife of James Nickerson, brought her craft of yoga to the Mankato community. She, too, was student-focused. I remember my daughter's graduation class at Wilson Campus School accepting no one else but Nita Nickerson as their commencement speaker.

James Nickerson, as president of Mankato State College, exuded energies that transcend the tentacles and define the legacies of Minnesota State University, Mankato, and institutions of Higher Education.

*Florence Cobb lives in Burnsville, Minnesota.*

**Cathy Collier**

*Printed with permission and submitted by Scott Hagebak with the following note: "Among the many things that I collected from that time period, I ended up with a journal of Cathy Collier's that was written for a class that spring. I think these three day entries best describe what happened surrounding the infamous bridge incident."*

*May 8, 1972*

Tonight, we listened to President Nixon's speech in which he declared his decision to mine the harbor at Haiphong and cut off supplies from China. The reaction of thousands will be seen tomorrow if the same rage and alarm that many of us feel is mirrored across the country.

By 10 p.m., we had 60 or more working on leaflets and signs at the Peace Coalition Office. Following phone calls and a trip to the town council meeting to round up more people, we numbered almost 200 when the meeting for strategy began at midnight at the Union. I called Roy Lashway, the Union director, to let him know that the Union would not be closing tonight, he said OK. Working until 4 a.m. on things needed for the rally, we felt the horrible strain of emergency. The whole night was full of working together, experiences and noting the dedication we had missed before.

*May 9, 1972*

Today's rally was extraordinary! The speakers were great and convincing. I'm sure the school and the state know we are serious.

We started the march down past Mankato High, calling to the students to come join us. Next we went through the streets of downtown and on to our destination at the intersection of Front and Main. Here, we rallied and gained spectators. When our crowd had grown, we divided into three groups, one to block the North Star Bridge, one to block the old bridge and 169 and one to stay at the intersection cutting off traffic between Mankato and North Mankato.

While at the intersection, I heard lots of different attitudes from townspeople and from our group. Father Rivers was very much for our cause and said "... I don't like marching any more than you do, but the war has reached a peak of moral and political absurdity." These talks went on for hours and, at the same time, walkie-talkie messages came in of what was going on at our other blockades. The city manager arrived and said we looked like a "panty raid."

As the day went on and tempers rose, a cement truck, business men and some housewives tried to run us over to break the blockade. By 5 p.m., two friends had been hit by cars and President Nickerson arrived, asking us what we were planning to do. Zeke and Toby explained about the decision to leave at 6 p.m. As time grew closer, the Nicollet County sheriff appeared on the bridge along with Nickerson. We could see cars and trucks backed up for miles. We heard on the radio that the sheriff's deadline was 5:20 p.m. Nickerson came back once more to the intersection and pleaded with us to call the people back before trouble began.

I suppose we all decided that we couldn't interfere as we watched the tear gas explode. We let the ambulances through and prepared first aid equipment. At 6 p.m. the police left, and after we came back together, we marched back to campus.

When we came back to the ballroom, we were angry and upset about the confrontation on the bridge. As the night progressed, there were bomb threats and tales of vigilante groups forming to show us that the community wouldn't stand for our tactics – everyone must have had some feelings of fear and anger.

The Union fed us, and the band Pepperfog was in town from Minneapolis and played, and we watched ourselves on the news. Following our student meetings, about 50 of us met with Faculty Senate members and the Student Senate VIPs. Such a ridiculous debate, it was full of heat and tension with everyone arguing their methods of ending the war or reaching Nixon. When we left, I felt sick inside at the faculty members' rudeness and their hate for Mitchell Goodman. They actually felt that he was the cause of every protest we have had. We gave them solid answers to their questions, but they hardly listened.

*May 10, 1972*

Today's rally was the best ever. Our numbers have really grown, almost 5,000 sat on the mall to listen. Students from Gustavus marched to Mankato and joined us. Zeke asked Bob McNamara from WCCO why he had only covered the violent aspect of yesterday. Many issues came out from the speakers such as the crimes and sexual assaults on Vietnam women, the black students' concern for Walter Reed being dismissed from his job, Eber Hampton speaking on the prejudice of this institution, faculty members pleading with us to keep the march peaceful, arguments between Goodman, Mundahl, Lofy and Hess about the war and the same personal hassles they went into last night. There was lots of concern and frustration in deciding which way was best to show our antiwar concern. It came down to two choices, going back to the bridge or to march silently with the faculty and the majority of participants. I decided quickly that there was little to gain by going back to the bridge, so we went with the silent march.

We marched two by two downtown, up Front Street to Madison Avenue and up to Madison East. We expected to rally there and decide if we would go back to the bridge, but the marshals, mostly faculty, herded us like cattle on back to campus. There were a lot of upset people. It was a peaceful march, as we wanted, but with little free choice at all.

Tonight, I realized that 5,000 people and sore feet just don't make headlines. I wonder if anyone noticed at all.

*Cathy Collier lives in Mankato, Minnesota.*

**David Cowan '70**
**Facilities Services Manager, Minnesota State University, Mankato**

*Excerpted from transcripts of a discussion hosted by Jim Nickerson in 2005.*

I came [to MSC] in fall 1966 and graduated in the spring of '70, and then Kent G. Alm, who was the academic vice president, hired me as administrative assistant. And so I was there, certainly, in 1972 when we had the bridge takeover – not as a student, but as an administrator, spy. I'm not sure how that went down.

In my judgment, some of this stuff started in '68-'69, and it really didn't start to take off until we had more and more veterans showing up in our classrooms... They were walking around with their fatigues. They were talking the anti-war talk. I'm speaking about the veterans group that brought John Kerry here – Vietnam Veterans Against the War. Just their presence added a dimension that I don't think was there in '66, because there was very little talk about it then. Very little talk about it, I think, in '67. I think the momentum was there when they started coming back. They were starting to get out of their service in Vietnam. They were starting to show up at our campus. I'm sure at other campuses. It was talking to them and having them tell us that they were using tanks and running over babies and then throwing money out to the parents for the death of the kid. The drugs, all the rest of it, and ... if you knew a vet and he had war stories, if you get the war stories out of them, many of them didn't talk. But it was enough that they felt abused, and [on] a college campus, a number of them started to surface as leaders in the anti-war movement. And I was, at that time, on the fringe. We had our SDS (Students for a Democratic Society). We had other groups like that, but they didn't have the punch that a veteran had who could talk. And even if they didn't talk, their presence was there.

... [When John] Kerry came to campus and others came to campus in '69, '68 in the spring (we always did things in the spring), I think the demonstrations started to build in the spring of '69 certainly '70, the spring of '70, when we had a lot of stuff going on in the spring of '70. Absolutely. Kent State. Cambodian invasion. That's when Nixon, of course, went [to] Cambodia ... and ... the kids dying at Kent State, and they weren't always students, and the two kids dying at Jackson State, the black college. Then all hell broke loose.

I think we let some people go home early if the professor allowed. I can't remember what you called that at the time, but … it was a unique way to allow some people to escape, because we had demonstrations, as you recall, in and out of hallways. People were marching up and down hallways chanting all kinds of stuff.

Then [they were] trying to get people out of their classrooms, and it was a beautiful spring, we had great weather and great weather, a beautiful spring, and they had all these liquor stores with the cheapest wine available. Nice time to get a tan. Who knows what the reasons were that people went out, but Lord knows we had at least two demonstrations a week, it seemed. The size doesn't match what happened in '72, two years later, but clearly the spring of '70 was a benchmark. In my opinion, if the veterans weren't there, I don't think it would have picked up quite as fast. …

[We had] conscientious faculty and others who acted as marshals for these demonstrations … We had some political science instructors. … We had Vets Against the War [members as] marshals (and there were some big guys). They knew what they were doing …

[The police] made a few mistakes. They left a few liquor stores open around march routes. In '70, they learned to shut those down in '72, but people picked up on that because, as they would be marching by, people would run into Ma Farrell's liquor store and buy bottles of wine because you had to keep your spirits up as you literally, figuratively, but then they figured that if the demonstration is going by a liquor store on Front Street or something, you closed that. That was before the marchers hit, and they could never figure out why are they closed? It's in the middle of the afternoon. What's going on?

But in the beginning, they didn't do that. So there was always the risk where you have the alcohol, you have the wonderful music. People always had a guitar strumming around. We did have some people that were on the college payroll later in '72 and others that were Chair of Ideas holders.

Seventy-two was kind of, to me, the end of it. It was really '69 and '70 where it began. …

[Mitchell Goodman] was our Chair of Ideas guy. I remember when we went to the Faculty Senate. This was a big thing that Larry Spencer, Student Senate president at the time, and we pushed for the creation of a Chair of Ideas. Mitch Goodman may have been the first or the second. He was the first. We didn't know it was Mitch Goodman at the time because nobody knew the thing would be created.

One of the things that sticks out in my mind is that Faculty Senate meeting (and I can't remember the chairman of the Faculty Senate at the time. It wasn't

Charles Mundale; that was later), but anyway, people were marching around the Faculty Senate, somehow they got in[to] the room, and one guy had the kid on his shoulders, and he had the American flag upside down or in distress.

I don't know if it was Mickey Croce who then tried to grab it or slug the guy (he didn't slug the kid). I don't know if there were any assault charges, but we got the Chair of Ideas. The Chair of Ideas was created. How did we know we would end up with Mitchell Goodman who then served to be heightened and elevate the next round, the 1972 round, and Goodman was a provocateur, big time. ...

... How many of those thousands at any one of those demonstrations would we say that 40 percent were out there, as Mark [Halvorson] says, for the sun and frolic and 60 percent for the ideals? I think it was more like 70 percent were out for the good weather and 30 percent for the ideals. After all, you did get to skip class, and if the professor said anything, you'd just say, "Hey, I'm a principled person, and I'm against this terrible war." And what is he or she as a professor going to say?

... When the tear-gas canisters were being shot from the Nicollet County Sheriff's Department and they were shot into the crowd, I was there on the side with a City Council man, Dave Cummiskey at the time ... the canisters came into the crowd. The wind was blowing in such a way that some of the kids, even though the canisters were hot, picked them up and threw them back at the deputy sheriffs, Nicollet County, Wiebold's area. Not Blue Earth County.

Blue Earth County was good; Nicollet County was bad. That's the way we thought. The river separated us. They got a little whiff of their own stuff, as I recall, and then tear gas was everyplace. The wind changed, and everybody got it. End of protest.

*David Cowan lives in Mankato, Minnesota.*


### Lorraine Cuddy

I have lived in the Mankato area my whole life. My memories as a resident here during the Vietnam era were not so much ones of bomb threats and protest marches but rather of dealing with the daily routines and demands of raising two teenage girls.

I also was a volunteer aid at the hospital. I don't recall any disturbances there by the Mankato State College protesters.

My two daughters attended Catholic High School in Mankato. I believe they were somewhat sheltered from the Vietnam unrest that was going on at the Mankato State campus. Even though they went to an all-girls school, they did have close friends who went to war. They were not fearful of the college protesters. In fact, I think, sometimes, they wondered why they acted the way they did.

I guess, perhaps, if I had had a son who might have had to go to war, things for me would have been different. I would have had a much greater stake in the war and the protests.

My husband had a plumbing and heating business during those years. The Vietnam War did affect his ability to keep a stable workforce. We had a hard time keeping men. They were either being drafted or volunteering for the war.

I guess, as a whole, my family was mostly untouched by the Vietnam War and the unrest at Mankato State College.

I do believe President Nickerson did a good job in keeping things under control. I think if you give kids half a chance, they will work with you. They also need a chance to spread their wings.

*Lorraine Cuddy lives in Mankato, Minnesota.*


### Mary Dooley
### Professor Emerita of Geography

At the time students took over Old Main, we (the Geography Department) were having our regular department meeting on the third floor. It was interrupted by a knock on the door, and a student stepped in, saying, "Maybe you would like to leave the building; the students are taking over." And we left.

A little later, our graduate students presented us with a plan for the defense of the building. Each faculty member was assigned a military rank, the reverse of their academic rank.

*Ranks and assignments:*
Cpl. Anderson: distribution of propaganda media and materials.
Recon: upper campus.
Lt. Col. Apitz: paper blockade of the stairwells.
Pfc. Burns: security.
Pfc. Colakovic: interrogation and torture of prisoners.
Pvt. Davenport: diversionary tactics in the faculty lounge, and biological warfare.
Lt. Dooley: fix coffee and other womanly duties.
Capt. Girard: gas warfare.
Pvt. Goff: grunt.
Maj. Jack: land mines.

Maj. Morgan: stadia rod lancers.
Lt. Col. Rankin: suicide squad.
Col. Roscoe: signal corps (carrier pigeons).
Sgt. Smith: publicity.
Capt. Stoops: peace talks.
Maj. Thurston: logistics, weapons.

*All personnel will be issued:*
1000 paper clips and four rubber bands
10 rock samples
1 type "A" Exacto knife
1 stadia rod
1 copy of "The Geographical Survey" (for spit wads)
1 T-square
1 old wall map of Anglo-Egyptian Sudan
1 chili pepper suicide pill

FIGHT TO THE DEATH, OR UNTIL THE COFFEE RUNS OUT!!!
REMEMBER, PAX VOBISCUM, CAVEAT EMPTOR, SIT LUS ET LUS
FUIT, AND ALL THAT OTHER COLLEGE STUFF.

Otherwise, we had a whole series of bomb scares. Each office was supplied with forms for reporting details about the threats. We were asked to fill in such things as what were the exact words of a threat, and the specific building or area identified, was the caller male or female, describe the voice, etc. At first, buildings were evacuated until the area could be searched. Later, the police just searched the buildings as they were evacuated. As they came around, we usually responded: "Ho, hum, another bomb scare?" At one point, it was suggested that buildings were evacuated only if it was raining outside.

There were a few incidents of tear gas in buildings. I remember holding classes on upper campus with the traces of tear gas in the air. Having class under those circumstances was voluntary; my own response was to hold class, but student attendance was voluntary.

Finally, students were given the option of dropping out and taking the grade they had at the time. A few students took advantage of that option.

I do not know this, but it was reported that Police Chief Charles Alexander had his personnel out in force but not in uniform. The students usually recognized the cops, but the effect was more of protection rather than threat.

*Mary Dooley lives in Mankato, Minnesota.*

## *Dean Doyscher '69*

I was an anti-war activist on the campus during 1969 and 1970. I was an Army veteran and a senior majoring in urban studies. Since those years, I have gone on to success as a city planner, executive director of a regional planning commission and now president of my own development company.

I helped close down MSC in 1970 while working on my master's degree in urban studies. When the school closed, I was trying to complete all of the required credits. I took an urban planning job in Maine in the summer of 1970, and I have worked in that field since that time. I am pleased to submit a couple of memories. I have many, but thought these two may be unique.

I was drafted into the Army in September 1966. I served two years and re-enrolled at Mankato State in the fall of 1968.

I began a degree program in urban studies at the age of 23. Prior to the Army, my interest was in political science.

When I re-enrolled at Mankato State, I was totally opposed to the U.S. policy in South Vietnam. I had followed the political decision-making by President Lyndon Johnson and his Cabinet, and I thought the policy of the U.S. had no merit and was totally dishonest.

I had many friends who had died in the war, and I had many Army friends who served and came back with terrible stories. I listened and read everything I could about war in South Vietnam, afraid that I would be the next victim. Luckily, I did not have to serve in South Vietnam.

I have several memories about my anti-war activities. Since I had already served two years in the Army, I thought my credibility was a real asset to the effort. Many people were being discredited as "draft dodgers," afraid, and anti-American for not serving. I was able to overcome those accusations.

In the spring of 1970, I would meet in the evenings with "long-haired hippies" – that's what we were called – to discuss the next day's activities designed to disrupt the status quo of society. We could disrupt the college, so that was our target.

Our goal was to make authority figures question the power of government to carry out policies that were so plainly wrong, and to put the current power system under stress so that they might change.

I could not affect the White House or the Department of Defense, but I could affect Mankato State. If enough people protested widely enough, we could truly have a voice in stopping the war. We paid attention to the campus protests at the many universities, including the University of Minnesota and the University of Wisconsin. These efforts in Minneapolis and Madison gave us courage to continue.

Each morning, I would go to upper campus and enter a classroom building.

I would walk into any class and march to the front of the lecture hall. The bigger the class, the better.

I would shock the professor by my bold entrance to the front of his class. I would just start talking, no permission needed, about the real facts about the war in South Vietnam and not the official government version.

In some classrooms, the professor would engage me in discussion and, in other classrooms, the professor would try to throw me out. In either case, I stayed for 20 to 30 minutes and argue why we should shut down Mankato State.

After 20 minutes, I would ask the students who believed in social disruption to follow me out of the classroom. I was not always successful but, many times, students got up and walked out of class.

I would repeat this exercise three or four times each day, always going to different classrooms. I was not alone in this activity and could tell that the pressure to close the college was increasing.

My second memory is toting a wooden cross from upper campus down to Mankato West High School and over to the bridge. I remember the Mankato Police Department cars and staff leading the march, clearing the traffic and being totally supportive of the students. No harassment, only genuine help in our march.

People along the way were generally supportive until we got to downtown Mankato. When we approached Pappy's Bar about 10 to 15 men came out of the bar and began yelling profanity and threatening to fight like real men. One of the lines the men yelled was to "join the Army and do your duty, you chickens." I yelled back that I had already done my duty.

The Mankato Police quickly got the men back into the bar and no fighting broke out.

*Dean Doyscher lives in Mankato, Minnesota.*


### Carl M. Egan '67, '69
### *Professor Emeritus of Construction Management*

The words that come to mind as I reflect on the administration of President James F. Nickerson are leadership and vision. When he assumed the presidency in 1966, Mankato State College, like most colleges and universities in the United States, was struggling with in loco parentis. President Nickerson boldly confronted the issue at the October 26, 1966 State of the College address by challenging the student body to "analyze the opinions of all involved with the goal of reducing the college's responsibility" and find out the answer to the question "can we pull completely out of in loco parentis?"

On that occasion, he also expressed his confidence in the near reality of university status and noted that history was on the side of MSC. In a poignant statement, Nickerson articulated what it meant to be a university and the path to achieving that status. "We are the last state, along with California, to change its colleges to universities. We must do it with grace and validity and when we feel we have the strength."

Nickerson further noted that an elevation in status necessitated an attitude that higher education is a search for understanding rather than just vocational or professional training.

President Nickerson was true to the pledge he made to students (and faculty) in the early days of his tenure. He said, "My office is open to your representatives and spokesmen. It is a court of final appeal for violated rights and injustices. My office shall be a channel of getting and giving information." Nickerson pledged: "1) to listen and read carefully everything you have to say; 2) to inform you of changes being made and explain them; 3) to join in building a significant college or university."

My personal experiences are a testimony to the commitment President Nickerson made to the college and to the community at large. From the beginning, he set a tone for his administration that facilitated healthy dialogue. One demonstration of this was his endorsement of a faculty-student retreat held in February 1967. I had the opportunity to participate in that event along with 16 other students and 10 faculty members. We had candid discussions on stress, faculty and student apathy, class attendance and seating chart requirements, dorm restrictions, the grading system and city/college relations. At the closing session, four resolutions were adopted. The first, in my view, was most significant and underscored one of his leadership traits: "We support and encourage President Nickerson in his efforts to open up channels of communication on campus."

Early in 1967, a fellow student (Larry Anderson) and I approached the president about a new idea for marketing the college by enlisting students as ambassadors. We requested his blessing and support for a group of student volunteers that would spread the word about positive aspects of the College, its departments and faculty. President Nickerson immediately gave his endorsement and subsequently a group called Students for Mankato State was established. More than 30 students became involved in a student-operated speakers' bureau and presentations were given at numerous high schools and civic organizations in Minnesota and Iowa. Clearly, the president was confident in his position and willingly created an environment for students to grow and develop their own leadership skills.

During the summer of 1967, as chairman of the Student Senate's Housing

Committee, I worked with Associate Dean of Students Marie Bruce on a proposal to revise rules governing students living in dormitories. Our discussions focused on in loco parentis issues such as liberalizing the evening deadline for check-in and the elimination of the housemother position. These and other recommendations were submitted to President Nickerson that fall. All were ultimately accepted and phased in over the next two years.

There is no doubt in my mind that because of his gifted leadership, combined with a management style that fostered the development of people, not product lines, President Nickerson was able to effectively lead MSC through the trying times of the Vietnam era. While other colleges and universities across the nation, including the University of Minnesota, were struggling with violent demonstrations, massive destruction of property and, in one instance, the death of innocent students, relative peace prevailed at MSC and in the Mankato area. Noteworthy was the absence of a National Guard contingent to maintain order. President Nickerson kept the lines of communication open at the college and elicited views representing a broad spectrum of the community. These attributes, plus the empathy he showed for others, were the cornerstones of his presidency.

---

It was during the administration of President Nickerson that the Mankato State College Veterans Club was established. The number of veterans on campus was increasing, and many of them felt the existing student groups and predominant veterans' organizations were either ill-prepared or unwilling to address the issues they faced in adjusting to academic and civilian life. By and large, these nontraditional students were men and women returning from active duty in either the Cold War or the Vietnam War and were older than other students and even some of their professors.

On Feb. 23, 1967, fellow student Neils Neilson and I held an organizational meeting in room D-63 of the Science and Arts Building on the lower campus. More than 70 veterans were in attendance. The need for an alliance and a place to gather became readily apparent. Many felt out of touch with the political actions and demonstrations playing out on campus. Most simply wanted to get back a semblance of normal life and get on with their education and careers. Shortly thereafter, the Veterans Club was organized and meetings were convened every Tuesday at 9:30 p.m. at the American Legion post in Mankato. Elections were held and a constitution adopted.

The Veterans Club quickly grew to become the largest student organization at MSC. Its constitution contributed to that growth and foretold much about the stabilizing force the club would contribute to MSC during the Vietnam years. This had as much to do with what was not allowed by the constitution as it did with what was articulated to be the primary mission of the organization. It was to be a social and service club, not a political one. The endorsement or sponsorship of political parties or candidates seeking positions on the Student Senate or in the public arena was prohibited. The mission was to assist veterans with problems of adjustment to academic life and help solve issues of financial need and assistance. One of the articles of the constitution addressed the subject of discrimination. This was uppermost on the minds of many because they, or their fellow comrades in military service, had been denied membership in other veterans' organizations. The article stated, "Membership will not be based on race, creed, religion, sex or national origin."

The club meeting place off campus provided a nonthreatening environment where veterans could freely discuss personal or general concerns. True to its mission, the Veterans Club never engaged in demonstrations on or off campus. It did not take a position on the Vietnam War. It did, however, provide a place of refuge, support, understanding and healing for returning veterans to Mankato State College. It also was a strong advocate for extended and increased educational benefits for veterans.

What followed can only be described as a truly historic event. During the period from May 30 to June 1, 1968, Mankato State College hosted the charter convention that concluded with the founding of the National Federation of Collegiate Veterans (later names were National Association of Collegiate Veterans and National Association of Concerned Veterans). The fact this took place at MSC only 15 months after the organizational meeting leading to the establishment of the Veterans Club speaks volumes about the administration led by President Nickerson. It exemplified a culture he created, which embraced visionary thinking and bold action.

When I first approached Dr. Merlin Duncan, vice president for administration, in the fall of 1967 about the idea of a convention at MSC of veterans clubs for the purpose of forming a national collegiate veterans' organization, he responded with both a challenge and a pledge. He wanted reasonable assurance that there was significant interest in an entirely new and unique veterans organization and that if MSC held the event, delegates would come. On the condition there was evidence to support both interest and commitment, he assured me MSC would make available the facilities and administrators as deemed appropriate for a host institution.

I assumed the role of convention chairman and set in motion a major campaign to inform colleges and universities across the United States about the proposed convention. The Veterans Club selected "Administration and Alternative Policy Positions on Vietnam" as the convention theme, in keeping with its own policy of not taking a position on the war.

The convention was an overwhelming success. It was attended by 160 delegates, both men and women, representing veterans clubs from 33 colleges and universities. They came from 15 states as far away as Connecticut, New

York, Georgia, Texas and Colorado. Interest had been expressed by clubs at more than 80 colleges in 31 states, but some were unable to come. A wide range of views on Vietnam were presented via film ("Inside North Vietnam") and speakers (Gen. Maxwell Taylor, former ambassador to Vietnam; Mr. Girvan Griffith, U.S. Department of State; Mr. Douglas Head, attorney general of the state of Minnesota). These sessions were open to the public and were attended by many students, faculty members and townspeople. On the final day of the convention, the voting delegates ratified a national constitution in which Article II cited three objectives: 1) to help enrich and fulfill a student veteran's college career; 2) to encourage good fellowship amongst all student veterans; 3) to assist in any way possible within the limits of this association to make a student veteran's college life successful. It also included a nondiscrimination article identical to that of the MSC Veterans Club constitution. Officers were elected that day, and I had the honor of being selected president.

It was the birth of a new organization committed to helping veterans (approximately 675,000 were attending U.S. colleges and universities at the time) make the difficult transition from soldier to student, and secure the rights and benefits they deserved while pursuing their education. Mankato State College opened its doors to veterans across the nation at a time of heightening uneasiness and contention over the Vietnam War. These veterans were graciously welcomed to the College and community in addresses given by President Nickerson, Mankato Mayor Clifford Adams and Mankato Area Chamber of Commerce President Lee Snilsberg. It was also during this historic occasion – the first national convention of college veterans clubs – that President Nickerson chose to dedicate the new Memorial Library at Mankato State College.

*Carl Egan lives in Tuscaloosa, Alabama.*

### Claire E. Faust
**Emeritus Vice President of Administrative Services**

Of all the events that happened during the turbulent time of student protests of the war in Vietnam, the one that stands out in my memory was the march. This event had far-reaching implications even beyond the campus. Students, faculty members, officials and local citizens were affected then, and it still weighs heavily on the minds of those who were marchers or witnesses. My personal reaction at the time ran the complete range of emotions even though I had witnessed student rallies, protest signs, teach-ins, bomb threats and demonstrations for days.

On the fateful day of the march, I heard the participants long before I saw them on the mall between the library and the student union. This was the usual assembly place for all of the rallies that had taken place for days. I was in my office on the third floor of Armstrong Hall over-looking the mall. That morning, I was struck by the fact that this rally was taking place much earlier in the day than the others had taken place. Students were milling around some young men equipped with bullhorns. I could see students emptying out of the classroom buildings, the library and the student union. They were also streaming across the parking lots all headed to the point of the rally. Clearly this gathering had been planned and publicized well. The noise was growing in volume with loud recorded music and shouting, screaming students who obviously were making a lark out of the occasion. They were being herded together in some marching order and various commands were shouted through the bullhorns.

My first reaction: This is stupidity, they will miss their classes. Then I thought this will, in effect, shut down the College.

Then I had flashes of pity – how many of these people know what they are doing? Surely, they are simply taking a vacation from their classes and are being led astray by a few very vocal activists.

Many of the students were carrying protest signs with various inscriptions. Some were chanting various slogans, which often contained obscene words. Then I saw the ultimate disrespect. There were some in the lead of the group dragging a U.S. flag on the street. This made me very angry. I had taught young people all of my life to respect their country's flag. What right did this rabble have to show this gross disrespect?

Then the thought came to me – where are our police? Why are they not here to break up the mob? Then I saw one lone police car stopping oncoming traffic, but clearly they were not stopping the mob. In effect, they were aiding it.

As they marched by, I tried to recognize the faces of people I might know. All were strange to me. Then I thought – these people are the sons and daughters of good Midwestern parents who worked hard to fulfill their expectations for their children. All of them wanted their children to be good, productive, law-abiding citizens. They certainly would be ashamed if they knew their children were a part of this rabble wouldn't they?

What will be the response of the college administration? The faculty? The downtown citizenry? Will the news media cover this and give us the same notoriety that some other institutions have?

What motivated these young people to commit anarchy? What are the implications for me, a father, a loyal citizen, a teacher? What does the future hold for all of us? Will the future hold repeated incidents of this kind? Will the students ever feel compelled to rebel against authority for cause in the future?

After the crowd passed by and the mall became quiet, I turned to my desk with a heavy heart.

---

And now, after 30 years, I still feel sad when I think of that day and all that happened in our city. I hope and pray that students will never feel compelled to repeat this action.

*Claire Faust lives in Mankato, Minnesota.*

### Curt Fisher

*Based on a discussion hosted by Jim Nickerson on June 15, 2005.*

My wife Debbie and I came to Mankato in 1966, a critical time during the Vietnam War. Experiencing life on campus during this era was interesting. The feelings I had as a student were very mixed. I often wondered how the impact of being drafted would affect my friends and Debbie (my girlfriend at the time). I recall that the threat of being drafted was frightening and also remember the energy of the marches against the war.

What made the war most real and personal to me was the pipe bomb that was set off in Mankato's Law Enforcement Center. It was active destruction in a new building and its symbolism was very powerful. It really seemed to impact everybody in some way – though it touched us all differently.

Participating in the demonstrations was completely counter to how we had had been taught to live. I recall the demonstrations as really dramatic statements by the students because the culture was so different then – especially so in the area of discipline. We had strict rules on campus and guidelines that we adhered to. We followed the restrictions set by the College (getting the ladies back to the dorms before the housemothers locked the doors!). We also feared and respected the police and the law but the demonstrations were kindled by intense feelings of the environment we were living in.

The bridge demonstration was particularly memorable for me. It took place on a beautiful day – we all walked down the hill and gathered on the corner of Main and Front Streets. The crowd grew and moved onto the bridge, which caused a ruckus. I wondered initially whether or not I should be doing this – but the strong feelings of the war, its negative impacts on people seemed to support the energy growing with each demonstration. I remember feeling more solemn about our actions, about the group, about the symbolism and meaning of it all. I then realized it was a good thing.

*Curt Fisher lives in Mankato, Minnesota*


**Don Glines**

*The Awakening of a Community 1968-1973*

The Vietnam conflict, civil rights and women's rights movements, hippies and flower people, growth of free school, and more openness in male-female relationships were among the many cultural divisions that challenged people throughout the nation in the 1960s and early 1970s. Mankato, Minnesota, was one among the multitude of communities affected by these protests and changes in attitude. It no longer remained an isolated village 2,000 miles north of Dallas and 40 miles east of Sleepy Eye, but instead became a vibrant part of a changing society.

In Mankato, this awakening was led by Mankato State College (now Minnesota State University, Mankato) or, more specifically, by the open-minded, student- and community-centered, innovative college administration of President James Nickerson, Vice Presidents Kent Alm and Merlin Duncan, and Assistant Vice President Brendan McDonald. This group hired faculty open to new ideas and encouraged students not only to help restructure the College, but to become involved in improving the community, state and nation.

As a result, the students wanted to be heard and made it known through such activities as taking control of the administration building and closing the bridge over the Minnesota River until the city agreed to remove the monument celebrating where a mob had hung 38 Sioux Indians, even though Mahkato (Blue Earth) was originally Sioux land. They marched on the local school board in an attempt to preserve and expand the changes in education begun by the famous Wilson Campus School at MSC — hailed by the National Observer as the most innovative, experimental public school in America — yes, in little old "Mahkato" where all the area legislators were members of the conservative party.

During this time period, MSC also organized an experimental liberal arts program as a college-within-the-College, created the first master's degree in experiential education approved by the North Central Association of Colleges and Schools, and awarded a bachelor's degree in open learning through the

Studios for Educational Alternatives (the S.E.A. program).

My beginning 1968 role in all this was two-fold: to help develop these new efforts, but primarily to overhaul the campus laboratory facility to make it the "gooniest" school in America, turning it from extremely traditional schooling into a new learning model for the state and the nation. Starting with conventional K-12 students, Wilson expanded to include prebirth, infant, preschool and senior citizen, and the bachelor's and master's degree programs. The Christian Science Monitor described it as a smorgasbord school of 600 learners in a cradle-to-grave learning environment open 12 months a year for all who volunteered.

To achieve these goals simultaneously, I called state legislators – in a meeting with them – "a bunch of rinky-dinks." This, of course, made the headlines of all the newspapers and almost resulted in my firing. However, we persisted, and not only was the Wilson program approved and supported, but our efforts eventually led to five major changes in the state education codes. The state Department of Education was forced to give its blessing to all the Wilson experiments, including our refusal to use state tests, grades, grade point averages, required courses and other such badges of segregation.

The effort also forced President Nickerson to meet with 700 protesting parents, but once the program was understood, for those families who volunteered, it resulted in full acceptance of the desire for change in the traditional school structure and a waiting list for people wanting to enroll in this "gooney" program. Wilson students went throughout the community serving as role models for change. They had optional attendance and freedom to be most everywhere in town during the conventional school-day period.

Teachers had the same freedom and caused uproar when they first were seen at Michael's Restaurant for lunch, perhaps with a martini. When horrors were raised, the bank president, CEO of the mill, Chamber of Commerce president and department store manager, as examples, were asked why they were there at the same time away from their work, also with a martini. That ended the protest against Wilson staff and students being in the community during school time. The youth were a cross-section of Mankato: outstanding individuals going to university, those planning for non-college careers, physically handicapped students (as Wilson was the only one-floor school in Mankato) and unwed mothers and youth on probation, for Wilson accepted these latter learners who were rejected by the traditional schools.

Wilson students took college classes; even first-graders earned real college credits in such courses as Gymnastics I. High school age students earned as in such college offerings as home economics and chemistry. Wilson was the first school in the state to have a computer terminal, and thus helped advance the potential for a "technological revolution" in education.

The K-12 youth joined with college students to influence the community further by becoming involved with the City Council, volunteering in the local hospitals and retirement centers, calling attention to the need to improve conditions at the nearby state mental hospital and lobbying the Curriculum Committee and the Faculty Senate to approve more flexible programs.

Wilson and MSC were featured in numerous national publications during this era. Visitors came from almost all 50 states, Mexico, Canada and several other countries. Even the chairman of the State Senate Education Committee, a conservative originally opposed to the Wilson/MSC changes, eventually enrolled his son at Wilson. Canadian provinces related to the pioneering efforts in Mankato.

Much of the enthusiasm for involvement was based on the concept that if Wilson could successfully change, that could cause the College of Education to change, leading to further College change, and eventually to a new awakening in Mankato. In the education nation full of copycats, Wilson and MSC were originals.

This was a true Camelot period for Wilson and MSC, one that helped change the Mankato community forever. Unfortunately, a change in the leadership with the retirement of Dr. Nickerson, my departure from Wilson, a new dean of education who allowed change but would not lead, and budget cuts resulting in the closure of all laboratory schools were factors in a step back. However, the era of 1968 to 1973 changed forever the future of an awakened community, one no longer just 40 miles east of Sleepy Eye, but a major influence as a city in the state through the efforts and outcomes of the reformed institution.

All of the Wilson and related MSC histories, research, programs, evaluations of this awakening period are now documented in the archives (Wilson Campus School Archives and the Don Glines Archives) of Minnesota State University, Mankato, located on campus in Memorial Library. These prove the existence of that era of Mankato known as Camelot.

*Don Glines lives in Sacramento, California.*

### Arnoldus Gruter
### Former artist-in-residence, Mankato State College

*My Thoughts on the 1960s and 1970s at Mankato State College*

Perhaps there would have been a time that I would have looked back at the late 1960s and early 1970s with undivided satisfaction. Yes, I did my job as artist-in-residence, hired by the administration headed by Drs. James Nickerson and Kent Alm. Yes, I had a fine studio space at the student union. Yes, I had an average of 143 visitors daily who visited that studio, saw my work and asked countless questions. Yes, Mankato State College, as it was called then, at the time was arguably more a university then it has ever been since. When the Rotterdam Philharmonic and the Moscow State Orchestra played and the famous musical "Hair" was performed on campus directly from Broadway and when I created two major sculptures, "Waves" and "Chthonic," in addition to lecturing at other departments on the arts, Allen Ginsberg recited his poem "Howl" a few yards from the fountain to an audience of hundreds of students who visited my studio afterwards.

But it was also a time when students about to be drafted to serve and die in Vietnam asked me for advice – me, the immigrant from Canada and the Netherlands before that. Many of their fathers were World War II veterans and my liberators, their patriotic fervor deeply ingrained in their minds and expecting their sons to act likewise. The sons who would not submit to the American arrogance amply exhibited in Vietnam and add their number to the thousands who perished for nothing in that far-off country, their memory kept alive in Washington's Vietnam War Memorial, its shiny surface reflecting the faces of those who sent them there.

But my heart aches when I realize how little we learned from that experience as witnessed by the current events in Iraq. How their memory is besmirched by the stupidity, illegality and lies of our current federal government. More than 2,000 of our best have died trying to force our system on people whose customs predate Christ, our system which is still developing and incomplete. But time goes on, and perhaps one should not dwell too much on the past. But a little nostalgia should be forgiven of a person who marveled years ago at the sight of young people reacting against a bankrupt policy with genuine mass demonstrations, even if one disagrees with some of its aspects.

*Arnoldus Gruter lives in Mankato, Minnesota.*

### Paul Hadley

*The Chamber's Response to Student Unrest*

The Mankato Chamber of Commerce became aware of the "student unrest" by reading about it in the *Mankato Free Press.* The threat of a mass demonstration in the business district forced the Chamber's Board of Directors to meet in an emergency situation. Quite frankly, most of the board, after calling many of the businesses they represented, felt that the police, College guard and the sheriff's deputies could handle the few that most expected would take part. No one thought the number of participants that actually showed up to protest would be in such numbers. The total crowd, at the time of its peak, appeared to be over 6,000.

During the time between the newspaper story and the actual demonstration, the board met once. The consensus of men and women on the board at the time was that the Chamber should stay out of the situation and let the College administration, the police and the sheriff handle any situation that might arise.

Once the students started down the hill toward town, the Chamber office was inundated with phone calls from merchants, bar keepers and restaurant managers demanding we do something to keep the students from wrecking their places of business, driving away their customers and disrupting the traffic flow in and through the community. The phones at the Chamber office were literally tied up with in-coming calls long before the first students crossed Broad Street.

Chamber President Al Hassinger called another emergency board meeting. From that meeting, Dave Boyce, Chuck Fisher and Walter Johnson, all downtown merchants, were joined by Mark Halverson (head of the liberal People's Party) in a Student Relations Task Force. Their charge was to meet with representatives of the students, learn what their complaints against the merchants were and recommend to the board action to meet the situation.

The Student Relations Task Force named Dave Boyce chair, with me (executive vice president of the Chamber) as co-chair. Walter Johnson was the only one of the task force who was able to join me when the ordered meeting with the student leaders took place. Their first meeting took place during the actual closure of the bridges.

That joint meeting was set up by Jim Nickerson, president of the College, on a phone call from me. It was set up on the next day's afternoon after the establishment of the task force. Time was of the essence, and that is the reason others on the task force did not attend the meeting.

President Nickerson arranged for the meeting space in a room on the ground floor of the student union. I don't remember who attended representing the faculty. As no non-student appeared ready to chair the meeting, I assumed the chair position. Under the guidelines given me by the Chamber Board on the recommendations of the Student Relations Task Force, I opened the meeting outlining the hoped-for results (in effect, the purpose of the meeting and its protocol):

1. Anyone attending the meeting was to raise a hand if they wished to speak.
2. Speakers should make every reasonable effort to confine their remarks to the question under discussion.

3. The chair also gave a brief assurance that the business community appreciated the presence of the students on the campus of the College and the considerable business they gave the merchants of the community. A poll, taken within the past 48 hours by the business community, found not one complaint against the students. The same poll also found no one aware that the students had a gripe against the businesses of Mankato.

4. The Mankato business community was there for the specific purpose of learning what the students of the College perceived as problems with the business community. The Chamber was not saying that there were no problems, just that they were not aware of them and were there to learn what they were and how we could address them in an orderly fashion.

5. We hoped to prioritize the problems on the basis of the students' concerns, so we could know where the first efforts were needed to resolve the difficulties.

6. We also hoped that a plan of action would develop out of that meeting to handle the matter of greatest concern to the students first.

7. All attending were invited to participate in an orderly manner so that proper and accurate records of the meeting, the comments made and suggestions considered, could be maintained.

The points were prioritized by the students by secret ballots, counted by the students. They are placed here in that priority. I decided to concentrate the meeting on the number-one priority with a nod to their number-three priorities. They were, in reality, almost one and the same. Out of the discussion that followed, the students and business community agreed to set up a forum for the express purpose of giving the Mankato State College students an opportunity to tell the residents and business community whatever was on their mind.

The business community was to obtain the place for the forum, fill it with business and townspeople and assure an orderly meeting and presentations.

The students were to select and provide spokespersons for each major area of concern. I asked that they establish reasonable time constraints for each speaker and that they agree to take questions from the audience for not more than whatever time they felt would assure the meeting moving right along to give all speakers an attentive audience.

One student raised the question, "Who is going to lead the meeting, control the timing and content of the presentations?"

Everyone looked to me, so I suggested the business community provide the meeting's leadership, that it be a business person to which their leadership would agree.

The media raised the question, "What will the leadership do if one or more students attempt to take over the meeting or in some manner disrupt it?"

The question was directed to me. I suggested the students provide their own crowd-control persons with authority to remove disruptive individuals from the premises.

This suggestion was promptly vetoed by the student representatives.

I next suggested the Mankato Police have officers on hand.

This was also shot down promptly by the students.

"Perhaps the College police could do the job," was promptly met by another unanimous student veto.

"If we cannot provide properly trained personnel to control attempted violence, I suppose we will have to turn off the lights and invite everyone to leave the building. We have to provide for the public's safety and that includes the students as well," I said.

The discussion went no further, and everyone agreed that some form of regular meetings like the one just held must be established as soon as was practical.

The next evening's paper, *The Free Press*, hit the streets with the headline, "Hadley Says He'll Turn Out the Lights on the Students," or something like it. When I reported to work the next day, my phones rang almost steadily until we took them off the hook. The calls were almost all in favor of hanging me from the nearest tree at the least and firing him promptly and suing him for all he had at the worst.

My board held another meeting and only the cool heads from the Chamber's board chairman, vice chairman and other officers saved me and my job. They also saved the Chamber's good reputation. *The Free Press* refused to make a retraction or even balance out of the story with the full story of the meeting.

The meeting itself was held in the Methodist church downtown. More than 300 merchants, professional persons, faculty, college administration, city government and services personnel attended, and over half of those present were interested citizens. There were no police, sheriff's personnel or college security people present. The students were given ample opportunity to rant and rave if they wanted to. Surprisingly, they were orderly, presented their concerns and often suggested solutions, one of which has been met from time to time by the merchants: "Give the students a special discount to show merchant appreciation for the students' presence in our community."

However, a lot of good came directly from the meetings we set up with the students, the city's management and the business community:

1. A building inspection of all rental properties was instituted, forcing all landlords to bring their properties up to code or risk losing them.
2. The city ultimately licensed all rental units, making renting substandard

residences or apartments against the law.

3. We managed to persuade the worst landlord we had in town at the time to leave the community, taking with him the terrors of poor housing he foisted off on hapless students for several years.

4. The Chamber established a Better Business Bureau and officially managed it in full accordance with the national franchise.

5. Jim Nickerson and his successors were always asked to become members of the Chamber's board. Not all of them became members, but they were invited. Jim and his immediate successor were active and helpful board members.

6. A student was always on the Chamber's board with full voting rights and as a full board member.

7. The Chamber successfully introduced a new program of student housing by persuading homeowners with spare bedrooms to rent to students of all three institutions of higher learning in our town. Over 700 homes offered over 1,000 students housing for the next six to 10 years. Some are still doing it.

Like most North Mankato residents, my wife and I had difficulty getting home the night the bridges were closed by the students. One little sideline on the bridge closures, members of the Teamsters Union called the Chamber and offered to "open the bridges with a fleet of horn blowing, overpowering and threatening eighteen-wheeler trucks." A second offer came from the color guards of both the American Legion and Veterans of Foreign Wars organizations in our city to put a firing squad on the bridges with live ammunition to clear the bridges. Needless to say, both offers were rejected. The organizations were thanked but informed that we had everything under control with the State Police, local police and sheriff's officers. We didn't want another Kent State incident here.

In summary, no business lost more than a day of business. No damage to property in the downtown area occurred. No one was killed or injured in the downtown area. The incident left no scars and quickly passed into history and became memories of only a few old men and women who still reside in the beautiful little city.

---

Why did the student uprising take place when it did? What were its causes and was it unique to the campus and community within which it resided?

In answering the first question, opinion and comments made by students in their "presentations to the community" made it clear that a number of irritations and damning practices of the citizens of Mankato were the last straw.

The answer to the first question, why did they choose the time they did for their protest demonstration, lies in the fact that, at the time, the nation had already reached a crossroad in its political stance, that the press and the public it served had decided the war was, indeed, "unlawful," the result of the evil influence of the "military industrial complex." It didn't matter which political party was in the White House, the war was wrong in its origins, the nation's military leadership unstable and inapt in conducting it, and the politicians running both the war and the nation needed to be forced out of office. It was thought that the United States must cut and run, get out of the quagmire of Vietnam and bring the "criminal military" home. These dramatic changes in the political environment succeeded in stirring up all potential soldiers, the young men and many women, forcing them to choose between abandoning their homeland by escaping to Canada that obligingly greeted them with open arms and amnesty and going to college, whether prepared or wanting to or not. Most chose the latter; they escaped to the relative safety of the colleges and universities of all the states.

The WW II veterans' massive drive to get educated had wound down. Most schools had seen a dramatic drop in their enrollments. Buildings, staff and administrations that had expanded for the unexpected influx of veterans now had to downsize. They adjusted to the lower volume of students desiring a college education. Vietnam and the draft that manned our military forces forced a lot of people to rethink their future plans. To avoid the draft, they went to college while a few brave and misdirected souls chose Canadian citizenship as their way to avoid the draft. The sudden increase in the freshmen classes on almost every campus in the nation created the huge increase in enrollments. Housing them became a nightmare in almost every smaller community where a college or university dominated the economy.

The traditional "town and gown" attitude on the part of the community and educational institution prevented any meaningful dialogue in too many  towns and institutions. Mankato and North Mankato were no exceptions. The business community had never conducted any means of testing the student population's actual economic impact on the two cities. There were no established lines of communication between the business community and college administration. And there was no forum for handling college or college-student gripes and complaints for the institution or for businesses.

The third facet of the timing of the uprising started with the sexual revolution of the 1960s. The young men and women of the uprising were the little brothers and sisters of those who initiated the 1960s "live for today and yourself" and "if it feels good, do it" leadership. They were the first children whose families had raised them with no one home during business hours. The schools made no adjustments nor did anything to fill the vacuum of unsupervised time of millions of children across the country. Television, sex and/or drugs filled in for mom in far too many homes. The Internet, today's "babysitter" for the children of working parents, was only a tool of the military and a toy of the largest universities at the time.

The children who were in school, who revolted on those fateful few days, had already expressed their disdain for rules and regulations in a thousand ways. Dormitories and student housing were starting to allow co-ed living (alternate floors of boys and girls in Gage, alternate wings in McElroy, co-ed living experiment in Searing). Young men and women shared bathrooms, study rooms and even bedrooms at times in housing that used to be rigidly sex-separated.

The nation was becoming a permissive society, allowing living together in ways that were highly untraditional. Tolerance became far more than an ideal to achieve. It became a demanded norm by law, political pressure, political correctness and personal desires. Value systems of long standing in families were torn up in the collegiate environment and replaced with the 1960s' free love, anti-war, anti-establishment norms. Personal responsibility was diminished to the point of nonexistence in almost every walk of life.

The business community suspected and openly stated that the students were opposing the war in Vietnam. They hadn't a clue as to any other concern of the students. Those business people who had gone to college at some time in their lives still thought the rules they lived by in their years were firmly in place. They thought the students were motivated by the same things that had motivated them, the desire to get ahead, to get a good job and to raise a family in a manner better than their own had been.

The business community was wrong. The students had few, if any, of the same moral values the businessmen and women had grown up with. The students had no respect for their elders, their parents, or those in authority. Rules meant little or nothing to them. They obeyed only where the penalty for disobeying was great enough to outweigh their efforts to achieve happiness and harmony with the universe.

Their gripes startled the business community. Not one person attending the meetings from the business community had even an inkling of the problems the students faced. Those problems are listed below.

1. Mankato State College student housing was far short of what was needed.

2. Over half of what student housing existed would never be acceptable in any community in this country where the students were appreciated by the business community.

3. Over 25 percent of student housing, especially for men, was so bad it was, in fact, inhabitable. They listed the rental properties' shortcomings as:

A. Inadequate to nonexistent heating systems, forcing use of electric heaters.

B. Toilet facilities so filthy that even a dog would refuse to use them.

C. The absence of hot water and intermittent cold water service. The absence of a water heater or one that leaked so badly it was actually disconnected from a water source.

D. The presence of broken, inoperable and damaged windows; doors that would not close or could not be locked for privacy, making cold drafts inevitable. Repairs had to be made by students using their own money for materials.

E. Damaged and/or poorly repaired stairs, hand rails and treads, making many stairways into obstacle courses.

F. The absence of or unusable fire escapes from upper floors and almost every room above the main floor.

G. Electrical wiring that demanded extension cords resulted in overloaded circuits and forced some students to put a penny under the fuse to keep the power available. In this same vein, many students often had to pay the electric bill to get the power restored as the landlord had not paid it as originally agreed.

H. Inadequate hall and stair lighting made it necessary for some students to use flashlights of their own.

I. Damaged walls, many with holes right through them to the next room; little or no insulation to retain what little heat there was; and other structural shortcomings made living in some apartments a nightmare.

J. Plumbing that consistently backed up and overflowed.

K. No visible repairs and maintenance were made during the school year. What little was done was often done during the summer months when no tenants were in the building. Most such repairs were "Band-Aids" and not healing repairs.

L. The student housing office apparently did not investigate the conditions of the community-supplied housing they listed. The housing was not recommended.

M. The city had no means of enforcing the needed repairs and updating of utilities in the rental properties or was unwilling to do so. There was no recourse for the students to obtain any relief from the impositions placed on them by their landlords.

4. There was no apparent understanding of the economic blessings the

students brought to the community on the part of the government or business community.

5.      There was no source for correction, restitution or reimbursement for the students when they felt they had been had by some business in the community. Their problems were never addressed by anyone of the campus or in the business community.

6.      The attitude of sales persons, service persons and others who interfaced with students from the business community was definitely antagonistic, simplistically rude and most unsatisfactory.

7.      They felt that only a few eating places had any appreciation for their business.

8.      The only reason the students put up with it was a fear the College might expel them for bothering the faculty and/or administration with their problems. This fear was viewed universally as the main reason for the long-apparent silence.

9.      The war itself was never the problem; it was the fear of having to participate in the war that drove them to use the only tool available to them to express their fear in a manner the public would not accept. They knew most WW II vets, the persons calling the political shots, would never honor their refusal to serve. So the war became "unlawful," and the press agreed with them. Those students who spoke up about the unlawful war were far more concerned about being forced to join the conflict than they were about its lawfulness.

In summary, the student unrest was a full three years in coming. Kent State and the other major campuses around the country were already history when it finally came to Mankato. The students' housing situation should have been a source of community-wide shame. No citizen of the two cities, Mankato and North Mankato, would ever have permitted their own children to live in the degrading, unsafe and generally miserable housing a few greedy landlords controlled.

No aspiring city with any self-pride would have allowed such student housing to exist. It took outside developers to see the legitimate market for housing. Folks who had never heard of Mankato flocked to the city and new campus area. The developers had plans for apartment housing, specifically designed to accommodate two, three and even four students. The new complexes kept their costs down, recognizing the impossibility of students paying more than reasonable rent. They also recognized that a fully equipped kitchen was almost as important as the bathroom to the potential tenant.

These factors came together during that year, and came to a head a week before the demonstrations erupted.

Most cities with a large college or university did have safety rules and regulations at the time to protect student renters. Only progressively growing cities had building codes that automatically took care of most of the students' complaints. Many had tough rental-unit codes in addition, forcing landlords to maintain their properties properly and to keep all services up to code.

So, there is a distinct possibility that the old-school and old-money leadership of the area had stifled both cities' efforts to install a housing inspection and building code designed to protect all who had homes there, whether rented or not. There were very few that had specific rental housing codes.

Therefore, it is possible Mankato's experience is unique and that is why.

*Paul Hadley lives in North Mankato, Minnesota.*


### Scott P. Hagebak, '73
### Operations Director, Centennial Student Union, Minnesota State University, Mankato

*Excerpted from transcripts of a discussion hosted by Jim Nickerson on June 24, 2005.*

[In reflecting on Abbas Kessel,] the interesting thing as a student that didn't know him, but looked at him from a distance, [I thought] he was a very unusual person in so many ways. First of all, we had very few international faculty on this campus at that point in time. So he was unusual in that respect. Then, if you just looked on the surface, he wore suits that were tailored very oddly. He bought them at the thrift shop … He drove an old Mercedes Benz. I don't know how old it was, but … diesel that just kept running along. His house was painted black. His entire yard was a garden. There was no grass, which, of course, in Mankato was unheard of. Most of the plants were wild plants, and so, therefore, it was just weeds. Then this person would get up in front of 2,000 students at a rally and as everybody is getting wired and fired and ready to protest and he's the voice of reason that's telling all the students, "Think about what you are doing. This needs to be peaceful; if you want to have this be meaningful beyond today, then you need to do it in a peaceful sense."

… I think that, in retrospect, everyone that I know from that time period realizes that the things that happened on campus were not [Jim Nickerson's] fault, and [he] and [Mr.] Alexander, the chief of police, were the two most influential people in keeping the lid on this town. So many towns were getting blown up, and the demonstrations were turning into riots. We had march after march after march, and the biggest things that happened except for the bombing of the Law Enforcement Center – which I truly believe was [done by] an outside agitator – the biggest things that we had were some bomb threats and a confrontation with the Nicollet County Sheriff's Office when we crossed into Nicollet County on the bridge incident on May 10.

He had never dealt with those kinds of situations. That's the only time that there was … any real face to face problems against the police. … It's amazing to me, looking back, that we never really had those major blowups. We never had a student arrested during all those years. …

… One of the underlying things that went through that whole time period from a student's perspective was [we were] sitting in the middle of rural America in the provinces and what effect [could] we have on what [was] going on out there? We [had] our rallies, we marched on the Post Office, we cheer and we march home, and nobody takes notice. When Nixon mined Haiphong Harbor, and it looked like we were possibly going to go to war with China, that's when the students said, "We have to do something." It really became a strategy of [asking,] "What can you do that will bring this town to an awareness? They may not like it, but an awareness. We need to disrupt their lives in a peaceful way." So we strategically sat down and said, "There are three points of entry in Mankato. At that point, a lot of the highways that exist now weren't there, and we had Front and Main intersection, we had Highway 169 across the river and we had the North Star Bridge …

By closing those three locations, there was no way to cross between Mankato and North Mankato, and [that] literally brought the town to a stop. And so that was the intent. That was the plan. The intent was that we would sit at those [places]– we marched down as a group. We tried to go through West High School and pick up as many students out of there as we could, came down to Front and Main, split into thirds, had walkie-talkie radios and kept in contact with each other and put the three groups out there. The two groups that were on the Blue Earth County side had no problems, had no issues. The one group that crossed into Nicollet [County] were the ones that faced the issues, and we got national coverage. The very next day, another demonstration took place, and everybody stood in the center of the mall and said, "We don't want to have another violent confrontation, but we have to do something. What can we do?" And Abbas [Kessel] and Don Strasser and some of the other faculty and Charlie Mundale said "We need to do something to show that we care about the war and not about violence, but we need to do it in a peaceful way."

And so it was decided to have the silent march . . . 5,000 people [were] involved, marching two by two from campus, downtown, to Madison Avenue, up Front Street to Madison East, back down Victory Drive, back around Balcerzak and winding our way back around to the campus. It was absolutely silent. The march went on – at one point I was standing on Front and Madison and the head of the line was half way up the hill and the bottom of the line hadn't come around the corner down at Front and Main yet. It was just an amazing sight and got almost no coverage. . .

*Scott Hagebak lives in Madison Lake, Minnesota.*

### Tom Hagen

Abbas Kessel was watering a large passion flower vine in a 10-gallon Red Wing crock, the last of over 20 plants that lined the street side of the uneven sidewalk passing by his gray stucco house on Fifth Street. Although he lived in frigid Minnesota, he raised these lush tropicals through dark Minnesota winters, waiting for the warm and sunny June days that would bring them into bloom. His other plant passion, Minnesota wildflowers, filled the small space between the sidewalk and his house, spilling on to the boulevard. Hepatica, trillium, Dutchman's breeches, dog-toothed violets, May apples and dozens of others spread their leaves to catch the dappled sunlight, having already bloomed in April or May. The watering can, a two-gallon one, always looked a little too big for the diminutive Kessel. Perhaps it was just the oversized tattered jacket that came down over the knuckles of his two hands that gave that impression.

"Good evening, friend," he said with a smile and a characteristic tilt of his head to one side. "I'm happy you could come. I have something new to show you."

Inside the 1930s bungalow was a surprise. The walls had been mostly removed, leaving an open space uncharacteristic of similar houses of its size and style. The walls that were not lined with bookshelves and books and been painted eggshell white to better display the works of art that changed with the seasons or with Kessel's moods. Two of the living-room walls were windows, which were once part of a front porch, but in winter, they served as a retreat for his beloved plants. The little house had settled unevenly and the tilting floor was layered with oriental rugs, one on top of the other, so as that they covered the worn or frayed or threadbare parts that each invariably sported.

On this evening I had come to see the spectacular bloom of Epiphyllum oxypetalum. Startlingly white, the seven-inch bloom filled the night air with an exotic perfume. "To attract the moth that will pollinate it," Kessel said. "It only blooms for one short night. The blossom will be gone by dawn. It's called the night-blooming cereus," Kessel beamed. "How do you like it?"

Then there was the obligatory tea served in china cups of the same design Mrs. Walter Mondale had used in the vice presidential mansion in Washington, D.C. We sat on hand-made plywood chairs, painted flat black, that Kessel had designed and made to fit his small five-foot frame. I would sit awkwardly low to the floor, with my knees up nearly under my chin. These were always joyous visits. I would come to see a new flower in bloom, a new addition to his collection of ceramics or glass, or to have supper with Ruth, his old friend from the University of Chicago days. We talked about flowers or art, but rarely about politics or the academic world in which Kessel had immersed himself. Gustav Mahler often played in the background. These were aspects of Kessel few ever got to know well.

Later, I would learn about Kessel's involvement in the tumultuous Vietnam years, and see the pictures of the demonstrations, but not from Kessel himself. Kessel was always shy about these matters. I came to feel that he would have preferred to live in a less problematic time, but that the circumstances of his moment in history demanded the energies of a thinking and feeling man to address them. Address them he did. As his life approached its close, he became more melancholy. Mahler played more and more often on the phonograph.

He didn't live to see the collapse of Soviet communism or the death of the Ayatollah in Iran or the hopeful movement of its youthful population. Then again, he didn't live to see the silliness of "pre-emptive strikes" or what he would have seen as an American administration intellectually unfit to lead. He would have written long, carefully crafted editorials on these topics had he lived longer.

What is important to remember about Kessel's life is the metaphor. Kessel was a gardener. He cared about the tender plants that sat on the floor in his house through the long, dark winters. He watered and pruned them and occasionally there would be spectacular blooms and a call. To you and to me, he would say, "Good evening, friend. I have something new to show you."

*Tom Hagen lives in North Mankato, Minnesota.*


### Mark Halverson, '73

One of my pet projects was the Kent State-Jackson State Memorial which is up on campus today. With the assistance of a couple other people, I decided it appropriate to have a memorial. Bill Marek came up with the guts of the slogan that's on there now: "Hate, war, poverty and racism are buried here." Wishful thinking but I think that kind of summarizes the reasons for the Kent State and

Jackson State shootings.

The Student Senate – it wasn't even controversial – gave us a little money to fund this and it might not have even had a ceiling on it. They might have said just go ahead and do it. I had friends, high school friends going to the university up in St. Cloud who lived across the street from a quarry which produced monuments, so I called them and asked them if they could look into getting an appropriate monument. We didn't necessarily want something that looked exactly like a tombstone but there's a lot of variety of those. Within a couple of days they called me back and said, "well, you know what, we have just the thing here. Why don't you come up and get it?" I checked out a state station wagon and took four of my friends.

We drive up to St. Cloud and we pick up this granite monument, which is actually the one that's on campus now. That thing probably weighs 500 pounds and maybe more. We put it in the back of this state station wagon and it just bottomed it out. There were no shocks on the back and the back bumper was practically dragging. So, we drive it back from St. Cloud after having a little party with our friends and we get to St. Peter.

Some of my friends were from St. Peter and we said well, we're not in a position to do anything with this monument tonight. It was late. So we pulled into the driveway of the mother of one of the friends. For some reason I'm thinking it was February, but I don't know when it was. There was some snow on the ground so we got a sled and we're just dragging this big granite marker off the rear of this Mankato State station wagon. I think the cars just said State of Minnesota in those days rather than Mankato State College. But we got this big piece of granite halfway out of a state station wagon. We all look like we're hippie thugs, of course, and the St. Peter police drive by and stop and ask us what we're doing. We say, "we're going to unload this rock and leave it here for a while," and I don't know if they were perplexed or what, but they asked no more questions and just drove on.

We unloaded the rock, barely, and with the help of the sled moved it to the back of this friend's mother's house in St. Peter. It ended up staying for a couple of years, but that's another story.

Later, when we were talking about getting that thing engraved, I told Larry Spencer and Dan Quillan where we got the rock and they reached the conclusion that it was probably a stolen rock and I couldn't disagree with that. I don't know for a fact that it was stolen, but, you know, circumstantial evidence would suggest that these guys didn't broker. I think we paid them $100 for this rock that even in those days I'm sure would have cost a lot more. Maybe they purchased it as a reject or something, but I'm pretty sure they just walked across the street one night and grabbed it.

Dan in particular thought it would be terrible if we were to use this stolen monument as the Kent State memorial. I thought, actually, that if it was stolen that would be very fitting. But they said we can't use that, we'll get another rock.

Larry was friends with Steve Babcock at the time. Of course he ran for congress not too much later than that as "the democrat republicans can trust" which was a very discouraging thing at that point and time. He gave us a couple of small rocks and we took one over to New Ulm to have it engraved and we got it back and since it had been done in winter, we just set it up against the wall in the Student Senate office. One day one of us looked at it and we saw the word "buried" was spelled wrong.

We had two of these rocks so we took the other one and got it engraved. By then it was winter again, a year later at least, and we weren't going to put it in the ground so we layed it up against the Student Senate back wall. This was when Phase II of the Student Union was being constructed and one day someone bore through that wall with a jack hammer right where that rock was sitting and broke it. So the two not-hot rocks, the two rocks that had legitimate title (I'll say as a lawyer), clear title, one was spelled wrong and one was broken.

This was by now a year and a few months after the original rock was acquired so no one felt too badly about it, they figured if it was hot there weren't going to be any ramifications from it anymore so we said ok, go ahead and use that rock. We took it over and got it engraved. We had that sitting around again for a while. There was some campus committee that was in charge of every little thing. If you wanted to put a tree out in the mall you had to go through some particular committee, the name of which escapes me. And for quite a while we were messing around with trying to get this approved and we got kind of tired of that, so one spring day, this was two years later now, almost, in early spring, a friend of mine and I, and a couple of other people, went up with some hoes and shovels and we were starting to dig a hole right adjacent to the fountain outside of the Student Union, between the Library and the Student Union to put this rock in.

I can't remember who it was, it might have been someone from the Student Union staff, came over and said "well, you can't just do this." And we said "we've messed around with this long enough and we're just going to put this rock here." But they said "well, take it back, I'll talk to someone," and they got it done in pretty short order.

It turns out the committee decided it should go where it is now, in front of Armstrong Hall because a year before Kent State, I'm guessing (I don't think I was here then), at some previous point in time, they buried a coffin there in one of their anti-war protests. So they were saying that that's where this tombstone was going to go, on top of the coffin. We had that dedicated one day during the spring of 1972 when there was already a pretty good rally on the mall and in the

Student Union. These were almost daily things there for a couple of weeks.

It was Mitchell Goodman who made the speech. I think I have a picture of him standing by the rock dedicating it. A couple of other people spoke, too, but I don't remember who. But we'd finally gotten that rock in and within a few months the Mankato's Vet Club, not to be confused with Vietnam Veterans Against the War, put up their own Vietnam memorial across the way, kitty-corner from the Kent State memorial.

For the longest time I think Mankato State was the only institution with a Kent State memorial. Kent State didn't even have one until just a few years ago so it's a pretty unique thing and I would have to be almost certain that it's the only place with both a Kent State memorial and an anti-war memorial and what is basically a pro-war memorial.

The Kent State rock took a lot more doing than one would think including a lot of physical work, some bureaucratic runaround, the irony of it being spelled wrong, and then the second rock hammered by a jack hammer when it was sitting at the wall in the Student Union. So it was just destiny that the current rock should be there.

*Mark Halverson lives in Mankato, Minnesota.*


## John Hodowanic

My memories of what happened at Mankato State as we faced our reactions to the war in Vietnam are vivid – and painful.

Every war is always hell, but a war as unpopular as Vietnam made raw feelings ever more raw – among the faculty and staff but most especially among our students. It was they, after all, who faced the possibility of being drafted into a war many could not understand, let alone support.

And they weren't alone. The faculty had its pro-war faction and an equally outspoken anti-war faction. To my knowledge, there was no count of the number of faculty members who thought the war was a necessity and those who thought it was anything but. My guess, however, is that more faculty supported the war than opposed it, though those who spoke out were few and far between.

And I think it is fair to say that the administration was also of two minds about Vietnam: those who felt it was a necessary act of patriotism and those who thought it was a travesty. But most of the faculty, and most of the administrators, kept their feelings to themselves.

That posture, too, is natural. But the spokesperson of Mankato State – its president – was in no position to take no position. His responsibilities were to the faculty, to the students, to the community, to the State College System and, ultimately, to the state and its taxpayers.

As a thoughtful human being, Jim Nickerson was seriously opposed to the carnage in Vietnam. As president of Mankato State, Jim Nickerson was required to make sure the College was doing everything in its power to be what the state expected of it – to be the best house of learning possible, including how a college should act and react to a war that caused deep divisions throughout the campus, Mankato and the United States.

Many must surely remember attending a student rally on the campus that was largely and loudly a "Hell, no! We won't go!" rejection of President Lyndon Johnson's protestations on the United States' need to persevere and win the battle for Vietnam. But I also remember those students who were in tears at the thought of those who had already died in Vietnam and the countless others who faced the same fate. The powerful anti-war speeches of Professor Abbas Kessel gave some hope and substance to those who also opposed the war.

War is always hell. It always holds our feet to the fire, whether we support it or hate it. That was the great test the Vietnam War brought to the campus of Mankato State College – to its students, faculty and administration.

*John Hodowanic lives in Wayzata, Minnesota.*

### Bryce Lindsay

Curriculum Committee Action

The time was late in the spring quarter of 1971 (or 1972). This period remains in my memory because of the sometimes-violent student unrest related to the war in Vietnam. I was a tenured professor in the departments of Elementary Education and Educational Administration. I was also a member of the Curriculum Committee. The College of Education was searching for a replacement for Education Dean John Johnson, who was retiring that year. Dr. Jerry Kuhn from the University of Iowa was visiting the campus to interview for the position. He was invited to attend a special meeting of the Curriculum Committee. I believe Dr. Kuhn got an eyeful of the action that day.

Some violence had occurred that prompted the Curriculum Committee to address the problem of keeping the campus open. Several students spoke during the course of the meeting. Many expressed concern for their safety if they were to remain on campus during this turbulent time. I remember few details of the discussion that afternoon in Old Main, but I remember the decision to keep the campus open but to allow students who feared for their safety to take the credit and grade they already earned and leave campus two weeks before the end of the term. They also had the option to request a grade of "Incomplete" to be made up sometime later. I recall that a few of my students in elementary education opted for the early out.

When I returned to Armstrong Hall after the meeting that day, I found the front doors blocked by students sitting or lying on the steps and on the apron outside the doors. I recall being irritated by this action and determined to enter the building regardless of the block. To my surprise, the students parted enough to allow me to pass.

Highway Blockage

I had attended a meeting of the Lake Crystal Elementary School faculty on this particular day as a consultant to their study of a new organizational plan. On my return home, I found the Highway 169 south entrance to Mankato blocked. I was able to reach my home in West Mankato, however, by using Highway 66, which was not yet blocked. After arriving home, I walked to the Sibley Street underpass to see what was happening and found what appeared to be an organized blockade. I didn't recognize any of the students, if that was what they were, and did not stay very long.

My Opinion

I am a veteran of World War II and not in sympathy with the protesters. I did not support this behavior and saw it as primarily an exercise of power by the organizers of the students.

*Bryce Lindsay lives in Mankato, Minnesota.*

*Carl "Chuck" Lofy*
**Professor Emeritus of Counseling & Student Personnel and former Assistant Vice President for Academic Affairs**

*Addressed directly to Jim Nickerson*

When the demonstrators took over the administration building, you and Nita rarely left your office. You both spent most of your days and even your nights (sleeping on the floor) there. Your presence and that of Chief Chuck Alexander were the stabilizing center-posts around which the action swirled. Without you two and your understanding but firm leadership, the situation would very likely have hurtled out of control. I can still picture, as I watched from the windows of Old Main, a group of marching students noticing a pile of rocks along the sidewalk in front of the building. A few picked up rocks and started to hurl them at some police officers that were nearby. I gasped, alarmed that this could result in an experience such as had recently taken place at Kent State University, in which students were shot to death in a similar confrontation.

I remember Professor Abbas Kessel, a man of peace, addressing the crowds. I recall the long meetings of the Emergency Cabinet at all hours of the day and night. I can picture the scene on the upper campus as faculty and students poured out of the classrooms to gather to hear various speakers. I recall the then artist-in-residence (whose name slips my mind at the moment) stirring the pot of rebellion. Most of all, Jim, I remember you holding the center together by your leadership, your humanity and, especially, by your compassionate and calming presence. How grateful I was then, and am now, that you were our leader.

Over those years, on several occasions when I was down or discouraged or upset, I would walk over to your office and confide in you. You would listen gently and hear me out. And then you would always give the same advice, it seemed: "Take some time; step back a bit; and don't act until you have regained you perspective." It was all so simple. And it always worked. And it worked because you modeled what you counseled, especially in those days of upset. You helped us, on every side of the encounters, to find and keep our perspective. For that reason, the entire Mankato community will always be in your debt. Thank you, dear friend and mentor, for being the man and the leader you are.

*Carl Lofy lives in Minneapolis, Minnesota.*

## Judy Mans, '60
### Emerita Director of Alumni Affairs

I graduated from Mankato State College in 1960, an elementary education major who had also been editor of The Reporter. In January 1968, my husband, Jim, was on leave from the foreign service with the goal of finishing college. The GI Bill had been reinstated for men in the military during the late 1950s. We left the only student function we ever tried to attend being met by the beanie enforcer, upper classman David Cowan. A 30-year-old father of three was not about to don a beanie.

The plan was for Jim to be a student, Judy to find a job. Placement Office Director David Hendel took me to Ed McMahan, the director of special programs, who hired me. I signed the controversial loyalty oath, bought a faculty parking permit and became assistant in federal programs, a six-month position. Two years later, Jim Nickerson came to me (I hadn't ever met the man face to face before then) and asked me to fill the position of executive assistant to the president. I told him I would be gone in three months, admitted to being a lousy typist and that I wasn't available to work after 5 p.m. on weekends. He left. A little later, he came back, and this time we agreed that I would come across the hall as long as he understood that I was leaving in a few months.

April 1, 1970, the first week of the job, the president was gone, and my assignment was to write letters to the other candidates for my job saying it had been filled. That's when I looked at the hallowed president's desk and began the pattern of JFN's and my relationship for the next three years. Sort the mail: draft responses for signature on the top file, calendar items next, then action needed, and finally informational reading. Later, the reading material would be in the personal study just off his office, and there would be a file for action taken and one labeled "limbo" for things still needing action.

"Judy, you've to learn that not taking actions is taking action," he said. In desperation, we worked out the routine of daily calendar updates in triplicate: one copy for him, one copy for Nita and one copy for me; copies of invitations attached for Nita. We were thoughtful, respectful and trusting of each other.

This was the era of Vietnam, faculty and Student Senate empowerment, black student empowerment, the Open Meeting Law, the experimental college, hints of Title IX, the formalization of "town and gown" efforts, campus expansion. We were entering the down cycle of expanded faculty and student roles. All these found their places on the weekly agenda for Cabinet meetings with the vice presidents, their assistants and the assistant to the president, Judy taking minutes. What follows are anecdotal, personal memories of these times, not necessarily accurate or in sequential order.

MSC and downtown responses to Vietnam were at odds. Guest speakers

Jane Fonda and an Army general received equally hostile receptions on campus. There was no student apathy toward the war. U.S. troops entering Cambodia, Kent State, student activists and outside agitators all converged into a Kent State avoided through tense and forced collaboration between town and gown. The closing of the Main Street Bridge and the solidarity march down Highland Hill merged here. President Nickerson encouraged faculty and staff to join students staging the march, hoping to ensure it would be the peaceful protest it turned out to be.

All this and bomb threats, too. The top shelf across from my desk was lined with notebooks labeled "Bomb Threat 1," "Bomb Threat 2," and so on up. I can't remember how many there were. I do know the reaction to the first was quite different from later responses. The first time, the Executive Committee evacuated to the Newman Center down the street and the campus closed down. Later, campus would remain open and the president's office might be headquartered in Memorial Library. The president's office staff learned how to receive the threats, record them and activate the appropriate protocol. None of the callers were ever identified.

One day, when President Nickerson was out of town, there was a note under the door threatening another bomb. What to do? Other staff moved to other offices. The decision was made for me to remain in my windowed office for the day with the office door locked. I did ask what I would do if a bomb came through the window: "Pick it up and throw it back out the window."

Mankato State was one of the first, if not the first, campuses to have a Minority Group Studies Center, a response to black student activism on campus. In my memory, I can still see the group of confident, intense black students demanding to meet their president. He negotiated with them. In turn, they occupied Old Main cafeteria. JFN spent the night on campus, offered an ultimatum, and they left. Enter Mike Fagin as director of Minority Group Studies Center. Later to be named distinguished alumni, William "Corky" Finney and Cathy Clardy Patterson benefited from JFN's restraint from vindictive disciplinary action during these times.

There may even have been a dress code. In desperation, I put on a pantsuit that Jim had given me as a Christmas gift. Didn't mean to be assertive, it's just that it was all that was left in my closet that day. My first trip through the Registrar's Office, one of the women asked if it was OK to wear such attire on the job. "I don't know. I didn't ask," I said. But then, I went back to my desk and started to feel guilty. So I cautiously entered the president's office and asked if, indeed, it was OK. "Of course it is. It looks great," JFN said. After that, lots of pantsuits appeared on campus.

Later in his career as MSC president, James F. Nickerson had grown a beard and was being accused of having been downtown barefoot. Best he could recall was that he might have worn sandals in Madsen's SuperValu. At any rate, he and Nita were heading off for a much-needed vacation. Executive Vice President Alm's parting admonition to JFN was "be sure you come back without that beard." And when he came back, the beard was gone. Not long after that, he resigned as president of Mankato State College.

––––––––––––

*Judy Mans was also one of several participants in a series of conversations throughout 2005 with Jim Nickerson and contemporaries who were invited to share memories of the period of campus unrest. The conversations took place at Jim Nickerson's residence and were recorded and transcribed for the purposes of this project. The following except is from the April 28, 2005 conversation.*

I can remember the marches. And this is the part that some things are probably fading together, but we took one seriously enough that we moved up to … the library where your Cabinet was again, and Ed McMahon was a part of the group, but he wasn't up there. The marches were starting, and I was supposed to know where everybody was. Well, I can't find Ed McMahon. Old Main is supposed to be evacuated, and so I get on the phone and started ringing every office in Old Main that I can think of. And here, Ed McMahon answers his own phone in Old Main. Well, he was thinking about leaving. And I thought, "Why are you having us worry about you?" So we got him out of there.

And so here is this long trail of people walking down the hill. It's kind of like a religious pilgrimage, and I knew it was important, but how many years later two different people, Karen Winneke was in … the Residential Life Office at the time. In probably the late '80s or early '90s, she became president of the Alumni Association, and she talked about one of her proudest moments as an employee walking with the students down the hill and how important she felt in that whole human trail for keeping things calm. And then I went to a retirement party for a man in the Sociology Department … [It was] a homecoming event, and [they were] honoring their retirees. He [got] up almost with tears in his eyes, now this is at least 30 years later, and he said one of his most important moments of his career, again, was walking with those students to the lower campus. …

Yes, and that event angered the community, but it just – for how many years had that man worked at the College – and this was his stellar moment. Walking down the hill with those students.

And then the student press was just getting their teeth into things, and they needed to be in every meeting that happened. You finally decided it was an open meeting. Here's the Cabinet meeting again. Deb Gage comes in. Now, isn't that a privilege to be invited there? And [she came in] in a big hat, and she sat through the meeting knitting. I was so insulted. I had been editor of *The Reporter* and, you know, I was so insulted that she would do that. And so, before the next week, I went and I said to John, "I have a way to resolve this, if you promise not to laugh." And so, overnight, I learned how to knit, and I had this ugly floral hat that my sister-in-law had given to us in Hawaii, and I came in and whoever was there, I believe it was Deb, I sat down and I put my tablet next to me, and I started to knit. And then I would take notes, and then I would knit. I don't know what happened, but we never saw a hat or knitting there again. And, ultimately, they found out the meetings were boring, and they didn't come anymore. I just found that amazing.

I understand some people in war-torn countries now. Because we were not war torn, but you develop. Life has to go on. And so life went on. I can remember another bomb threat where there was a bomb, it was supposed to be in the auditorium in Old Main. There was something ticking and the whole big scare. Well, that time it turned out it was a clock in there. It becomes a part of life. …

We could have had another Kent State, and we didn't. It's the way I looked at it. … The school survived, but then we had another crisis because we had become the campus of protesters and so on. The enrollments went way down and then Kent Alm took the brunt as students didn't come, faculty had to be cut, and I think he took the brunt of something. I think that's why he left ultimately. …

… Doug Moore [the next MSC president] comes in. He's dealing with the aftermath of a lot of things, and the faculty still isn't happy and so on, and I don't know what I asked him, but it had to do with what does the faculty want? It doesn't seem as though there is anything that is going to please them. And he said, "Judy, you have to look at it like this," he said. "These are a lot of bright people that came here on their way to someplace else. This was their stepping stone. And they got stuck here because, all of a sudden, the mobility that your intelligentsia had for moving from place to place was lost." The openings weren't there, and that was so helpful to me. They were good people …

*Judy Mans lives in Brainerd, Minnesota.*

### Charles Mundale, '50
*Retired Executive Director of the Minnesota Center for Corporate Responsibility*

We hardly need a reminder about the selectivity of memory, so I hope my recollections of only three incidents during those tense days of protest against the Vietnam War can serve some other, more useful purpose, showing perhaps how seemingly small acts led to larger outcomes or illustrating what was meant in those troubled days by "keeping the lid on."

I.

The story I have probably told most often is set on the upper campus mall. A platform and big-box audio equipment had been set up between the library and the student union. A large crowd had gathered; loud, angry music provided sound bridges between loud, angry speeches. Meanwhile, President Nickerson and his "Crisis Cabinet," staying close to the action, had been meeting in the library. As president of the Faculty Senate at that time, I was a Cabinet member. When the meeting was over, we came out of the library and stood in front of the main door, listening to the speeches. After a particularly incendiary speech, President Nickerson said, "Somebody has to get out there and counter that." His elbow nudged mine.

As a political science teacher and "campus politician," my negative sentiments about the war were fairly well known, both to students and to fellow faculty members. But it was also known that I did not favor the disruptive tactics being urged by a small but vocal group, a group that included students, a few faculty members, and – it was claimed – outside trouble mongers. I was no more than a few sentences into my remarks when one member of this group rushed the stage and pulled the plugs on the audio system.

The stratagem produced not the roars of approval the fellow was no doubt hoping to hear but just the opposite. "Let him speak. Let him speak," people shouted. The students, apparently, were looking for a more temperate way to express their feelings. I tried to offer just such an alternative. I cannot recall exactly what I said during those few minutes after the audio system was reconnected, but I do remember that I endorsed the march they were planning, and I urged them to march in silence. "Your silence will be heard," I argued, "to far greater effect than noisy shouts."

The next day, after the long, mostly silent, march through Mankato, as I was entering Morris Hall, a student said to me, "You made a lot of enemies yesterday." The student standing next to him immediately interjected, "You made a lot of friends, too."

II.

During the week following the "incursion" from Vietnam into Cambodia, a tactic that aroused intense unrest on campuses all across the country, activity on the campus was also especially volatile. Students began cutting class to participate in various anti-war activities. Some began demanding that they be allowed to take incompletes or even drop classes after the drop deadline without having it show on their records. Some faculty members sided with the student demands; others opposed them. While this was happening on campus, someone – never, I think, identified – set off an explosion at the new city jail that was still under construction.

It is a measure of the intensity of feelings created by these developments that a meeting of the entire faculty seemed in order. As chair of the Faculty Senate, I presided. Many members of the faculty wanted to respond to the students' requests to declare what one faculty member characterized as "academic bankruptcy" for that quarter, so they could devote their energies to the anti-war movement. Many faculty members also wanted to distance the activity on campus from the incident at the new jail. After some frank discussion, the faculty voted to approve waiving the drop date. My most vivid memory, however, concerns the resolution regarding the explosion at the jail. I had had a role in drafting the resolution, and I'm sure that's why I recall so clearly what happened. Professor Cyril Allen, who was chair of the History Department, proposed we amend the sentence in the resolution that stated "we regret" the incident to read "we denounce" it. It was, of course, an important and significant improvement, as well as an apt example of democratic process.

III.

Mankato experienced several protest marches during the Vietnam crisis. One of the tactics associated with those marches was the "sit-down," in which participants would simply sit down at some key location like a bridge or an intersection. The incident I most vividly recall was at the intersection of Main and Second streets near downtown. The entire intersection was filled with protesters. Traffic-as-usual was simply not possible. I was there but remained standing as I moved among the sitters.

So far, so good.

Then, down Main Street and heading for the Minnesota River bridge came a semi truck. The driver pulled his vehicle right up to the crowd. No one moved. I looked around, wondering what might happen. A few yard to my left – yes, I remember it that specifically – I saw it: a student holding a brick behind his back. Would he heave it at the truck? I moved closer and closer to him. If he made a move, I would try to stop him. Suddenly, a man was on the truck's running board.

Mankato Police Chief Alexander thrust his arm through the cab window, his hand holding his badge within inches of the driver's face. "Listen mister," he declared in a loud voice, "I'm the chief of police in this town, and I'm telling you to back this damn thing out of here right now." The man complied.

I have no idea what happened to that brick, but I know it was not thrown at that truck.

*Excerpted from transcripts of a discussion hosted by Jim Nickerson on June 15, 2005.*

[What sets Mankato] apart was that nobody got shot here. Nobody got into fights, well maybe not quite nobody. There was a little conflict, but no one ever got hurt … While things were in a sense coming apart at the seams on campuses all over the country, we got by, we managed. We had our protests, people got it off their chests and no blood was shed. So what made this different? Why did this happen in Mankato?

*Charles Mundale lives in Minneapolis, Minnesota.*


### Lee Nordgren, '49

I was a combat veteran during World War II and stayed in the Naval Reserve during the Vietnam War. I also had started a business downtown in 1946.

I recall debating Dr. Kessel on campus — he referred to himself as a Persian, then. Then [I recall] a time when a large group wanted to tear down the flag at the Post Office. Then again, when we heard that "people" were going to come downtown from the lower campus and burn us out.

*Lee Nordgren lives in Mankato, Minnesota.*


### Dwain Petersen
### *Former Director of Institutional Research and Professor of Education*

Two memories still come to mind from those days. I remember when we were asked to take shifts in the president's office throughout the night to try to discourage students from occupying that office as they were doing at Harvard and other colleges and universities throughout the country. I took my shift and spent some boring nights in Old Main. I did not want any excitement and was happy to be doing my part.

At that time, I was director of institutional research and ran an attitude survey at registration utilizing item sampling. We would randomly select six items out of a pool of 150 items and get students' views of the "environments" of then-Mankato State College. Attitudes of our students were similar to other colleges in our niche, and the administration said it was interested in our findings.

The other memory is when, during a demonstration, our son had to get across town for a piano lesson. My wife drove a little Karman Ghia similar to President Nickerson's and took him across town avoiding the demonstration. This son is now a playwright in the Twin Cities and has included this incident in one of his plays ... His memory is, of course, enhanced by speaking of the flowers emblazoned on the Ghia and how his mother threatened to move our sons to Canada if they were threatened by the draft. That was no idle threat, and I was tormented by the fact that, at the time, I was an active naval reservist and was serving as an air intelligence officer in my Naval Air Intelligence Reserve Unit in Minneapolis. I was greatly relieved when the draft was ceased, and I was able to continue my Reserve career and retire as a commander in the Naval Reserve.

*Dwain Petersen lives in Mankato, Minnesota.*

### David Phelps, '72

*Chapter 6 from the book in progress,* Tie Died Generation

In the spring of 1972, the United States seemed at a crossroads. A presidential election was heating up. The war in Vietnam would not go away. The nation was deeply divided. The atmosphere at Mankato State College was no different. Events seemed to be spiraling out of control. Discourse was growing increasingly heated. The relationship between the College and the community was on tenderhooks. Frustration was ample.

In early April, as George McGovern won the Wisconsin primary with 29 percent of the vote on his way to the Democratic presidential nomination and a lopsided defeat, President Nixon ordered additional bombers to South Vietnam as the north launched an Easter offensive below the demilitarized zone. The editorial page of the *Daily Reporter* was incredulous. "Events of the past week should awaken those who have fallen into the growing category of Americans who think the Vietnam War is nearing an end," the newspaper stated. "The current North Vietnam offensive drive has brought action back to a pace not seen for some time. ... President Nixon's presumed hope that the Vietnam War would not be an issue during the 1972 presidential campaign has been all but erased. And that is good, since until all American troops are home from South Vietnam, the war demands to be an issue that has to be resolved."

As tensions rose with the authorization of U.S. bombing near Hanoi and Haiphong, the holder of Mankato State's Chair of Ideas began to make his presence felt on campus and to attract the attention of the residents of Mankato who were not used to his East Coast forcefulness. In an open letter to students April 17, Goodman wrote, "I came to Mankato because I was told this chair (of ideas) belonged to the students and it was meant to 'challenge the attitudes and participation of students and faculty alike.' Challenge. But how do you make that challenge in the face of widespread indifference to any ideas or actions? (Is it indifference? Or is it a sense of helplessness?) Time is short."

A nationwide student strike was called for Friday, April 21. Bad weather forced Mankato State's strike activities into the student union where 400 attended. Speakers included Bob Corbett of the Vietnam Veterans Against the War, Mankato Mayor Vern Lundin, Rita Gallagher of the women's liberation movement and an elderly Mankato woman, described by rally promoters as "a 70-year-old peacenik from World War II."

Strike day got off to a shaky start when liquid tear gas was dumped on the stairwells in Old Main, Armstrong and Morris Halls, forcing the buildings to evacuate. At the student union, President James Nickerson addressed the strikers and warned that incidents like the tear gassing would be counterproductive to their cause. "I regret the impact of the constructive actions will be dulled by those who demonstrate in an unacceptable way," Nickerson said. But Goodman was at the rally, too, and clearly wanted center stage. "If students are going to insist on keeping classes open, maybe we need a little tear gas to wake them up," Goodman said.

Lundin, a popular church-going mayor whose son John had served in Vietnam, warned the protesters to keep their activities lawful and to be respectful of differing points of view. Lundin, much like Nickerson, was walking a tightrope between disillusioned students and increasingly angry city residents. "I, too, would like to see the war end tomorrow if possible," Lundin said. "Some people do not like to see the desecration of the flag they've loved all their lives. Some people still respect the responsibilities of all the elected leaders of our country."

Nickerson's mail was beginning to reflect the growing divide between his campus and the community. One Mankato resident wrote Nickerson, "I would like to register a complaint with you in regard to the disruption of classes by the so-called 'peaceniks.' I feel you are derelict in your job as a college president and have not done enough in regard to curbing and discouraging this type of activity. Students who want to get an education cannot do so if you allow these hoodlums to disrupt classes by tossing tear-gas grenades into their classrooms. If a situation like this would have come up when I went to school, the disruptive element would have been well taken care of by school officials and students alike. People like you who condone this permissive type of atmosphere should not be heads of educational institutions."

Nickerson, to his credit, personally replied to letters such as that one. In this instance, he wrote, "Your opinion is respected but I cannot agree. First, classes were not forceably disrupted by students. 'Peaceniks' as well as hawks deserve a hearing. Those who dissent are not by definition hoodlums. We have no evidence against any persons who may have been involved in the tear-gas incidents. I must choose between the policing of thought and suppression of peaceful demonstration inferred in your letter and providing a campus which recognizes the necessity of hearing all sides, the right of opinion and argument no matter how unpleasant and offensive. History will write which of us was closer to the truth."

In that atmosphere, the College and the city of Mankato were about to enter the most turbulent month either had ever experienced first hand.

---

On Sunday, April 30, Mankato's two VFW posts, the American Legion post and the National Guard held a "Loyalty Day" parade through the heart of Mankato, along Second Street from Lincoln Junior High to the National Guard Armory. The procession was supposed to include 30 units. Two additional units were not invited but joined anyway.

The MSC Vets for Peace organization along with the regional branch of the Vietnam Veterans Against the War decided to tag along. More than two dozen protesting veterans marched in the parade, wearing their military fatigues. Students lined the route and shouted "Peace now" as a truck converted to look like a railroad engine carried World War II veterans with a loudspeaker blaring the "Stars and Stripes Forever."

In front of the Post Office, which was along the parade route, demonstrators sang the John Lennon ode "All we are saying, is give peace a chance." The protesting Vietnam vets walked by with their fists raised above their heads. Emotions ran high. At one point, a World War II vet punched a demonstrator for carrying an American flag at half staff.

On Wednesday, May 3, college protesters conducted a torchlight march from the upper campus mall to the Post Office, as Mitchell Goodman continued to alienate the mainstream. In an interview with the *Mankato Free Press*, Goodman suggested that Mankato State "is a place heavily loaded up with conservative faculty who only want to continue the old routines, from what I've heard."

The protests continued on Thursday with a warning from Abbas Kessel and a shot at Goodman to keep matters nonviolent. "America has traditionally been a nation of violence. Anyone who commits an act of violence is responsible to society," Kessel said. Goodman characteristically attacked his critic, "Everytime I speak, Kessel comes up and confuses the issue. Closing down the university is not an act of violence."

More than 800 students took part in the upper campus rally. After the speeches, the students marched down the hill to Old Main and the office of Nickerson. As they marched, the protesters chanted, "What do we want? Peace! When do we want it? Now" and the slogan that moderates worried would alienate the rest of the community, "One, two, three, four. We don't want your fucking war!"

Nickerson smiled as the protesters marched past his office. The group then marched through the lobby of the Blue Earth County Courthouse one block to the east of Old Main. Although Front Street was supposed to be off limits for this demonstration, the students walked down the middle of the street anyway and then headed for the Post Office and filled its lobby. Goodman urged the students to enter the second-floor offices of the Selective Service, telling them they had a legal right to look at their files. By the time the students broke through the door to the second floor, the Selective Service office was closed. Students then responded with a sit-down strike on the lobby floor, causing a look of alarm on the face of Police Chief Charles Alexander who by now was present at most student demonstrations to make sure police response was measured and appropriate if things got out of hand. Alexander was openly respected by the college administration and begrudgingly by the demonstrators for keeping order. He took precautions to assure there would be no needless head bashing on his watch.

Following a quiet weekend, activities heated up the week of May 8 after President Nixon ordered the mining of all North Vietnamese ports and stepped up the bombing campaign in the north. On Tuesday, May 9, the *Daily Reporter* printed a page-one map of Vietnam with the bold headline, "STRIKE, STRIKE, STRIKE, STRIKE, STRIKE." A petition circulated by the MSC Peace Coalition read, "I don't believe there is an enemy in Vietnam. If, as our government says, there is an 'enemy,' I hope they win." In an editorial, the campus newspaper wrote, "Again we have been asked to strike. Again we will support that strike. But most important, again we are forced to strike. A strike at MSC, in itself, won't change Mr. Nixon's mind. But it is one of the few alternatives open to the American public to register their displeasures and should be used as such."

Town and campus tensions were stretched to the limit. The atmosphere was explosive. There was talk in Mankato's blue-collar bars of retaliation against the protesters, particularly Goodman, whose anti-war and anti-establishment rhetoric pushed the envelope for them. To the working men and women of town, the protesters increasingly were viewed as pampered college students led by an East Coast Svengali.

Tuesday began with a bomb threat to Old Main, telephoned in at 6:45 a.m., effective at 10 a.m., Nickerson decided to evacuate the building and move his Crisis Cabinet to the Memorial Library on the upper campus where it could be closer to a scheduled noon rally. Goodman appeared before the Cabinet and demanded a commitment from the College to take a position as an institution on the war. Vice President Kent Alm wouldn't go for Goodman's proposition. Alm said individuals could take a position on the war but could not expect the College to support, sponsor or protect them.

Off campus, authorities went on full alert after discovering heavy damage at the under-construction Blue Earth County Law Enforcement Center on the west end of Front Street. Sometime before the city awoke, a bomb blast fueled by upwards of 30 sticks of dynamite shattered the predawn Mankato quiet, blowing out a wall of the facility and causing extensive interior damage totaling $300,000. Suspicious that the bombing was tied to the anti-war protests and the Old Main bomb threat, Mankato police wanted the FBI's assistance in investigating. The bombing shocked the town and reduced its waning patience with the anti-war protesters.

At noon, Goodman took center stage at the rally on the upper campus mall. Under a clear blue sky with warm May temperatures, he told the students that Washington only responds to power, and the only power held by the students was their ability to shut down the college. Nickerson addressed the rally as well, sensing the growing restlessness of the students. "I pray we don't meet brutal violence abroad with brutal violence at home," he told the rally.

At 1 p.m., 3,000 protesters marched down the hill to the heart of Mankato at Front and Main streets. There, Goodman urged students to bring traffic to a standstill as a way of bringing the war home to residents. More than 1,000 students then moved across the Main Street Bridge over the Minnesota River into North Mankato and at 2 p.m. took control of Highway 169, the main north-south artery through the communities.

A massive traffic jam resulted as protesters held their position on the state highway for more than three hours. Local law enforcement authorities from Nicollet County, North Mankato and the State Patrol assembled at the north end of the student-controlled highway. Barricades were erected to keep the students from spreading; 50 helmeted officers stood on the other side with nightsticks in hand.

At 4:45 p.m., the State Patrol called Nickerson, who was with his Crisis Cabinet at the upper campus library, with word that the crowd would be dispersed by force, if necessary, in 15 minutes. The trooper told Nickerson he could have one last opportunity to urge the crowd to depart peacefully. Nickerson hustled to the highway, grabbing student leaders Larry Spencer, the Student Senate president, and Mehr Shahidi, along with him.

Nickerson twice took a police-provided loudspeaker and urged the students to leave before authorities forcefully attempted to remove them. Spencer took the bullhorn and told the students to follow their convictions but be prepared for the consequences. A new deadline was set by Nicollet County Sheriff George Witty. Protesters said they would leave at 5:45; Witty gave them until 5:20. At the deadline, Nickerson made one more plea, ending it almost apologetically, "I'm sorry it's working out this way. Take care of yourselves, kids, and God bless you."

When students refused to leave, the brigade of law enforcement first fired fake tear-gas bombs into the agitated crowd. When that didn't work, authorities followed with real tear-gas canisters. Protesters responded by throwing cans and rocks at the police line. For 20 minutes, the ruckus went on with police entering the crowd with mace and clubs. Backed up cars and trucks, most with agitated drivers, began to inch through the crowd. Some of the protesters jumped on the hoods. One student was hit in the leg by a vehicle. Meanwhile, the State Patrol came to the aid of one driver when students attempted to drag him out of his car. At 5:40, Goodman made his first appearance at the roadblock and urged students to retreat and regroup at Front and Main. By 6 p.m., traffic on Highway. 169 was flowing.

Nickerson aide John Hodowanic and Kessel joined the protesters at Front and Main and urged them to go home before anyone got hurt. Goodman had different thoughts. "To keep your self-respect as a human being, you have to be in this street today," Goodman told the protesters.

Lucian Smith, a Vietnam vet, told the marchers that their activities were becoming counterproductive. "You're pissing off the wrong people," Smith said. "They have nothing to say about the war policy." Goodman would have none of that kind of talk. "Here's someone who's completely helpless and hopeless," Goodman said of Smith. But, lacking organization and leadership, the crowd began to thin out and was gone by 7 p.m.

Police Chief Alexander was clearly frustrated by the day's events and the growing activism of the anti-war protesters. "It's just a mob," he told *The Free Press*. "The leadership can change 10 times in 15 minutes."

At 8 p.m., Nickerson convened his Crisis Cabinet and met with Alexander, City Manager Bill Bassett and Tom Kelm, chief of staff for Gov. Wendell Anderson who dispatched Kelm to Mankato as events appeared to be spiraling out of control. Kelm wanted to call out the National Guard, although the governor was less enthusiastic about that prospect. Even top Guard officials, wary of a Kent State repeat, were reluctant to use their troops, many of whom were the same age as the protesters. Another rally was expected Wednesday, but no decisions were made on how to handle a repeat of Tuesday's event. Even as the Crisis Cabinet was meeting, Goodman and the loose-knit protest leadership were planning for the next day with Goodman urging civil disobedience.

When the *Daily Reporter* hit the campus Wednesday morning, it contained an editorial that asked, "What happened yesterday?" It went on, "The strike that began peacefully ended in violence. Something that has never happened in Mankato occurred Tuesday afternoon. The event yesterday was indeed unfortunate. The confrontation between protesters and the law officers brought out much ill feeling on both sides. Whether the measures taken by authorities were appropriate (i.e. tear gassing, mace) is questionable. But in an instance, it changed a demonstration against the Vietnam War to an establishment-student showdown of the past ... No one group or individual can be singled out for the incident yesterday. But an underlying factor is the Vietnam War that refuses to go away and President Nixon's decision to follow a course of force to end the war."

Again, overnight violence wracked Mankato. Using bolt cutters, someone broke into the motor pool of the Mankato Army Reserve unit at the intersection of highways 60 and 169, two miles west of town. The unknown intruders placed packages of dynamite under the hoods of two five-ton trucks. The first bundle exploded around 5 a.m. and destroyed one of the trucks but the force of the blast dislodged five sticks of bundled dynamite in the second vehicle. Nonetheless the first explosion was strong enough to damage several vehicles in the motor pool. The hood of the destroyed truck flew 150 feet and landed on the roof of the reserve building. Capt. Clark Meyer, company commander, said the lost truck was worth $24,000.

Anyone glancing through the *Daily Reporter* that morning did a double take upon reaching the arts and entertainment section of the newspaper. Arts and entertainment editor John Enger penned an editorial in the section, an unusual place for opinion other than critical reviews. "This week's art and entertainment section has been considerably shortened because, quite frankly, there is nothing in my eyes entertaining about what is going on in both the world and on this campus," Enger wrote. "Peace, brothers and sisters, and we'll see you in the streets."

The *Mankato Free Press*, representing the mainstream of the city, said in an editorial that day, "Cool heads must prevail in a city under stress. Mankatoans more than ever before in the long history of the war are being tested on the homefront for their resiliency, cohesiveness and understanding."

The noon rally on campus drew 3,000 students, including several hundred from nearby Gustavus Adolphus College in St. Peter. Strike leader Zeke Smith was on the podium when he sighted WCCO television reporter Bob McNamara in the crowd with a camera man. WCCO was the CBS affiliate in Minneapolis and had the most-watched newscasts in the area. Smith felt McNamara had sensationalized Tuesday's strike activities. He asked McNamara why he had reported only the "bad" aspects of the demonstration. An angry McNamara, clearly uncomfortable with the attention focused his way, replied, "We reported it like that because that is what we saw."

Black leaders used the forum to demand the immediate reinstatement of education professor Walter Reed, but Nickerson declined to commit to a deadline for his final decision on the matter. But the main disagreement among the assembled students was whether to participate in another day of civil disobedience, advocated by Goodman, or protest peacefully with a silent march through the town.

"You're all ambassadors of peace," urged Marc Karson, chair of the Political Science Department. "It would be ironic if the thing you hate the most (violence) is the thing you became." H. Roger Smith, a popular urban planning professor, urged the students to take their peaceful message to local community groups like the Kiwanis and the Rotary Club. Goodman derided the silent march idea. "It won't make a damn bit of difference," he told the crowd.

The rally ended at 1:20 p.m. when the college turned off the sound system. As the students began marching down the hill, the civil disobedience group of about 300 broke ranks and headed toward Mankato High School, where several students had been disciplined for joining early protest marches. "Let them go," the dissidents shouted outside the high school. "Do you like being in jail?"

The splinter group rejoined the silent march at Byron Street for a few blocks and then broke off again and headed for Front Street, chanting, "We don't want your fucking war." When they reached Front and Main, they were uncertain what to do next. An effort began to reoccupy the Highway 169 overpass, but the highway had already been shut down by state troopers to avoid the disturbance of Tuesday. As surveillance aircraft and helicopters circled overhead, the marchers reversed themselves and moved to the other end of Front Street where Highway 169 passed over Park Lane. The marchers were greeted with more troopers at the Park Lane overpass and soon moved out, but not before letting the air out of one trooper's squad car tires.

The silent march, with Nickerson among the protesters, covered seven miles and lasted three hours. H. Roger Smith, acting as a march marshal, told the students that town residents "don't know how to react to peaceful silence, especially after what happened yesterday." The march snaked up Madison Avenue to the Madison East shopping mall, a growing center of the city's retail presence. From there, it went along Highway 22 and back to campus. Along Highway 22, an agitated Goodman caught up with the marchers. "Do you like being tricked?" Goodman asked a group of women marchers. "You're just following Nickerson's parade. You have to do something with more impact."

Nickerson felt more in control Wednesday. When he was called to the Highway 169 overpass Tuesday he didn't have a plan for diffusing the situation. But Wednesday, he kept protesters focused and peaceful. At the end of the silent march, he praised the students for staying on the designated route. "I'm proud of you for that, and I believe in you," Nickerson said.

But relations between the town and campus continued to deteriorate. A hand-written note, signed only by Tom, Mike, John, Pete and Oscar, arrived in Nickerson's office during the week. It said, "We are a group of World War II vets. Some of us work in the postal department, but most of us travel in several states at our jobs, and we learn first hand from the hard-working taxpayers about the low-down un-American cowards called potheads and slobs, creeps, etc., that go to school not to learn to live like good Americans but to riot and demonstrate against the citizens that made this great land possible. Some of us saw the creeps at the Post Office, and it was sickening to see and learn that these so-called students has stuped [sic] that low to disgrace the tax-paid institutions. God bless America if they are to vote in this type of radicals."

Wednesday evening, the Mankato Chamber of Commerce held a community forum at the Inn Towne motel to discuss the war protests and the campus atmosphere. Goodman was in attendance as was Mark Karson, the political science department chair. Karson told the forum that Goodman's path of civil disobedience was counterproductive and alienated city residents. City Councilman Herb Mocol said the community was polarized to the point that he feared for Goodman's safety. Goodman said the community was "dead." He said demonstrations and a strike at Mankato State would have a national effect.

After the meeting ended, Mocol approached Karson and asked him to visit a few Mankato bars so Karson could get a clear understanding of the polarization he'd mentioned earlier in the evening. They hit the Rathskeller and the VFW where Karson heard patrons talk about "getting" Goodman and "dismembering him." Shortly before midnight, Karson and Mocol ran into Nickerson at the Inn Towne parking lot. Karson asked Nickerson to meet with Goodman to explain the graveness of the situation. Karson also suggested it might be wise for Goodman to leave Mankato.

Karson then went to Goodman's apartment to discuss ways of reducing tensions in the city. Goodman expressed interest in going to Washington, D.C., for the coming weekend's huge anti-war rally. Goodman said he'd be gone about five days, but he wanted no restrictions placed on his return to campus. Goodman also asked if the College would pay for the trip.

Thursday, May 11, would be another trying day for Nickerson and the college. Nichols Hall was evacuated and closed at 11:15 a.m. because of a bomb threat; Morris Hall was evacuated and closed 45 minutes later for the same reason. Karson tried vainly to arrange a meeting with Nickerson and Goodman, but Goodman couldn't be pinned down for a time. Nickerson, meanwhile, was meeting with Bill Bassett, the Mankato city manager and Chief Alexander to discuss how to handle future protests and marches. They'd soon get more practice.

The now-daily noon rally was relatively tame until about 50 students in the civil disobedience camp broke ranks and started a march down Val Imm Drive ostensibly for Front Street. Alexander met the group at the foot of the hill and allowed them to proceed with the assurance that this was a peaceful march.

But upon reaching the intersection of Front and Walnut, the gang of 50 decided to backtrack to Old Main and do their demonstrating there. Goodman was not with them. The protesters decided to occupy Old Main and forced their way into the building at 3 p.m. They blocked one exit with chairs and furniture and ordered noninvolved students, faculty and staff out of the building. *Minneapolis Tribune* photographer Kent Kobersteen was escorted out as well. A photographer for the *Daily Reporter* was told his camera would be broken if he didn't put it away.

Nickerson remained in Old Main. He paced up and down the corridors trying to keep the situation under control. His aide, Hodowanic, told the protesters to "play it cool." Fifteen minutes later, riot-equipped police arrived at the administration building to a jeering crowd of now 700 that had gathered on the front lawn of Old Main. When police entered, a fire hose was turned on them but the event was quickly over. No one was hurt and the building was cleared by 3:30.

But things were still ugly outside Old Main where Goodman was now present. Some in the crowd were pumped with adrenaline, but deep divisions within student ranks over the style of Thursday's protest were widening. When one student confronted Goodman to criticize his leadership and insinuate that Goodman was using a father image to his advantage with female students, Goodman blew up and slapped the student. Standing nearby, Abbas Kessel said indignantly to no one in particular, "There is your prince of peace."

A Pete Seeger concert Thursday evening had a cathartic effect on a week of rancor and bitterness. About 4,000 attended the concert, including many city residents.

But Nickerson and Goodman had yet to meet. Nickerson suggested a 9:30 p.m. meeting at his office after the concert and said he would ask Chief Alexander to attend, although Nickerson forgot to call Alexander. Karson remained the go-between, and Goodman again expressed concern about his safety. Karson and Nickerson waited until 10:50 p.m. for Goodman, but he was a no-show. He later said he had called the president's office around 9 p.m. and was told Nickerson was not in.

On his way home for the evening, Karson decided to stop by Goodman's apartment once more, where he found Goodman on the phone with Alexander asking about threats against him. Goodman was angry when he learned that Alexander had not been invited to the meeting earlier in the evening, even though Goodman failed to attend. He told Karson that Nickerson was attempting to manipulate him and wasn't overly concerned about Goodman's safety.

Goodman's tactics during the week of May 9 clearly were wearing thin. The Friday editorial in the *Daily Reporter* was headlined, "The acts of few tears strike apart." In the body of the editorial, the newspaper stated, "Don't think for a minute that we have slid to the right in our beliefs about the Vietnam War. Please do think before you are led into something that can accomplish nothing and further alienate the community. We can help end the war. But in doing it, it makes no sense to create another one here in Mankato. We must all stay together and continue with the struggle of ending U.S. violent aggression through peaceful means. Otherwise, you are as guilty as the Nixon administration we are so uniformly opposed to."

On Friday, another noon rally was held on the campus mall, but attendance lagged behind the previous rallies, in part, because many students went back to their hometowns for the weekend and usually left on Friday. As the rally leader, Goodman urged protesters to go into classrooms and urge students in class to come outside and protest the war. About 15 protesters went into Armstrong Hall to interrupt classes but failed to generate additional support. The rally ended at 1 p.m. As Goodman and Karson were leaving the function, a student approached Goodman and told him to go back to California. Angered, Goodman called the student an asshole and told the student he should go to Vietnam.

The disruptive week was not quite over. At 2 p.m., a group of 100 protesters marched down the hill to Old Main to stage a sit-in. They told Nickerson and college employees to leave the building. Nickerson refused but agreed to let the students conduct their sit-in if there would be no violence. Goodman was only intermittently involved, stating later in the afternoon that he no longer was going to negotiate with Nickerson about the scope of anti-war protests. Along the front balcony of Old Main, protesters hoisted a flag with a peace symbol and hung the American flag upside down. Inside, dogs ran about as protesters prepared to stay for the weekend.

On Saturday afternoon, Goodman arrived at Old Main to request a body guard in light of rumored threats against him earlier in the week. Nickerson was sitting in the building's vestibule with one of his administrative staff, Dean Scott, when he was told of Goodman's demand. Nickerson agreed to meet with Goodman and asked Karson to be there. During the meeting, Goodman became notably agitated and charged Nickerson with a lack of concern over Goodman's personal safety. Nickerson's security staff said their resources were too strained to assign someone to Goodman, and the request was denied. Protesters left Old Main at 8 a.m. Monday, May 15, concluding a peaceful weekend of occupation.

On Tuesday, May 16, the day presidential candidate George Wallace was shot and paralyzed in a botched assassination attempt in Maryland, about 400 students conducted a peaceful candle-light march through downtown. Parade organizers, learning a lesson from the previous week, obtained a parade permit from the city and allowed Mankato Police squad cars to lead the protest. Students knew city tensions were high, but they were yet unaware of the warnings that had been given to Nickerson and Karson from the mayor about the barroom talk of doing something to Goodman and his followers.

On Friday, news of the potential for vigilantism surfaced in a story in the *Daily Reporter* in which Goodman claimed that Nickerson and Karson urged him to leave Mankato because of death threats and that his salary would be guaranteed. In the same story, Nickerson aide Hodowanic said it was up to Goodman whether to leave or stay. Karson denied making a deal with Goodman.

"I told Goodman I thought he was hurting the town," Karson told the student newspaper. "Over a long period of time, many of the town's people had come to oppose the Vietnam War, but I felt that Goodman's advocating of civil disobedience was polarizing the community. I think it was causing people to lose sight of the Vietnam War and causing them to call for law and order."

Karson then told of meeting with 75 Mankato men in a bar the week before and hearing talk about their intention to confront Goodman and students if protests got out of control again. Goodman said Karson was trying to scare him out of town. "I think he was just trying to scare me," Goodman said. "He told me that he had heard someone was talking about dismembering me, and you don't tell someone that another person is going to dismember you unless you're out to scare them."

Goodman's influence on campus clearly was waning. A staff memo sent to Nickerson during the weekend sit-in noted that student participation in the demonstration declined as the weekend wore on. The memo suggested it was time to wind down the protests and take advantage of Goodman's decline in popularity.

"The president has gone more than the last mile with the strikers, and, I would argue, they know it," the memo said. "The leadership of Mitchell Goodman has seriously (or joyously) eroded. More and more students see him for what he is ... a self-seeking, slithery snake who is using the college and its students for his own personal motives."

It had been a trying two weeks for Nickerson. His office correspondence revealed the wide range of emotions the protests had evoked. One student wrote, "I do not support the protest. I do not feel you can end war and violence with violence. People are not going to listen when there is destruction to property and to human life. I hope to pass these views to some of my fellow students in hopes that they do not want violence. I write this small note to let you know there are still students at MSC who want to achieve peace. I do not know what to do about the situation at hand right now, except to let you know and others how I feel." An elementary school principal in nearby Mapleton wrote, "Your 'Chair of Ideas' (held by Goodman) could better be named 'Chair of Communist Ideas.'… If we continue to have such 'soft' leadership as you are giving, the Reds will take over the world."

But Nickerson also had his supporters for his guidance of the campus in such an unsettled and unplottable chain of events. One area resident wrote, "How wonderful it is to have men of goodwill in a world so full of hate – you have been a tower of strength to the community and I thank you for keeping us from a Kent State – I hope the hateful critics will only spur you on to bring unity to our town."

Near the end of May, Goodman addressed a group of 200 to offer his reflections on his spring quarter at Mankato State College. "What is it that has caused this reaction to me that has a kind of hysteria?" He called the atmosphere on the campus and in the town "a witch hunt climate." For Goodman, as he prepared to leave the Chair of Ideas, "The lowest blows ever struck on me in my life came here at Mankato State."

The last anti-war rally of the spring quarter drew just 200 and involved a march to a small manufacturing company called Kato Engineering. Protesters targeted Kato Engineering after learning it had a $98,000 contract with the Department of Defense. Karson told the students their march would be pointless. "They make motor engines, not B-52s," he told the students. But the 200 went anyway, and when they arrived at the company, the plant manager appeared and told the protesters that Kato Engineering's contract with the Pentagon was for building hospital generators.

On Friday, June 6, 1,200 Mankato State seniors graduated from college to enter a world full of confusion, a nation divided, a future unclear. Those who were freshman four years earlier had seen life-changing events. They had observed and participated in one of the most unsettling periods in U.S. history, capped by a just-finished month that seemed to grip at the moral fabric of society.

In that four-year period, a sitting president declined to seek his party's nomination for another term because of his role in an increasingly unpopular war. The Democratic National Convention of 1968 turned into a riot as nightstick-wielding policemen battered heads in Chicago's Grant Park. Bobby Kennedy and Martin Luther King were assassinated. Richard Nixon was elected president. Woodstock and Hendrix changed rock. Charles Manson defined the term "cult." Berkeley became synonymous with radical fringes. The gay culture stepped out of the closet. We put a man on the moon. "The Godfather" became a film classic as did "The Exorcist" and "Easy Rider." Sonny and Cher and Archie Bunker were introduced on the small screen, along with "Sesame Street" and "60 Minutes."

Students burned draft cards. Women burned bras. And in Mankato, 13,000 students and 40,000 city residents watched as the spiraling dissent, the cultural shifts, the fragile politics and the battered national psyche came together in a town that was the fictional home of Betsy and Tacy, two innocent schoolgirls from childhood literature. From the fall of 1968 when homecoming still was important, to the spring of 1972 when tear gas hung in the air and protesters barricaded highways, streets and buildings in opposition to the war, the students, faculty and administration at Mankato State had their own niche in transforming the United States.

Those sitting in the fieldhouse for graduation that day were the sons and daughters of World War II vets and stay-at-home moms. Many were the first in their family to get a college degree. Now those students were heading out into an unsettled world to become accountants and teachers and journalists, to become members of the establishment about which they had deep reservations. Some would go into politics to keep up the fight for social justice and peace and equality. Some would go into politics and become disillusioned. Some would be defined by the events of their college experience. Others would quickly forget what they had just witnessed in their quest for a paycheck.

Fittingly, the centerpiece music chosen for the commencement ceremony and performed by the MSC Concert Wind Ensemble was a commissioned piece titled "The Riots of Spring."

Nearly 40 years later, Nickerson would reflect on that month of May in 1972 and conclude that it was, all in all, a positive reflection of the American way. It was "democracy in action," Nickerson determined.

"We were all struggling there, but, to me, it was the best of times in the sense that democracy really came alive. Teaching democracy is in the textbook. This history actually happened. It just isn't in the book; it actually happened. For one of the few periods in our history, democracy became a living thing," Nickerson recalled as he tried to put meaning to one of the most tumultuous times of his long career in higher education.

Today, there are two memorials on the campus mall where students gathered in the early 1970s to argue about the morality of war and racism, chide the establishment and hope for a more perfect world. One memorial honors the student lives lost at Kent State and Jackson State in 1970. It says, "Hate, war, poverty and racism are buried here." Fifty yards away, near Memorial Library, a red granite monument shows a dove with an olive branch in its beak and an M-16 rifle, stuck bayonet first into the ground with a soldier's helmet hung on the gun's stock carved with the word VIETNAM. The monument reads, "For those who fought for it, freedom has a taste the protected will never know. 1959-1975."

*David Phelps lives in St. Louis Park, Minnesota.*


### Dan Quillin, '72

I came to Mankato State in the fall of 1969 with an associate of arts degree from Metropolitan Community College in Minneapolis. I was a young person in transition. My social awakening was stimulated by great teachers, thoughtful books and a number seven draft lottery number. A Pell Grant and college loans gave me my opportunity to go to Mankato.

Like many of my contemporaries, I wanted to make a difference and believed my generation would. Starting out as a Dorm Council president at Mankato State in the fall of 1969, I was elected to the Student Senate in the spring of 1970. By the fall of 1970, my peers elected me speaker of the Student Senate and, in the spring of 1971, I became president of the Minnesota State College Student Association.

These were both exciting and stress-filled times, whether you were the college president or trying to be a student leader. Dramatic events on the national scene and on campuses throughout the country were unfolding, affecting our everyday lives.

On the national scene, the war in Vietnam affected us all and was a central issue in our lives. This was the age of the 18-year-old vote, Kent State, Jackson State, the invasion of Cambodia, re-escalation of the bombing of North Vietnam and the mining of Haiphong Harbor. The war on poverty, riots in urban ghettos, Black Power, Earth Day, long hair, the cold war, the Cuban missile crisis, the bomb and nuclear holocaust were fresh in our minds. We were not far removed from the assassinations of King and Kennedy, the march on Selma and George Wallace. As students, on average, we were 13 when John Kennedy was assassinated and 18 when King and Bobby Kennedy were murdered. These events formed the lenses through which we viewed the world. We saw in the Eugene McCarthy anti-war presidential campaign that perhaps … we could make a difference. We read about the Berkeley free speech movement and started to think about student rights and our role in the college. Perhaps more than most generations, we thought we could do things better than our predecessors and fix a society that threatened and troubled us deeply. There was a touch of arrogance to our thinking.

Locally, students demanded and were being given a larger role in campus governance. We weren't interested in running homecoming. We had bigger fish to fry. We wanted to make a difference in how our society and our communities were being run, and the campus, for better or for worse, was our laboratory.

Activists had two channels for action: ad hoc anti-war student protest groups or trying to make elective channels responsive (i.e., student government, local and national elections). While the goals were similar and there was crossover participation, leaders were different as were their philosophies and their degree of alienation. Philosophically, the differences revolved around means and ends and how to change the society. What were the best means to achieve common ends? Could the ends justify the means? On our best days, these groups were allies in a common cause; … on their worst, they despised and distrusted each other's motives. Wrestling with these questions brought us moratoriums, student strikes, protest vigils, marches, occupations, disruptive civil disobedience and finally to the edge of violence in the spring of 1972.

*Campus Governance*

As 18-year-olds who were about to be given the right to vote and who were being sent to Vietnam, we wanted and expected to be treated like adults … even if our behavior sometimes fell short of adult expectations. We pushed back Victorian rules that had governed dormitory life for preceding generations. We demanded that we be treated as adults and that dorm rooms should, in effect, be our apartments. Barriers regarding separation of the sexes and visitation rules were not totally abandoned but were largely liberalized. Laws and rules that inhibited our rights such as prohibitions against liquor on campus earned our contempt at a time our peers were given responsibility for fighting and dying in a war we disagreed with.

Campuswide, we felt we were making inroads. Many would learn the ropes from those who came before us, such as David Cowan, who would go on to become a college administrator. We expanded the student role in college governance. We pushed the envelope by advocating the abolition of the "F" grade, evaluating faculty with the "blue book" and demanding voting student representation of the College Curriculum and Personnel committees.

We supported and actually developed mini-courses when the College needed credit hours to avoid financial problems stemming from a plateau in student enrollment. We set up book exchanges and day care services. I remember being an advocate for a unicameral college governance body, joining the faculty and students in one legislative body, and advocated for the idea in the college magazine, and on the College Constitution Committee in the winter and spring of 1972. I also remember developing the content for two mini-courses, "Students'

Involvement in the Age of Campus Revolution" and "Speed Reading."

We pushed the College on affirmative action. With the help of an enlightened College newspaper with a succession of thoughtful student editors who reported and editorialized on our activities, by the spring of 1972, the Student Senate was no joke, and 20 percent of the student body would vote, which was an all-time high.

On the state level, we became players with the State College Board through the Minnesota State College Student Association (MSCSA). As the first president from Mankato State, I recall we succeeded in passing a number of policies, including getting student workers paid every two weeks instead of once a month. To the chagrin of most of the college presidents, we pushed the liquor-on-campus issue as a student rights issue. Finally, an exasperated President Robert Dufresne from Winona State voted against it, saying "I oppose sin in all its evil manifestations."

Bit by bit, our foothold became stronger. Articles on the organization's successes appeared in the *University of Minnesota Daily* and Twin Cities dailies, as we either were invited or invited ourselves to legislative hearings or got invitations to the governor's inaugural ball. (We did not go!)

Today, MSCSA has evolved into a mature organization with a quarterly newspaper, an executive director, legislative lobbyists and its own foundation. The early days were not quite so heady. ... I remember driving through a November snowstorm to Moorhead State College to convince their skeptical Student Senate not to withdraw from MSCSA for some petty, long-forgotten reasons. A day does not go by that I don't take pride in what that organization has become.

Student government in those years was a melting pot of left-wing radicals, black power advocates, traditional fraternity types and a sprinkling of independents. Running a meeting in a fair but effective matter and getting results was a skill we honed daily. To this day, my comfort level in preparing and running an effective meeting was not honed in any classroom but through the hundreds of meetings as a student leader at Mankato.

By the winter and spring of 1972, we were politically engaged outside of campus as well as on. Working with students across the state, we pushed Project 72, which was an effort to mobilize people ages 18 to 21 for precinct caucuses and the fall vote. Giant precinct caucuses on campus and in town made us feel we had real power and helped nominate George McGovern for president. Locally, the impact was significant as we nominated and elected Dave Cummiskey state representative on a shoestring budget of $2,800 and 36 hand-painted lawn signs defeating five-term incumbent Gus Johnson.

*The War and the Spring of 1972*

The war would be an overriding issue that would be with us throughout my college years. It was a wave that grew on the Mankato campus throughout the period of 1969 to 1972. In spring of 1970, Nixon invaded Cambodia and, on May 4, 1970, the Kent State tragedy occurred and the student peace movement had its first martyrs. In the spring of 1972, it seemed to be getting only worse. It made no sense to us. It was clear we were losing the war. We did not buy the domino theory. Innocent Vietnamese were dying. A young Vietnam veteran against the war named John Kerry was asking, "How do you ask a young man to be the last person to die for a mistake?"

In April of 1972, in response to a spring offensive by the North Vietnamese and Viet Cong, President Nixon renewed bombing of the North for the first time since the Johnson administration, with unprecedented intensity hitting Haiphong and Hanoi. ... This was not "winding down the war," as he had pledged, but was an escalation whose consequences seemed ominous. Nationally, statewide and locally, a student response that would be the strongest campus reaction in the nation's history was inevitable.

*Post Office – the Prelude*

On April 25, 1972, after an evening rally at the student union, an around-the-clock protest vigil began at the downtown Post Office that would run 19 days. My recollection is that Larry Spencer, Student Senate president, and myself started that vigil as an act of frustration and anger. My recollection is we had nothing more than a pair of sleeping bags and a pair of signs that voiced our displeasure. Others soon joined us, and television stations and local radio stations began coverage. I remember a variety of responses from the community; ... while some responded angrily to yet another protest, others brought cookies and coffee or joined us to swell our ranks. I remember being interviewed by the local radio stations and being asked how the community had responded. I responded that the people giving us the peace sign outnumbered "barnyard gestures" by a 2-to-1 margin. The vigil would continue to May 4, the anniversary of the Kent State tragedy. The vigil ended with a torchlight march from the campus to the Post Office. This became the prelude to the two weeks that would rock the campus.

*May 4*

The following day, Thursday, May 4, a rally was planned by anti-war groups for the mall to honor the Kent State and Jackson State students and to try to shut down the campus as a ultimate act of civil disobedience. A headstone was to be placed commemorating the Kent State and Jackson State students.

## The Kent State – Jackson State Memorial

The history of the memorial headstone located at the center of today's upper campus is a story within a story. The original memorial headstone and footstone combination was purchased by the Student Senate in 1971 to commemorate the first anniversary of Kent State and Jackson State. The original memorial stones consisted of a headstone and footstone, both made of a modest orange and brown stone. The original combination contained a spelling error in the footstone. For that reason, it was never installed. The stone containing the error was sent back to the cutter, and it was reinscribed with the spelling error corrected over the summer of 1971.

By fall, some of my fellow student senators, led by Mark Halverson, had shovels in hand and were anxious to arbitrarily and unilaterally place the stone memorials with no campus approval. As the story was told in the *Mankato State Reporter,* I convinced them that if this was to be indeed a permanent memorial, we would have to get the College administration to sign off. Reluctantly, they agreed.

It took several months of negotiations with the administration and Ira Johnson, director of campus planning, to get approval for the site where the memorial exists today. But by that time, the winter of 1971-72 had set in and installing the memorial in frozen ground was not possible. This resulted in us selecting the second anniversary of the Kent State-Jackson State incident, May 4, 1972, and planning a moratorium rally on the upper campus mall as the dedication ceremony for the memorial or what Mark Halverson would later refer to as "Pandora's rock."

However, just a few weeks before the dedication, as fate would have it, both the headstone and footstone met their untimely demise. ... Both stones were leaned up against the west wall of the Student Senate office when a construction worker working on the student union addition drilled a hole through the west wall of the Student Senate office, strategically hitting and drilling a hole into the headstone. Still planning to proceed, despite the newly drilled hole in the headstone, the final *coup de grace* came a few days later when the footstone was knocked and broken in two by accident by student Sen. Bill Kolbinger while entering the Student Senate office.

The placement of the monument was to be the central activity of the May 4 rally. We were distraught about the situation. Through some minor miracle, Mark Halverson and Student Senate President Larry Spencer were able to acquire, at the 11th hour, a large, beautifully polished stone with the inscription chiseled perfectly into the rock and, as they say, the rest is history. The monument was dedicated before a rally of a thousand students Thursday, May 4, 1972. Today, 34 years after the event, it stands as a piece of history of the campus. The story of the stone was chronicled in the May 5, 1972 *Reporter.*

That day, after the mall rally, a group of 200 students marched down to the Post Office, occupied the Selective Service Office and did some minor damage. The students passed a hat to pay for the damages and left the building by 6 p.m.

To some of my contemporaries, simple protest was no longer adequate confrontation. Chair of Ideas Mitchell Goodman pushed for more dramatic attention-grabbing actions. He and Abbas Kessel would set off some classic mall debates as students, faculty and administration would disagree with each other on anti-war tactics and strategies in the days that followed.

*May 8*

Nationally, things went from bad to worse. Nixon went on national television Monday evening, May 8, announcing the blockade and mining of all North Vietnamese ports. Nixon's speech was like throwing fuel on a growing fire.

The issue now on campus became one of tactics. Large, dramatic but peaceful protests to win anti-war converts received strong competition from those arguing for more dramatic civil disobedience and attention-grabbing events that could shut down a campus, town, state or country.

*May 9*

After a rally on the upper campus mall on Tuesday, May 9, riled-up students marched to the high school and then down Front Street to Main, where they sat down and occupied the intersection. A large portion proceeded to the Main Street Bridge and Highway 169 which they locked down until 5:30 in the afternoon, when Nicollet County officials removed them using tear gas and mace despite President Nickerson's best effort to talk them off.

Regrouping that evening, calmer heads were determined to make both a powerful anti-war statement the next day but not lose control of the situation, as had been the case Tuesday. My recollection is that, in the absence of a better plan, there were strong fears that Wednesday could bring violence. A silent march was planned for Wednesday with faculty and student marshals orchestrating. This was not a unanimous plan. We knew some would view this silent protest as a cop-out. Returning to the downtown intersections, the Main Street Bridge and Highway 169 to renew the confrontation was the action that some wanted.

*May 10*

The day began with 500 students marching the 12 miles from Gustavus College in St. Peter to join 2,500 students at noon at the upper campus mall. After impassioned speeches, 3,000 students, four abreast, extending nearly a mile in length, began a historic march down the hill through town. It would be the single largest student protest march in the school's history. I remember President Nickerson joining us. I am not sure if it was politically a good idea for him to do so, but his solidarity with us on that day was important to many of us. I think it was probably his way of re-enforcing what he believed to be an acceptable form of protest and a much-better alternative to the blocking of Highway 169. I was one of the many who spoke that day to the crowd urging the silent protest option over the confrontation at the Main Street Bridge. I remember being a student marshal with a red bandana on my arm and a bullhorn.

At one point, at the intersection of Byron and State Street, those who were not satisfied with a silent march began screaming for changing the direction of the 3,000 students, trying to redirect it to the main downtown intersection and Highway 169. I remember the scene at that intersection as if it were yesterday. My more radical brethren yelling for students to go one way (toward downtown's main intersection and Highway 169), while I stood next to them with my bullhorn imploring them to remain on the designated route! While some 200 defected for the downtown bridge and Highway 169, for the most part, the bulk of students stayed true to the course and returned to the upper campus.

With tensions at an apex Wednesday evening, a group of students and townspeople met at the Inn Towne motel and formulated a joint call for a combination peace-and-prayer rally the next evening at the upper campus mall. The entire Mankato community was invited and Mankato businesses were asked to close their doors from 6 to 7 p.m. Thursday evening, May 11.

*May 11*

Early Thursday afternoon, anger flared as 150 students marched down the hill and approximately 80 occupied Old Main. A civil servant inside Old Main, feeling trapped by angry students, called police and indicated that there were lives in danger. Police responded by breaking into Old Main and physically clearing the building. The arrival of police on campus fired the anger of some students to new heights.

*May 12*

On Friday, a group of 100 students occupied Old Main peacefully throughout the weekend, leaving Monday, May 15.

*May 17*

A second meeting between students and Mankato businessmen was held at the Inn Towne motel to discuss opening channels of communication between the college and the community over the anti-war activities that had occurred. During the meeting, I asked the businessmen to help raise funds to send people to Washington to express their views about the war. At the same meeting, the group decided to ask KEYC-TV to provide a half-hour of air time to discuss the war and talk about the events that had occurred on campus and in Mankato during the previous two weeks. I would later moderate that program, which aired May 23.

On that same day, 23-year-old Dave Cummiskey would declare his candidacy for the legislative seat occupied by 78-year-old Gus Johnson. I, Dave Cowan and Jim McDonough would make it our summer and fall's work to elect Cummiskey.

*May 23 – Postscript*

As part of the effort to heal the rift that these events caused between townspeople and the college, KEYC-TV provided a half-hour special May 23 titled "The Week They Brought the War Home." Brad Theissen and I wrote the script, and Brad assembled the film footage. I was asked to moderate the program with a guest panel consisting of Student Senate President Larry Spencer and anti-war activist Rita Gallagher representing the students' point of view. John Hodowanic represented the College administration, and George Leland, president of the First National Bank of Mankato, represented the townspeople. That evening, we went through the events that had transpired from April 25 through May 12 including a discussion of the philosophy and tactics used.

The final days of spring quarter 1972 were spent negotiating the best deal students could obtain relative to academic options for those who had participated in the student strikes of the spring of 1972.

*Dan Quillin lives in West St. Paul, Minnesota.*


**Beth Sageng, '78**

In May of 1972, I was a sophomore at Mankato State College and still a teenager. I was busy trying to wrap up spring quarter. I was majoring in psychology and was not skipping many classes despite the intense politics sparking activity all over campus. With the anniversary of the Kent State killings coming up and the Vietnam War showing no signs of abating, the tension was starting to show a serious edge. Demonstrations were occurring on campuses all over the country.

The lunatic fringe on both sides was burning buildings and inflicting violence on students. Nothing like that had happened at Mankato State. A lot of people were starting to get together in larger and larger groups around town to discuss the war, gathering on the mall at upper campus and meeting in church basements and bars.

I was not into violence and not in favor of violent demonstrations, but I wanted to do whatever I could do to help stop that war. It wasn't that I was not patriotic or did not support the troops. I love my country and the troops were us – by that time. We all had friends and relatives who had been killed in Vietnam.

The government had no answers and no plans to get out. It was very serious for the males, because if you were not in school, you got drafted into the Army. Besides, the war had been going on for roughly 20 years, which was my whole life. One of the first things I remember seeing on our new television … was Buddhist monks setting themselves on fire in Vietnam to protest the war. Fighting and body counts were on the news every day of my childhood. I felt like it had to stop, and that I had to do whatever I could to help. I decided to participate in the big march on May 4 but not to participate in any violence. The Vietnam Veterans Against the War and Dr. Abbas Kessel, a political science professor at MSC, influenced me, as well as did the increasing violence of the demonstrations at other campuses. It felt like it was now or never to join together and make our voices heard.

We walked downtown from upper campus, and I ended up by the Main Street Bridge. Highway 169 went over the bridge at that time and Main Street turned into Belgrade in North Mankato. This was blockaded by their finest law enforcement. I walked up the bank to the highway and saw students crowded on the bridge as far back as I could see up to a line on the north end of the bridge.

Opposing the mob were the sheriff and highway patrol with cars amassed three abreast towards the demonstrators on both the north and southbound lanes. There was yelling going on, and the tensions were extremely high, but not out of control. I worked my way around to check out different areas. Some of the drivers of the blocked vehicles were frustrated because it was supper time/quitting time, but there was no violence that I could see. I had no idea at the time what was going on with law enforcement, Dr. Nickerson and college officials or the townspeople, or of the actual number of people involved. I was simply participating to the best of my ability in this march to demonstrate our opposition to the war. I was surprised when it made the national news since there was little violence. I like to think that everyone who demonstrated against the war in Mankato or other locations in some way helped bring it to an end.

Now my daughter participates in demonstrations against the war in Iraq. As a mother, I worry. But I am proud of her courage and integrity, and support her efforts to uphold the right to protest, which is in grave danger today. When it becomes up to the citizens of this country, as a last resort, to protest in the streets again to make our opinions known, we need to exercise this right or it will be lost as many others have been.

Peaceful public demonstrations of opinion are fundamental to our ability to change public policy when all else fails. It is up to the average citizen to use it or lose it.

*Beth Sageng lives in Mankato, Minnesota.*


**Louis Schwartzkopf**
**Professor of Physics**

*Addressed directly to Jim Nickerson*

Jim, I write this in response to your request for a piece from me on my experience with the riots of 1970-1971, when I was at Berkeley. But in thinking about it, the story I want to tell predates this somewhat. It is the story that, to my mind, is the most important to tell from this period. It took place during my first or second year as a graduate student, so in the 1967-1969 time frame.

It started with one pivotal event that I remember clearly during my first year as a graduate student in physics at University of California, Berkeley. My first two years at Berkeley, I lived at International House. It was the custom of many of the students to watch the "CBS Evening News with Walter Cronkite" in the great hall after our supper. The Vietnam War had been going on for a while, and there was usually some war news every night. This particular night was different and much more memorable: Walter Cronkite announced that the government had eliminated graduate student deferments, an action that had implications for many of those in the room, particularly the young American men.

Reaction on campus was immediate. I remember meetings held in the LeConte Hall (one of the physics buildings) auditorium, filled to capacity, with speakers explaining the options available to us; enlisting in the Air Force or the Navy, waiting to be drafted, going to Canada. Other than knowing that I had no interest in fighting in the war, there was no clear choice for me. How I managed to avoid service is another story, but simply a digression here. What I want to tell you is what happened at the Oakland Induction Center.

The Oakland Induction Center was a major point of embarkation for draftees to be sent to Vietnam. It was the last place where they were sent before they were shipped overseas. The draft had been going on for some time now, but with Walter Cronkite's announcement, it occupied a much more central part of the attention of the students. One day while walking through Sproul Plaza (the main plaza in the central part of campus), I saw among all the other student tables one with a sign announcing a rally. In large letters on the sign was the statement: "We're going to shut down the Oakland Induction Center," with dates and other details.

I should explain my political state of mind at the time. I had graduated from Lincoln High School in Lincoln, Nebraska, in 1963, then gone off to Massachusetts Institute of Technology in Cambridge, Massachusetts, for my undergraduate work in physics. Life, for me, in both Lincoln and Cambridge was good. I had no reason to doubt what I had learned in school or what my parents and friends and family had reinforced, that the government was there to serve the interests of the people. Policemen were your friends. Even though the war in Vietnam was a terrible thing, our leaders in Washington must know what they were doing, and must have good reasons for going to war. It's true that I attended a tuition riot at MIT, but it was really rather civil – the rioters did nothing more than surround the president's house and chant (with considerable relish, actually), "seventeen hundred dollars is too (expletive) much!" Shortly after, the crowd dispersed. It had made its point. The police were there, but their main role turned out to be to help the demonstrators cross Massachusetts Avenue, the main arterial between two parts of campus.

What happened at the Oakland Induction Center was considerably different. My friends and I did not attend the rally, but we saw the news report about it on television that night. There was a solid mass of people, mostly of college-student age, sitting about eight to 10 deep, in front of and blocking the doors. Then the police came. They came in small groups, one or more wading into the sitting students, swinging their police clubs at them. I do not remember seeing demonstrators running away. What I do remember is the young people sitting there with looks of terror on their faces as the police kept swinging, and it went on and on. I thought, "Why are the police attacking the demonstrators?" There was no provocation other than that of sitting in front of the door. There was no sign of discussion between police officers and protesters. There was simply the onslaught of the attack on the sitting demonstrators.

The scales fell from my eyes. I never saw the government in the same light again.

*Louis Schwartzkopf lives in Mankato, Minnesota.*

### Ruth K. Schwickert

Mankato has been my home since 1946. My husband and I raised four children here, we owned a hardware store and roofing company on Front Street.

Looking back on the Vietnam Era, especially those turbulent years here in Mankato with the College demonstrations and protest marches, I do so with strong feelings of patriotism and little sympathy for the war protesters.

My husband had been a captain the Navy. Both he and I strongly believed in the ideas of serving our country and being patriotic citizens. My own son had enlisted in 1969 and was stationed in Korea. Even though our hardware business was never affected by these demonstrations and we personally did not feel threatened by the College protesters, we still could not condone their actions.

I remember the day student demonstrators blocked the highway. Some friends and I were playing bridge at the Century Club. When we tried to get home, we found the highway blocked. Fortunately, I know an alternate route, and we got home without incident. We were not afraid but more annoyed by the whole thing.

Today, looking back on those times, my feelings haven't changed. I still disagree with the actions of the MSC students and still believe we have a responsibility to serve our country.

*Ruth Schwickert lives in Mankato, Minnesota.*


### Mehr Jay Shahidi, '74

The spring of 1970 was a turbulent moment in the history of America. The war in Vietnam had expanded to encompass the whole region of Indochina. The tragedy of death and destruction was growing at a dizzying pace affecting the very fabric of America. More and more, young Americans were being sent to the front to kill, to die and to come back home damaged. Something had gone wrong with America and the result was superbly tragic. That was not supposed to be the case. America was intended to be good and lead humanity to ever-new heights.

America's body politic was angry, frustrated, guilty and revengeful. The misguided and mean policies of the most powerful government in the world combined with the greed of the powerful wealthy elite was bombarding the innocent and tearing up American democracy. The youth of this country were rising up to the atrocities and injustices of "the Establishment." So much was happening inside the crucible of social change that even the most astute observer of the American experience was baffled. Despite all the sadness and frustration, much of the change produced positive results: the civil rights movement, environmental movement, women's movement, just to name a few. America, in short, was boiling and transforming at a rapid pace.

America's turmoil was active in Minnesota, too. Thousands of young college students were protesting the war and rebelling against "the Establishment" at Mankato State College. Sometimes, the demonstration of their anger got out of hand and brought uncivil behavior, disruption and destruction to the campus and the community. The protesters, the women's liberation advocates, the civil rights and environmental activists had many kinds and types of leaders. One man among them shone brilliantly. He advocated peace through nonviolence, discourse and entreaty. He led the marchers but pleaded for civility and calm. He was small physically but enormous mentally. He wore old clothes and did not show off his degrees and accomplishments. He learned insatiably and taught unequivocally. He was a true scholar but not an armchair intellectual. He wrote to editors and those of authority, and he called for change peacefully. He was indefatigable. His name was Abbas Kessel.

The first time I heard him speak was that spring. He criticized the U.S. policy in Vietnam eloquently and bravely. But he did it with historical evidence and facts – much of it from the government's own records. He said the U.S. government had misled and lied to its citizens about Vietnam. That there was not credible evidence that the Vietnamese had provoked the United States into the war. That this war was planned and promoted by certain industries that profited from it financially. That it was a futile war, which was damaging the U.S. reputation around the globe and would be detrimental to America in the long run. That the money spent on the war would create a deficit that would become an enormous burden for generations of Americans in future. That the French had mistakenly gotten involved there and had paid a dear price. And now America was more and more burying itself in a war it could not win and, had no legal or moral right to fight. He urged the angry audience to become outraged, to protest the war, but to stay peaceful and civil. He called on us to struggle for peace without disrupting the education and work of other people. To keep our cool when provoked by the supporters of the war. To prepare and present our case against the war to audiences with facts and logical analysis. To never give up hope for peace and creation of a more just society.

During the next two years, as the war and its consequences got worse, I heard and saw Dr. Kessel many times. He became the icon of peaceful protest on campus largely because of his amazing intelligence. But also because of his high integrity, unwavering commitment and unpretentious demeanor.

Kessel was unique. With a rare courage, he exuded passion with utmost sincerity. He spoke the truth as he found it, not to please or appease anyone. An immigrant from Iran who had become an engineer at Berkeley and a political scientist at the University of Chicago, he amazed the listener with his knowledge of both physical and social sciences. He was a Renaissance man. He had been a researcher and public speaker for the powerful Chicago Council on International Relations. And then, he had applied at a remote college in 1966 to teach political science.

"I wanted to get away from the big city and all its pressures," he once told me. Some people at the Chicago council had become displeased with his blunt and to-the-point style. He had criticized the U.S. policy in the Congo, Iran and Israel/Palestine. He had called for reduction of military spending and more aid for developing the Third World. He had implicated the U.S. government agencies with overthrowing certain foreign governments and assassinating their leaders. And, way before President Eisenhower, he had warned us against the encroaching power of the "military-industrial complex."

Dr. Jim Nickerson, the president of Mankato State College, had hired him. Later, they had become good friends who liked and respected each other even though Kessel did not spare Nickerson in his intermittent critical essays and articles he wrote about education, college administration and the future of America. Nickerson also marched with Kessel at the front line of most anti-war marches. "Only when large numbers of citizens unite and express their opposition to this carnage through these marches and rallies" would the fiasco of Vietnam come to an end, I recall him telling me.

And that turned out to be the case, as he professed, by the end of 1972. The two shared their vision of non-violence and peaceful change. Neither, though, was a pacifist. Government, order, defense and police forces were ingredients of good government. But democracy and the Bill of Rights, they believed, should be the guiding lights of the people of America. No government, no president, no Johnson or Nixon was above the law. The presidents were designed, by the founding fathers of America, to be servants of the people and work for the people. Both men also believed in public education and liberal arts. They strived for the development of the "total person," not just a robotic technician. Music, flowers, history and colors were part of one's education.

After the United States pulled out of Indochina in 1973, I received the ultimate honor of getting to know Dr. Kessel as an advisor and later as a friend. Life does not give you that kind of chance often. Behind the plain exterior resided a person of incredible kindness, generosity and love for life. During the war, he often bought one-page newspaper ads which were almost completely black in color with a short statement at the bottom reading: MOURN THE WAR AND TELL NIXON SO. SEND THIS PAGE TO HIM. Kessel honestly mourned the war. Millions of lives would have been spared if we had heeded his call earlier on and rushed to the streets to oppose that malicious assault on human life and dignity. That lie which was stuffed down the throats of American people.

Kessel was an artist and naturalist. He loved Darwin and Mozart. "When George Bernard Shaw died," he wrote once, "I cried. … I cried again when Pablo Picasso died." Kessel took upon himself to speak out about life, liberty and the pursuit of happiness, just as the Founding Fathers of America had wanted. But he also considered it his duty to speak up about the ills of the society and devoted his life to devising remedies and actions that would alleviate human misery.

He was a powerful mind yet remained a humble man. He made his own furniture and grew his own prairie of wild plants around his tiny house. When I visited him for the first time in his living room on a cold Christmastime night, I was flabbergasted by his large and varied collection of books. Even the wall of the stairwell was covered with shelves. He possessed an eclectic collection of pieces of art, including some his own creations. Kessel was indomitable in his pursuit of knowledge and truth.

He affected my life so drastically that few days go by in my personal and professional life when I don't think of him or his utterly profound words of wisdom. He wrote in an article on Henry Kissinger that "no one was indispensable" and no one should have "near-absolute power." His time on this planet was well lived. He greatly enriched my college. He felt lucky to have had the opportunity to come to America but never forgot the plight of the millions desperately struggling to have a fraction of the prosperity and freedom enjoyed by him. He deeply cherished and honored his chance to be a teacher. And, he gracefully received death from cancer at the age of 69 in 1988.

---

When a giant of a man, Dr. James F. Nickerson, the war-time president of Minnesota State College, Mankato, asked me to write a passage to possibly be included in the manuscript of his memories, I felt moved and honored. When I came to the United States of America in 1968, as a foreign student from Iran, I could not imagine the possibility that, someday, I would become a student leader at a 14,000-student college campus and serve as a senator, vice president and president, which gave me an unusual opportunity to get to know and work with amazing educational leaders, especially this extraordinary man.

I discovered Jim to be a great educator. He touched and affected my life in a way I had not thought possible. In public and private meetings, in conducting the management of the College, in his speeches, and in his demeanor, I saw a thoughtful, creative, compassionate and deep individual who loved education, civility and peace. Originally, I went to Mankato to study for a degree in economics. I met and learned from several great teachers. But Mankato opened

my horizon and outlook. It enabled me to get to know myself better. Most of
what I acquired there, which helped formulate my social and political views,
was not possible to experience in classrooms only. Jim created conditions in
Mankato that allowed me to learn how to become an activist. He led us to
become a cosmopolitan institution. He brought in many top-notch faculty and
staff members. Arnoldus Gruter was our artist-in-residence. Music and theater
departments flourished. Abbas Kessel, a peace activist graduate of the University
of Chicago, was hired, and computer science became a major. We began to
compete with the University of Minnesota. We evolved into a national college.
The likes of Ted Kennedy, Ralph Nader and Jane Fonda were now willing to visit
us, and presidential candidates often made Mankato their forum.

In spring of 1972, at the height of the Vietnam War and the ensuing domestic
turmoil in the United States, Jim appointed me to his Crisis Cabinet, a group
he had organized from the ranks of the faculty, staff, students and townspeople.
Our mission was to advise him as how to deal with massive student protests
against the war at our campus. MSC, in 1970-72, was at the forefront of angry
national opposition to a policy that would soon kill almost 58,000 Americans,
maim nearly half a million more and cause the death of millions of Indochinese
– most of them bystanders.

For three nights in a row, I remember, Mankato became the first news item on
national nightly news broadcasts, when the legendary Walter Kronkite described
the actions of the student protesters in and around Mankato. Even though, by
far most opposition were expressed peacefully, we experienced civil disobedience
by some, and violence by others. Overall, Mankato remained vibrant but calm,
compared to many other major colleges and universities. I give my gratitude for
that calmness and civility to many teachers, students, community leaders, and
college staff members. But most of the credit should go to one person – Jim
Nickerson.

As president of a large college in a small town, he worked brilliantly, skillfully
and tirelessly to listen to our grievances, march with us, talk with us, shout
with us and hope with us. He met with protest leaders, gave them the bully
pulpit, promoted nonviolence and became the true leader of our campus
movement against the war. He also supported our civil rights movement and
our environmental movement. By being one of us, by representing us, he gave
strength to our collective resolve, subdued violent tendencies and pulled the
rug from under those preaching violence against "the system." Jim stayed on
campus, engaged, open and available. He diffused tensions and the potential for
violence through his charming personality and passion for justice.

During those years, Jim endured enormous pressure from some townspeople,
community and government leaders and his superiors who wanted him to deal
with protesters harshly and resort to more police action to identify and expel

their leaders. Jim tolerated the heat and kept moving. He showed foresight and courage. And the result of his policies and actions enabled Mankato to come out of the war era relatively unscathed, kept the College functioning, saved our collective investment and prevented injuries and death. Yes, he convinced the police and the National Guard to stay away from the campus.

On one occasion, I recall his office contacting me to meet him immediately upon the occupation of Old Main by a splinter protest group. By the time I reached the building, the police had come to evacuate it. He persuaded them to leave quickly. And there were no injuries, damages to property or arrests. Jim let the protesters stay in the building overnight. He also stayed there with his staff. This was another brilliant example of diffusing tensions by being there and granting the angry protesters a forum for expression.

By 1972, U.S. involvement in Indochina had gravely damaged this country's prestige abroad and was tearing the domestic fabric apart. Jim recognized this and worried about the loss of American democracy and internal freedom. He feared America, which he truly loved, could become a police state. He felt very responsible for the safety and well being of "my students." Such a feeling manifested itself the day he stood on the bridge of Highway 169, barricaded by protesters, and used the loud speaker of a sheriff's car to urge and convince the protesters to leave peacefully. And, they did. We all did. Without a police raid.

That day on the bridge, I was standing behind Jim. It was one of the scariest moments of my life. We were between protesters sitting on the bridge on one side, and the security forces, weapons at hand, ready to move in on the other. For a moment, I thought a clash was inevitable. Jim asked the sheriffs to give him some time. They did. He asked Larry Spencer, our Student Senate president, to also speak to the crowd. He did. And, we all left the bridge. That day, I learned from Jim the power of inclusion and respect. He usually asked us student leaders to join him in his efforts to neutralize explosive situations. He included the other side in his plea for calm, and he always spoke with respect for all.

Despite the sadness and tenseness of the war years, Jim never lost his indomitable optimism, his commitment to education and his zest to build MSC into a multi-faceted, multi-cultural and intellectual environment. At a meeting of his staff, requested by me, to discuss the possible information on an international center on campus, he said MSC was becoming an international institution and he appointed a staff member to study the feasibility of such a center. Later, that center was organized in the form of the International Student Office.

Jim strived to bring about a system that could provide a well-rounded education to students, not just vocational training. During his tenure at MSC, the number of majors programs and specialties offered grew significantly. His later work, at the American Association of State Colleges and Universities, to enable enlisted military men and women to study for academic degrees, is a testimony to his philosophy of education.

Jim is still at it. He has never given up, despite personal and family sickness and setbacks. At 95, he is as sharp and alert and full of life as then. He is socially and politically engaged. He has not become a dogmatic or fearful person. On the contrary, he speaks and behaves ever more openly and freely. Perhaps it is because, today, he is not at the helm of a large institution with all kinds of responsibilities to bear and groups and individuals to satisfy. I find Jim to be a social scientist with a scientific mind, an artist with terrific managerial abilities and a scholar who can form concrete solutions to abstract problems. He has truly been an inspiration to me. He and his elegant wife, Nita, became dear friends of mine later. I visited them at their home in Washington, D.C., and benefited from their knowledge and social etiquette.

At a large gathering in 1971, at the student union, a teacher, angry at the protesters, told Jim that "a teacher's job is to teach and a student's job is to learn. There is no room for protest against the government." Jim responded by saying, "I cannot quite agree with you. This institution must be for more than just teaching and learning."

Indeed, Jim led MSC into a center for social and political interaction and community development. After the U.S. withdrawal from Indochina in 1972, MSC faced a significant decline in enrollment and revenue partly because some of the 2,000 or more veterans and those avoiding the draft quit school, partly because of declines in the rate of population increase and the economy, which were national trends. Jim, however, received much of the community's blame, which claimed this decline in enrollment was because of his softness toward the protesters. He tolerated enormous pressure before resigning as president in 1973.

I did not get the opportunity in life to attend an Ivy League college, but I journeyed through a unique and tantalizing crucible named MSC. I wept for Vietnam and mourned for the dead. I grieved the damage to Earth and its living organisms caused by this wicked and vicious war. I hoped and resolved to do all I could to prevent another one. Yet, despite all the sadness, anger and frustration, I loved my years at MSC. I loved the experience of Jim Nickerson.

*Mehr Shahidi lives in Minnetonka, Minnesota.*

*Scott Shrewsbury*
*Professor Emeritus of Political Science and Law Enforcement*

I joined the faculty of Mankato State in 1965. At the time, there was little to indicate the campus would soon be in the throes of intense, and sometimes turbulent, political protests – or that I would be caught up in them. But as the war in Vietnam continued to escalate and as students became more aware, a small group of campus activists grew into a movement that confronted the institution with challenges it had not faced before.

As a political scientist specializing in international and comparative politics, with an emphasis on Southeast Asia, I had a professional interest in the same issues that worried the student activists. With my own inclination toward political activism, I was personally engaged by what engaged them. As a young instructor, close to them in age, various students gravitated toward me for support and advice.

Anti-war activities at Mankato State can be divided into two overlapping periods, with 1968-1969 as a dividing point. The first period saw conventional political activity. It was characterized by teach-ins, organized debates and speeches to campus and community groups. Teams of well-dressed, clean-cut anti-war students canvassed neighborhoods, spreading their message across Mankato. Membership in political clubs, especially the Young DFL, grew by leaps and bounds.

During 1968, attention turned to presidential politics. Much time and energy were expended to promote the candidacy of anti-war Sen. Eugene McCarthy. At mock political conventions on campus, he won the Democratic nomination. Mankato State students went to Indiana and Wisconsin to work with the McCarthy forces. "Be Clean for Gene" was the slogan of the day. Anti-war students, faculty and sympathetic townspeople organized to win the local precinct caucuses for McCarthy. They were so successful that, a month later, in coalition with pro-McCarthy nuns from Good Counsel and the political organization of North End grocer Herb Mocol (who later became mayor), they wrested control of the Blue Earth County Democratic Farmer Labor Party from a pro-Humphrey group.

During the 1969-1970 school year, anti-war activities on campus took on a different tone. Students appeared to turn away from conventional politics and toward a more demonstrative style. It was a style characterized by theatrical gestures, confrontation, intensity of emotion and even despair. Although student leaders remained committed to nonviolent tactics, there was increased concern that some protest activities would turn violent or would provoke violence from others.

Several factors came together to create this sharper tone. First, the idealism of "Be Clean for Gene" gave way to the cold reality that political efforts had failed: Nixon the "hawk" had become president. Second, large numbers of anti-war veterans returned to campus from Vietnam. Their idealism had been severely tempered by experience. Vietnam Veterans Against the War brooked no nonsense and were unimpressed by academic rank or authority.

Third, the anti-war movement underwent a predictable evolution. Over time, especially a time of increasing frustration, any movement can be expected to divide into factions, each following its own agenda and preferred set of tactics. More radical factions will emerge and accuse moderates of selling out. Factionalism will make the movement, as a whole, harder to control. Instead of a unified leadership, there will be conflicting sets of leaders, often working at cross-purposes.

Fourth, Americans were bombarded each evening with violent television images from the war. Some people, influenced by the "legitimate" and official violence they saw around them, came to think violence was the norm.

I have many vivid memories of those turbulent days. But, I have limited myself to recounting only three episodes. Each episode comes from the post 1968-69 period and each underscores the forces and tensions that were at play.

### The Survivors of Pearl Harbor

Late one afternoon, I was reading at home the *Free Press* account of a huge rally held on the upper campus mall to protest the invasion of Cambodia. A parade of students, faculty, staff and townspeople had given speeches criticizing this latest outrage. I was pleased that the reporter had accurately quoted from my speech. I had proclaimed that Nixon didn't understand much about Cambodia and Southeast Asia if he thought the invasion would hasten an end to the war. I predicted the invasion would widen the war and culminate eventually in a communist Cambodia.

The phone rang. I answered as a harsh and raspy male voice exploded into my ear, "Are you that Shrewsbury up at that college?"

"I teach at Mankato State," I replied.

He persisted, "Are you that Shrewsbury that spoke in the newspaper today and said the president don't know what he's doing in Vietnam?"

"I spoke at the rally," I admitted "Who am I speaking to?"

"Never mind who I am," he responded, "just say I'm an irate citizen."

"Yes, we're irate citizens," I heard a female voice in the background say. "And we don't like what him and them other professors said about our president and the war."

"We're taxpayers," the man continued, "and we shouldn't have to pay our taxes to you and all them others traitors up at that college."

His diatribe continued for a few moments. The woman echoed his sentiments and interjected complaints of her own from time to time. I listened, thinking if they vented their rage long enough, they would settle down, and I could find a way to end the "conversation" on a more cordial note. But as they continued, their anger fed upon itself and became more intense.

Finally I interrupted, "I'm sure a lot of people agree with your point of view and you have a right to express it. But I also have a right to express my views."

The man paused for a moment before he calmly said, "We don't have all them students to talk to, and *The Free Press* wouldn't listen to us."

"Why don't we meet where we can discuss this at greater length," I suggested.

"I don't know how we could meet," he said doubtfully.

"Tell him to come to the group," the woman interjected. "We'll all talk to him. See how he likes that. He'll have to listen to other people than all them students and professors."

"What group is this?" I asked.

"The Survivors of Pearl Harbor," he answered. "We meet every month at twelve."

My mind raced, searching for reasons why I couldn't walk into that lion's den. "It's hard for me to get away from campus," I said lamely. "Why don't we find a time you two could come to my office? I'll buy you a cup of coffee."

He paused. I suspect he was trying to find an excuse not to walk into his own conception of a lion's den. In the end he just said, "We might do that," and hung up.

I was sure I would never hear from them again. I was right, but I often wonder what would have happened if I had ventured into the lion's den and had talked to the Survivors of Pearl Harbor about my reasons for opposing the war. Many days, I think I missed a golden opportunity. But then ...

## A Day with Congress

Dan Welty and I sat in the office of Minnesota Congressman Ancher Nelsen, waiting for him to meet with us. It was mid-afternoon, and we were nearing the end of a whirlwind set of appointments. Less than 15 hours earlier, we had been sitting in an auditorium watching an emergency meeting of Mankato State's Faculty Senate.

For several weeks, tension over the war and anti-war demonstrations had been growing on campus and in the community. In the midst of the usual round of rallies, sit-ins, marches, bomb threats and class disruptions, an explosion had wrecked the new Law Enforcement Center downtown. Although, as far as I know, no connection was ever actually shown, many were quick to link the incident with the campus anti-war activities.

The Faculty Senate was fearful that tensions on campus might soon reach a breaking point. After discussing several strategies to alleviate the situation, the Senate prevailed upon Dan and me to fly to Washington early the next morning. Our mission was to inform the members of Minnesota's congressional delegation of the campus sentiment. It was a symbolic gesture to demonstrate that something constructive was being done.

By the time of our appointment with Rep. Nelsen, we had already had lengthy conversations with Sen. Walter Mondale and Rep. Don Fraser. We had had shorter meetings with staff members from the offices of Sen. Hubert Humphrey and Rep. Al Quie. For the most part, our reception had been cordial. Mondale and Fraser had been particularly sympathetic to our message, agreeing that what was happening at Mankato State was similar to what was happening on campuses throughout the state and the country. Dan and I emphasized that the vast majority of student protesters were peaceful and sincere. The politicians agreed with that characterization and hoped that it would remain that way.

Congressman Nelsen soon arrived and invited us into his inner office. Surrounded by examples of his woodcarving hobby, he told us how proud he was to represent Mankato and Mankato State. He had been in Congress since 1959 and felt he had always tried to do right by the College. He listened attentively as Dan and I described the effect the war was having on campus. He gently reminded us that he represented more than just students and faculty dissatisfied with the war. He understood the frustrations students had about the war, but he also understood why many people were frustrated with the behavior of the students.

He noted that the academic community tended to be more hostile to him than did the general public. "This is particularly true of some of you professors," he said. "There is this guy at Gustavus who is always after me."

Turning his attention to the damage done to the Law Enforcement Center, he said that many of his constituents were encouraging him to make an issue out of student activists. He would not do that, however, because it would add fuel to an already bad situation. "I promise you, I will not try to make political hay out of it."

He then changed the subject to his woodcarvings, showing us his favorite pieces. As we made our way to the office of Rep. John Zwach, our last appointment of the day, I remarked to Dan that I was surprised at how much I liked Ancher Nelsen. Since coming to Minnesota, I had always worked for and voted for his opponents.

Our meeting with Congressman Zwach was equally cordial. He was the most friendly and "folksy" of all the legislators we met that day. Throughout our discussion, he was philosophical and deeply troubled by the war and what it was doing to the country. He wondered if anyone could ever find a viable way out of Vietnam. He was sad that the country had become so divided and hoped Mankato State would avoid the violence seen on other campuses. At the end of our conversation, Zwach prevailed upon his aide to drive us to the airport since the hour was getting late and he didn't want us to miss our flight back to Minnesota. Another nice Republican, I thought.

On the return flight, Dan and I discussed whether our day with the congressional delegation had accomplished anything. I doubted if such a hastily arranged mission would do much to make the increasingly frustrated student demonstrators feel better about the prospects for the war ending. Dan agreed but suggested our efforts would make the congressmen feel more positive about the campus demonstrations and the commitment of faculty and administration to do everything possible to keep them peaceful.

As we flew back to Minnesota, we were unaware that folks on campus had been trying all afternoon to contact us to request that we spend a couple more days in Washington. They wanted us to be an advance team to arrange for the arrival and care of a number of students who would engage in their own lobbying efforts. In the end, by working with Rep. Fraser's office (and perhaps Sen. Mondale's), arrangements were made for a contingent of Mankato State students to spend some time in D.C.

Many months later, after the turmoil had subsided, Rep. Nelsen was on campus to speak before an American Government class. I encountered him on the steps of Morris Hall. He yelled a greeting, remembering my name. As we were shaking hands, he said, "I kept my promise, didn't I?" I had to think back for a moment to our conversation in his office and his promise not to make a political issue out of the campus disturbances. "You certainly did," I replied.

*Kessel at the Post Office*

The anti-war rally had materialized in front of the Post Office just after dusk. At first, the large crowd of students, several faculty and sympathizing townspeople were mostly quiet. Some carried candles, which made their flickering faces stand out against the gathering darkness. I was with several colleagues on the outskirts of the assembly and could dimly see a speaker's platform far down the street, over to my right.

As one speaker followed another, some in the crowd appeared to become more restive. Notes of concern turned into anger and anger to rage. I gradually concluded it was possible for this demonstration to turn violent. As if to confirm my growing concern, I suddenly heard glass shattering. Someone had hurled an object through a nearby window. A rumor quickly spread through the throng that there would be an attempt to march to the armory and attack it.

As elements in the crowd were becoming more and more unruly, a diminutive figure took the platform. It was my political science colleague, Abbas Kessel (who preferred to be called simply Kessel). Kessel agreed with the activists that the war was wrong in almost every sense. He had expressed his views in numerous *Free Press* articles, lectures and campus teach-ins. There was no question that he agreed with the demands of the demonstrators, but he was uncomfortable with demonstrative politics. He felt that reasonable discourse would eventually prevail over the murky sources of bad judgment. Kessel was blessed with a keen intellect and expressed himself in clear, crisp statements.

On this night, he exhorted the crowd to refrain from excessive actions. He was deeply fearful that demonstrations could easily be transformed into violence. Violence would be bad for the anti-war message. He told the rally, "The man in the White House would like nothing better than to see you react with violence." Periodically, a smattering of boos and catcalls would greet Kessel, but the vast majority of his listeners heard him with respect.

I was proud of my colleague that night as I was to be proud of him throughout those days of campus turmoil and afterward. Many on campus and in the community misunderstood Kessel's role during the campus protests. He was mistakenly seen as being at one with the demonstrators, an instigator of protest. Many people did not realize that Kessel preferred orderly dialogue and discussion. But if demonstrations were inevitable, he intended to do everything possible to make sure they were kept peaceful and constructive. He was a gentle man and a man of peace. He performed his role with dignity and courage.

At the conclusion of the rally, the original plan had been for the demonstrators to march up to Old Main to continue for a while with protest songs. But an ugly chant spread across part of the crowd, "Go to the armory, Go to the armory!" Others shouted, "No, no, go to Old Main!"

The largest part of the crowd headed up the hill toward Old Main. But a sizeable group followed those who were moving headlong toward the armory. I, along with other faculty members, debated whether to go with the majority to Old Main or to go with those headed for the armory. We decided that maybe those on the way to the armory could be dissuaded from carrying through with the plans of those hard-core agitators up front. Along the way, we admonished those around us to follow Kessel's advice to avoid violence. We pointed out the immediate danger of attacking the armory and the possible long-range consequences.

As the protesters drew close to the armory, a remarkable thing happened. The body of the crowd slowed, then stopped and gazed at the structure before them. Four or five people had advanced to the shadow of the building and urged the crowd forward. I held my breath. It seemed as if an invisible wave floated across the would-be mob. Almost to a person and without a word, it turned, faced up the hill, and slowly made its way to Old Main. There, we listened to folk and protest songs, participated in sing-alongs, and eventually dispersed. Aside from the episode of occupying the bridge and downtown streets, this was the closest I came to seeing a peaceful demonstration turn into wholesale violence.

I remember looking back toward the armory after the demonstrators had gazed deeply into themselves and decided not to become a mindless mob. I saw a handful of shadowy figures, one of them in a long, dark overcoat, trudging dejectedly in the opposite direction. I did not know who they were. They may not have been Mankato State students at all. Eventually, there were rumors of outside agitators coming to campus. And, of course, during those times when paranoia lurked just below the surface, it crossed many minds that those young men may have worked for some government agency or other. Such agents provocateur were not unknown in those days and under those circumstances.

*Epilogue*

I will close by making three observations about those days of campus protests at Mankato State. First, the anti-war activities were not the only conflicts bubbling on campus at that time. Those were the days when students began to actively demand autonomy. They sought to throw off the old idea of *in loco parentis* and demanded to be treated as adults. They wrested control of their own campus organizations and publications. The controversy over "Herbie and I" in Plaintiff magazine gave us our own free speech movement. Students won inclusion on curriculum and other decision-making bodies. Agitation over the nonrenewal of an instructor led to turmoil similar to the anti-war protests and resulted in the creation of the Chair of Ideas. Demands for equal treatment and opportunities for minority students exploded with an intensity that paralleled and intersected the anti-war activism. The demands of women for equal treatment and recognition had to be addressed. And toward the end, we saw the birth of the environmental movement on campus.

Second, I personally witnessed two episodes that could easily have led to a tragedy like Kent State. One was the day the bridge and streets downtown were occupied. The other, involving the armory, I recounted above. That these and many other episodes occurred without bloodshed can be attributed to various people. There were talented student leaders committed to nonviolence. They did the hard work of organizing demonstrations so as to maintain control and to minimize disruptions. There were faculty members, like Kessel, who consistently and constantly cautioned that violence would be morally wrong and self-defeating. Above all, were the roles played by C.D. Alexander, Mankato's police chief, and President James F. Nickerson. They were under great pressure to "crack down on those students." They heard such voices from both campus and community. That they did not heed those voices is to their everlasting credit. By ignoring those who counseled violence, they avoided bloodshed. They handled the protests with courage and understanding. I was particular proud of President Nickerson at the time, and my admiration for him has only grown as the years have gone by.

Third, we should not look back upon this period through a lens of negativity. The times were, indeed, difficult – sometimes fearful and dangerous. They were often frustrating. But, the campus was alive with conversation, questioning and concern. How many times, when I was an undergraduate during the late 1950s, did I hear my professors complain about how complacent we were, how unaware, how apathetic? And, how many times later in my career as a professor, when students had turned inward and had become imbued with the ethos of me-ism, did I miss the exuberance, dedication and commitment of those anti-war activists?

*Scott Shrewsbury lives in Minneapolis, Minnesota.*


### H. Roger Smith
### Professor Emeritus of Urban and Regional Studies

The country was in a state of turmoil over the war in Asia, especially Vietnam. Our foreign policy was still one of imperialism and meddling in the interest and governance of nations across the globe. Nixon was lying to the country and the world, yet was still being supported by a significant proportion of the electorate as we watched, through the medium of television, thousands of young men and innocents being killed or mutilated by the horrors of napalm, Agent Orange, artillery blasts and the machines of modern war. "The war" was uppermost on the minds of the nation and the world. Nevertheless, it was not a popular war as we were lead to believe by the Nixon administration. More and more of the electorate and the disenfranchised were beginning to question the value of this conflict that seemingly was based on bogus body counts and headlines that continued to make us believe that the light at the end of the tunnel was symbolic of the imminent end of the war and not the onrushing locomotive that could destroy us all.

The war certainly was a focus and garnered much of our attention, but President Nixon was literally managing these times. The grand manipulator, through his administrative management of the media, had literally divided and conquered the electorate by diffusing the Asian conflict as a focus by subdividing our attention between the environmental crisis, women's liberation, the war on drugs, racism and "the war." The analogy of 1971-1972 and today with our war in the Middle East, with our war on poverty, war on terrorism, war on drugs, et al., is easily recognized. We are truly a war-based society seduced into fighting all manner of wars that cannot be won and will never realize a victory.

Closer to home all of these issues were also a focus of campus life and the greater community as well. Great changes were occurring in both campus and community. The old T.C. on the hill was no longer a teachers college but had become recognized as a full-fledged Minnesota State College or MSC. The Crawford Years, under the presidency of Dr. C.L. Crawford, were now behind us. The College was in the process of being transformed by way of a new era of leadership under the guiding hand of Dr. J.F. Nickerson as president. The town, itself, was in a state of total transformation with the demolition and destruction of the core of the community under the urban renewal program. An entirely new venue for shopping had emerged on the hilltop, with a new state-of-the-art shopping complex known as Madison East. Like the campus itself with two distinct locations, one on the hilltop and the original campus in the valley, Mankato was being bifurcated.

Minnesota State College enrollments had literally soared to unprecedented heights with numbers exceeding 14,000. The College was marketing itself to a much larger market and region than at any earlier time and was attracting minority students and many foreign students to the campus. Co-ed dorms were becoming a part of campus life, much to the consternation of many local residents.

Under Dr. Nickerson's leadership, many new programs were emerging to accommodate and recognize the transformations that were happening in the world and especially in higher education at that time. A Task Force for Change was initiated that gave students, administrators and faculty an opportunity to shape the College in such a fashion that it gave the campus a way of dealing with rapid change rather than simply relying on a fixed body of knowledge. The chancellor of the Minnesota State College System noted, "There can be no innovation without critical self examining (sic). It is only by reassessing our priorities, closing down the less important in order to open up the more important, that we will be able to respond to realities and to continue quality education." The Task Force for Change was created to help find the "more" in "more important." A sense of community was beginning to emerge, and students and faculty realized they had a role in shaping the process of change. Innovation and involvement were now encouraged thus facilitating the process of change.

Under the guidance of President Nickerson and his "North Dakota Mafia" made up of vice presidents and deans, new attitudes toward the places of students and faculty in those changing times became manifest by encouragement of innovation and change. Essentially, the administration was becoming one that looked for values in new ideas, and instead of asking why, they offered, "Why not?"

Risky new ideas were being tried throughout the campus. An experimental college with an experimental curriculum and co-ed living was given sanction and encouragement by the administration. New curricular components were being initiated on campus, i.e. women's studies and peace studies. Innovative programs, such as the Chair of Ideas, were initiated to invite thinkers and philosophers who offered a different perspective on contemporary thought to come to campus and spend time with the campus community and the community at large. An artist-in-residence position was created with a venue in the Centennial Student Union to allow young people and others to visit with the artist to learn about and see art being created and displayed. Mini-courses, a curriculum of short-term single-credit classes was initiated to attempt to save faculty positions that were cut due to a sudden six percent drop in fall enrollment. Courses on topics such as gunsmithing, guitar playing, yarn making and the sociology of bars (booze) were tried and were somewhat successful in helping generate the credit hours necessary to retain threatened faculty positions.

Yet another innovation was a five-week "hands-on" experiential learning environment focusing on urban issues in remote places such as Mobile, Alabama; Portland, Maine; Portland, Oregon; San Francisco and Boston. One full week of the tenure was when the student participants were dropped off at the bus depot in Boston or San Francisco with only two dollars in their pockets and their social security cards. The purpose of "Plunge" was to expose to the participants first-hand to the experience of being homeless and disenfranchised in the urban place.

What was happening was truly a time of transformation and change. The preceding is nothing but an example of the many and varied efforts that were being instituted in both the community and within higher education itself. Most importantly, these innovative action experiences gave the students and the faculty a place and a role in shaping their futures. The fundamental key to much of the successes of the time was that students knew they could offer ideas and be heard. Students began to realize they were empowered and, for the first time, they knew it was OK to dissent. They became aware of the implications of their decisions. Though they were empowered to make change and take control in the transformation of their futures, they also could see the consequences of their actions.

All the ideas and programmatic components that were reshaping campus life were important to varying degrees to all of those in both the campus community and the community at large as well as the nation. Many of these changes were not popular and were generating a significant negative response. Sometimes change and transformation are perceived as threatening and contrary to popular thought and understanding. Some components of the community and the region were severely threatened, especially by the questions that were being raised about a war that many of them had been seduced to believe was important and justified. Words like hippies, commies, pinkos, weirdos, faggots, fairies and freaks were in some local minds synonymous with the MSC student, and everyone knew what they meant. Not only was the campus split but so was the community at large. "The war" was either black or white. There was no gray.

Suddenly, "the war" began to take on an even greater dimension than in previous times. Students, church leaders and some local residents began to have teach-ins, be-ins, sit-ins and laugh-ins in the student unions. This was wonderful fodder for the media, and they exploited it, especially in the community. Letters to the editor denouncing the campus leaders, administrators, students and other young people appeared daily in *The Free Press,* and there were calls to "throw the baggage out," especially that Nickerson man.

The voice of dissent was not just in Mankato. The force was nationwide. Actually, it was worldwide in the truest sense. People were outraged that we were fighting a war in which we should never have been involved, and at a huge personal cost to all. (Is there an analogy to the present lurking here?) Some of the local population was literally considering "going up there and bashing a little sense into those &%#$@ people up there at TC." Demonstrations, marches, teach-ins and sit-ins were going on all over the country, and Mankato State was simply one cosmic component of the growing dissent as more and more organizations were emerging either for or against the war.

In the spring, things really started to come to a head. A three-day teach-in was planned. Students were told to skip their classes and participate. Organized efforts on the part of the anti-war element of the campus were organized to go into classrooms, disrupt the classes and encourage both faculty and students to participate in the anti-war teach-in. These efforts were nonviolent although sometimes confrontational, to say the least. Many faculty encouraged their students to participate, and walk-outs of classes were common. A lot was said and a lot of empowerment was earned, but nothing violent ever was a part of this effort. When compared to the marches, demonstrations and rhetoric on campuses across the nation and here in Minnesota, the MSC campus community was very much involved and committed yet peaceful and nonviolent in almost all respects.

Finally, in mid-April, a demonstration and march was scheduled. Protest-oriented activities with speakers and some entertainment were planned for out on the mall in front of Armstrong Hall. The day before these events, a number of students fashioned a Vietnamese "hooch" out of sticks, rope and bark on the mall and were planning to sleep in it. During the early morning hours, some unknown dissenters who did not agree with the prevailing posture of their colleagues against the war went out and threw an accelerant on the hooch and torched it. No one was injured, but the burned-out hooch immediately became a symbol, and while the crowd gathered and listened to the speakers, i.e., Abbas Kessel and others, several of the demonstration and march organizers fashioned a makeshift cross out of two charred and still-smoking sticks from the burned-out hooch. It was this cross that led the march into the valley, past the high school and into the downtown.

At some point in time, a rather large crowd of onlookers, some for but most against the war, had gathered along Second Street at Main and an incipient confrontation began to take place with considerable argument emerging not just from the marchers but from the onlookers as well. No police presence was apparent though Police Chief C.D. Alexander and his men were nearby and were in communication with selected participants via walkie talkies. One of the most outspoken groups that thought the march was nonsense came boiling out of Pappy's Bar threatening to beat the "living shit out of the bunch of turds." The crowd was huge but did not respond other than with verbal discussions of the group's parentage, bodily make up, chromosomal deficits and sexual preferences. Though threatened, there was no violence.

Finally, without any intervention other than by those speaking the voice of reason, the march split up with some of the students turning back to City Hall and the Post Office and the others went off ostensibly to the hilltop. At the Post Office/City Hall, things became more heated. The flag of the United States was both a symbol of democracy and of the imperialists' war. There was considerable talk of tearing down the flagpole and marching through downtown. Either one or a combination of both was a potential detonator that could have resulted in serious violence to both property and public safety. Nevertheless, the police presence was very subtle, and though tempers were beginning to flair, the crowd still did not erupt or get out of control. The Post Office was of course a powerful symbol with its flag and connotation of the imperialist thinking of the times. But it was also inviolate. More peaceful and thoughtful minds prevailed and focused the group's attention on the Mankato City Hall and its flag.

Demands were flying and, finally, Bill Bassett, the city manager, came down and spoke briefly to the ostensible leadership and finally agreed to lower the flag, dip the colors and return it back up the flagpole upside down. The upside-down flag is the international symbol of distress. Though far removed from the burning or destruction previously demanded, the international distress symbol in front of City Hall and its associated symbolism diffused much of the fervor of the crowd. With this statement made, the crowd began to dissipate itself to more salubrious venues such as The Square Deal and Schulte's Bar.

Much of the credit for this peaceful and positive demonstration must be given to both Police Chief Alexander and City Manager Bill Bassett for seeing what might have happened and allowing this simple yet symbolic statement to diffuse the energy of the crowd and allow the day to end on a peaceful note. It is to the credit of some of the campus and community leadership that this event was permitted to occur. This simply symbolic act helped divide the sentiments of the crowd and thus diffuse what might have been a very serious demonstration of violence and destruction.

Though not personally involved in any of the off-campus demonstrations, it should be noted that Dr. Nickerson's efforts through his staff and faculty and the forward-looking programs they guided had set the stage for these demonstrations. The empowerment he had given the students on the MSC campus gave them a responsibility for thoughtful and nonviolent acts against the College or the community.

The march on the Post Office was only one public demonstration of many people's anger and frustration with the Mankato community. There were separate instances on both the Main Street Bridge and the North Star Bridge. The demonstration on the Main Street Bridge resulted in one act of violence by Nicollet County sheriff and the North Mankato police. The tossing of tear-gas bombs was directed at the student marchers to cause them to disperse and permit the flow of traffic to resume. (This, if you remember, was how the violence at Kent State erupted and quickly escalated into the murder of four young people.) The same kind of escalation could have as easily occurred on the bridge that April afternoon, but, again, the resolution on the part of the students was to continue their protest but refrain from further violent confrontation.

The purpose of the incidents on both the Main Street Bridge and the North Star Bridge was, of course, to bring to the attention of the community and users of the bridges that they could not simply ignore the protests and rhetoric of the times because "most of that was up at the College and was a student issue." The blockading of traffic and the closing of the bridge on Highway 169 brought all that mid-afternoon traffic to a dead halt. Suddenly, those people who were now at a dead stop were experiencing the anger and frustration the students were feeling about the war. In this case, their anger and frustration were directed at the young people on the bridge not at the war, yet the message was clear. People were angry. It was warm and most cars were not equipped with air conditioning. Drivers began to open their windows, and dialogue was initiated. The young protesters were not there to hurt anyone. They wanted the public to hear the message and feel the inconvenience of losing mobility.

There was a lot of anger on the part of the victims of the shutdown, and there were many threats made to the participants. Several marchers, in acts of nonviolence learned in large part from the voter registration marches in the South, lay down behind the wheels of semi trucks to keep them from backing up and plowing their way through the marchers. (It is interesting that so many of the tactics that were initiated over the outrage and indignation of the truckers there on that bridge that day were used only a few months later when the expressway systems of many states, not the least of which was Minnesota, were used by these same truckers to shut down the interstate highway system in protest of rising fuel prices. What goes around comes around, it does seem.)

Finally and without incident, the North Star Bridge takeover ended. The point was made without violence. Traffic began to move again and the participants dispersed, but the point had been clearly made and, of course, the media made the best of it. Once again, these people had acted in a thoughtful, albeit not-always-rational manner yet without violence on their part and no property damage. The only thing that really got hurt that day was a lot of community and personal pride. Nevertheless, in spite of the one incident on the Nicollet County side of the Main Street Bridge, all the participants reacted and responded in a thoughtful and nonviolent manner. There were contingencies in place by local law enforcement officials, the National Guard, the Minnesota State Police and civic leaders to call in support to meet any violence with even more violence. How easily this could have turned into another Kent State University or Berkley.

Again we find that the sensibilities of Police Chief Alexander, Col. Paul Meyer of the National Guard, Paul Hadley of the Greater Mankato Area Chamber of Commerce and many others representing the business community, churches, schools and the faculty, staff and students of Minnesota State College kept a peaceful situation peaceful by not yielding to the temptation to meet the marchers with force of power and of numbers.

In retrospect, it is clear that those were truly the times that try men's souls. These were certainly days of significant transformation and change. Tests were made and, generally, we all passed with flying colors. Nothing remains the same for long, and change is inevitable and, hopefully, we as a nation would have learned from the experiences of a senseless war in Vietnam and the indignation and outrage of people who are allowed to question and dissent. And here we are again demonstrating once more that only fools permit stupidity to reign when they do not learn the lessons of history and doom us to repeat them again and again until we learn. (Thank you, President Bush?)

Today, we are once again in desperate need of more people who are willing to dissent and stand up and question. (Thank you, Cindy Sheehan)

*Excerpted from transcripts of a discussion hosted by Jim Nickerson on June 15, 2005.*

...The war became the center of [the campus unrest]. I think you all remember the big issue before the war on the campus was race. It was the integration of the college that was taking place then with all those problems, and there [were] protests at that time in regard to the College not moving fast enough to deal with the issues that racial integration was producing and that, of course, happened nationally. That was a situation nationally, and then the war just eclipsed that and absorbed that. It's not unlike what happened before the Civil War where we had all the reform movements, but it was the antislavery movement, the abolitionist movement, that eclipsed all the rest and became the issue that's with the nation.

... Really the training ground for the young college-age national leadership of the anti-war movement was the civil rights movement. And that was kind of a preview of what was going to happen on this campus while we were working through that. I remember the time, first there was Kent State and the reaction on the campus to that, and then there were the killings at Jackson State. I remember Bob Cobb [Florence Cobb's husband, professor of Health Science] asking me if I would go out on the mall and speak and at least try to show that we were as concerned about the deaths of those black students at Jackson State as we were about the students at Kent State.

... [Nickerson's] philosophy of a calm, gentle guidance rather than an absolute, "this is the way it is and if you don't like it, pow," was really, I think, the key difference between Wisconsin and Kent State and a lot of other places in Mankato.

... I'm not sure that, right now, we are seeing a lot of change. You think about the '60s, man. We murdered a president, we murdered Martin Luther King ['70s]. We lost Martin Luther King, we lost Bobby, Malcolm X, and that was just one symbol. Go to something that is a real common denominator. We went out of that very structured kind of mode of entertainment we call it [inaudible]. We didn't touch anymore. We had the Beatles, and there was just a huge upwelling of change. Some of it very powerful social change and others insignificant, but when you look at the whole era of Vietnam, it generated the women's movement, it generated the environmental movement and we had Richard somebody-or-other-knucklehead that exploited that along with the war and tried to divide the country. In some ways, I think he was successful.

*H. Roger Smith lives in Mankato, Minnesota.*

## Lee Snilsberg

It was difficult for me as a 50-year-old man in business for 20 years and a veteran of World War II to watch students from Mankato State demonstrating against the Vietnam War. This type of action was foreign to my way of thinking, and I didn't understand it. I was concerned that the students might get out of control as so many demonstrations in other places had experienced. Mankato was a peaceful town and this action made me and other downtown business owners fearful of what might happen. It is fine to disagree with our government, but not at the expense of some innocent bystanders. That is what the students were doing on the street and in Old Main.

Downtown business was hurt by the blockage of normal traffic. Fortunately, the citizens, police and college administrator performed in a cool-headed manner in every confrontation with large crowds of demonstrators. President Jim Nickerson was referred to by some as the "barefoot president" because of his down-to-earth style and dress. He had a way of keeping his contact with the students at their level and giving them breathing room, which resulted in a peaceful solution to the demonstration. It was a scary thing to see hundreds of young people blocking traffic to the Main Street Bridge and, luckily, no one was hurt.

I, for one, will always remember how well the College administration and police cooperated and how it really brought this community and the College closer together. It was the start of College and community cooperation that has improved ever since and is an important part of our university town today.

*Lee Snilsberg lives in Mankato, Minnesota.*


### Larry Spencer, '73

*Addressed directly to Jim Nickerson*

I reflect on this period of my life as a high point. It shaped me in so many different ways. I developed skills and abilities that have stayed with me throughout my life.

I feel like I knew of your character before I even enrolled at MSC. My older brother, Mike Spencer, attended Mankato State College and left in 1967 for dental school. He had friends in the student government like Steve Albani. Back in 1967, he told me about this really great college president that initiated the first student protest against Dow Chemical by placing a private call to one of the student leaders that subsequently triggered the first campus protest.

I first ran for Student Senate as a vice presidential candidate in spring of 1979. The ACT ticket was headed by Pat O'Neill, an affable Irishman. I was recruited by Dave Cowan to run against Tim Murphy. Dave Cowan orchestrated the ticket and placed me on it as new blood in his dwindling political machine.

The traditional Greek system dominated campus life was still well organized. I was known among liberal Democrats and had the blessing of the anti-war movement. We were defeated, and a traditional campus veneer blanketed campus life.

Tim Murphy was hesitant to appoint me to any position in the committee system so I created my own action committee that dealt with discrimination against students in public services and housing. Our first target was the Mankato Citizens Telephone Co., which insisted on the convenient practice of charging students an extra-large deposit for phone service. We researched the state law and discovered the state tariffs prohibited discrimination in the application of rates and service. We retained an attorney and prepared to file a complaint with the Railroad and Warehouse Commission, which had the applicable state jurisdiction. The phone company quickly lifted its policy and promised to rely solely on credit reports in determination of security deposits.

We then moved on the human rights ordinance to prohibit discrimination against students in housing and public accommodations. Dave Cowan assisted in the effort to grease the skids with the local establishment, and the ordinance was adopted.

The fall of 1969 brought a gathering storm of anti-war activity. The first large local protest of the war occurred at Mankato. A moratorium was observed with a series of anti-war teach-in sessions and the first anti-war march. The following November, the campus dispatched buses and a fleet of cars to Washington, D.C. for the November moratorium march on Washington.

I recall traveling to Washington, D.C. with four students in a VW bug. We arrived in D.C. along with 500,000 other protesters. The town was packed with protesters. One of the events was a 40,000-person, single-file candlelight march past the White House, and the name of each American soldier killed in Vietnam was called out. The March lasted 24 hours and well into the night. The next day, the March began. Pennsylvania Avenue was not broad enough to contain all the protesters, so the bulk marched up the Mall at the end of the designated parade permit in order to participate in the speeches.

A more-militant anti-war demonstration was planned for May, 1972. The call to action was endorsed that summer by the National Student Association, and a winter conclave was held in Ann Arbor Michigan in 1971. As was typical, a Mankato State College station wagon filled with long-haired unkempt students drove to the conclave. The next May, groups of students attended the May Day demonstrations in D.C. A far-more-activist agenda was planned, and the D.C. police were prepared for any altercation. The White House was surrounded by city buses as barricades; the fountains were full of naked counterculture enjoying a warm spring-day dip in Dupont and other circles.

I remember being with a young Mankato student newspaper photographer as a crowd squared off with D.C. police. The crowd dropped back and formed a line to taunt the police and return tear-gas canisters. The police formed a row and proceeded to march into the crowd. I stood in the ever-narrowing gap as my photographer crested his photo journal. I pulled him from the crushing jaws of police batons and dragged him gasping for breath into a nearby door to the Smithsonian as chaos engulfed the street.

That fall, the Black Student Union staged the first sit in at President Nickerson's office. Jim Nickerson diffused the situation with negotiations.

The impending draft hung over the entire male student body like the sword of Damocles. The Selective Service had a policy of requiring colleges to recertify that a student was in good standing and progressing toward a degree. The form need to be certified by the director of admissions and submitted annually to the draft board. Mankato had the unusual policy of giving the form prestamped with the admissions officer's signature to the student. It was left to the student to complete the form and submit it directly to the draft board. This policy resulted in keeping many students from being drafted into the armed services. I always suspected this policy was the result of Jim Nickerson's influence. The following winter, I took off the winter semester, and the practice of self-reporting took on greater significance for me.

Any young opinionated or alienated faculty member found a ready audience in the student populace and those who were attracted to the greater campus environment. Barclay Kuhn was a professor steeped in a tradition of Marcuse and Marx, seasoned with excess use of marijuana and drugs. His unorthodox teaching style did not blend with an ultimately conservative History Department. They elected to not renew his contract. His posse of campus radicals and core Students for a Democratic Society moved to establish an experimental college in an old Main Street building. He then proceeded to bitterly protest his dismissal. Demonstrations followed and a compromise was sought. His core group wanted to save Barclay; my goal was to open the retention and tenure process to student input. Both goals were more that the faculty was willing to concede. Dr. Nickerson allowed the students to fund their own Chair of Ideas, which was established too late for Barclay to assume. Mrs. Nickerson recruited a candidate for the first chair. Al Huong, a tai chi master and dancer, provided a cultural focus to the campus. The revolutionary nature of the position came full circle with the appointment of Mitchell Goodman, known from the Chicago Seven trials. The chair was finally defunded by the Student Allocations Committee when the administration used it to extend the tenure of their friend and house art mentor, Arnoldus Gruter.

I was elected to the Student Senate the spring of 1971. The character of the student body had become increasingly political. The campus was in the midst of

George McGovern's presidential campaign. New hope was breathed into students engaging in the political process. The students registered to vote in ever-greater numbers and turned out to the precinct caucuses to elect McGovern delegates to the county and 2nd Congressional District Convention. The participation record of students for the previous election cycle was completely overwhelmed.

The demonstrations and anti-war movement continued to grow in strength. The invasion of Cambodia renewed the smoldering anti-war sentiment. The immediate effects of the headlines were disbelief and despair. Three other students and I decided to make an individual statement and pitched our tents on the federal courthouse (Post Office) lawn. Soon other students began to join us at the courthouse until the lobby was full of students, and we effectively closed the courthouse. That evening, a group of students led by Mitchell Goodwin gathered at the courthouse. After a rousing speech by Goodwin, and mesmerized by torch light, they began a march through the town. They loitered at the armory site before proceeding to the Federal Building. One student had prepared a Molotov cocktail and hidden it below his trench coat. He tried to entice other students to break windows of the armory so he could send the burning projectile into the building. Unable to recruit an accomplice, he made his best effort to direct the explosive toward a window. It burst into flames on the stone face of the building, and the crowd moved on to the federal building.

There, Abbas Kessel confronted the group with an intellectual plea for nonviolence. It was interesting to see one diminutive man capture the attention of a mob and disburse it.

The next day, the larger crowds gathered at the federal courthouse and then moved to the main intersection of Front and Main. Angry motorists were caught in the traffic snarl before alternate routes could be established. One truck driver actually plowed into the crowd of students. He stopped, and people let the air out of his tires, insuring that the traffic blockade was complete.

The next day, the crowd moved to blocking Highway 169 in North Mankato. President Nickerson called a meeting of his Cabinet, which included Dan Welty, Faculty Association president; Nickerson's vice president Ed McMahan; Joyce Stenzel, the Student Senate vice president; Mehr Shahidi; and myself as Student Senate president. Tom Kelm, Gov. Anderson's chief of staff, was on the speakerphone to address the group. He told us the governor was prepared to do anything to end the blockade of 169. Until this time, the nondoctrinaire Democrat had done little to recognize the displeasure of the anti-war sentiment within the Democratic Party. I saw it as an ideal opportunity to request the governor take a public stand against the war. I asked Mr. Tom Kelm if the governor was prepared to make a statement against the invasion of Cambodia and personally urge the boycott of the federal telephone tax, which was the only revenue enhancement that Johnson and Nixon had established to pay for the mounting war costs. Kelm had another plan in mind and said the governor would not endorse any civil disobedience, and that he was prepared to order out the National Guard to clear the highway and establish order. Dan Welty, a conservative Republican, broke the stunned silence after Kelm's threat by stating passionately, "My God, my son is on that bridge. We will not have another Kent State in Mankato."

The Cabinet meeting quickly adjourned and reassembled at the Highway 169 and Main Street intersection. Jim Nickerson gave a short speech requesting the crowd to disburse before the police attempted to use force. I gave the second and last address. Recognizing the gravity of the occasion, I urged a nonviolent response and encouraged people to follow their hearts and consciences, and then promptly joined the sit-in and awaited the response by the local police and state troopers.

The response came quickly. The order to disperse was not heeded, and the North Mankato Police and the Blue Earth County Sheriff's Department proceeded to tear gas the crowd as well as trapped motorists, spray mace in the faces of nonviolent protesters who sat on the ground and wield batons to clear the crowd. The students had an opportunity to escalate the incident. A beverage delivery truck with an armory of glass pop bottles lining the exterior was caught in the traffic. The students began to hurl missiles at the advancing deputies. They were restrained by the other students who had already begun to fall back from the advance of the police.

The next day, an even larger crowd gathered on campus. A group of student leaders and faculty gathered to discuss the day's event and the next day's planned demonstration and subsequent protest march. The moderate leadership appointed a small army of marshals to guide the march as well as a scheduled list of speakers. At the end of the rally, and before the march plan could be presented to the crowd, a psychology professor, Eber Hampton, cut the cord to the microphone resulting in the end of the discussion and a premature exit of the march. The parade marshals fell in along the body and in the lead. The parade route was long, and the demonstration was large. The marshals were disciplined and several attempts to break away and lead the demonstration to the highway were frustrated.

The campus was in a state of upheaval. Activists were calling for the cancellation of the spring semester. Probably more students needed the credit hours to graduate. Like Solomon, Jim Nickerson exercised a sweeping compromise by giving both sides their due – those who needed to complete the semester were permitted to take their finals and others were permitted to take an incomplete, which would be expunged from the record within a year if not completed. The protests in the last week of school faded out and the semester ended with a graduation.

The attempts to turn the protests into an incendiary situation were not defeated. Several days later, someone dynamited the completed-but-not-yet-occupied regional Law Enforcement Center. Although it did not implode, the building was structurally compromised and was a total loss. Despite rampant rumors, no one was implicated in the crime. Most students did not know about the crime, and discussions of the event were never held in public or in private.

I do recall meeting the general contractor celebrating that evening at Michael's Restaurant. I asked if he was disappointed that his year of effort had been destroyed. He was celebrating the anticipated change order to demolish the building and start reconstruction.

The following fall the student enrollment dropped at the campus. It may have had to do with the displeasure of parents at the idea of sending their students to Mankato or with the elimination of the draft threat to the majority of the male population. Fewer students meant less money for the institution, and a series of last-minute retrenchments were declared that would result in the layoffs of the newest and younger faculty. The Student Senate, feeling the success of the previous strike action, called for yet another strike. President Nickerson was aghast and dispatched Vice President Ed McMahan to meet with student leaders.

The rash action and damage was undone by a joint plan to establish mini-courses, which commenced that fall and winter term. The Curriculum Committee review of new courses was suspended, so that professors were free to submit and rapidly receive approval for a series of special one-credit studies of unique or in-depth material. From a special course in community journalism to a pub crawl through the bars studying the effect and impacts of alcohol on society, courses were approved and conducted. They would happen early to mid-term and increase the number of credit hours, thereby plugging temporarily the funding shortfall while other budget-cutting measures could be explored.

Jim Nickerson led the campus to recognize a voice for the ultimate consumer of education, the student. He slowly restructured the College governance system of faculty-dominated committees to include students in all aspects of campus planning, parking, admissions policy and curriculum development. The administration was an agent for change, and the students grasped the concept and often supported administrative measures over a more recalcitrant faculty. Nickerson established a President's Cabinet that included student representatives. I insisted that no student should serve alone on a committee as the sole spokesperson, and two positions were added to his Cabinet. He let the Student Senate make all the student appointments rather than making recommendations to the faculty or administration. Little progress was made in matters of faculty hiring, firing or promotion.

His support of students was repaid on more than one occasion. Toward the end of his career, the struggles with Chancellor G. Theodore Mitau over local campus autonomy were reaching a crescendo. The chancellor was attempting to build a centralized state system and smelled the opportunity to force Nickerson from his position. A new evaluation of the campus had been completed and was critical of Mitau's centralization and diversion of system resources. Dave Cowan, now in the administration, cooked up a scheme to request a document of identical weight from the chancellor's office. He leaked a copy of the yet-unreleased study to the Student Senate. We requested a document from the chancellor's office of identical weight, and placed the report in the dated stamped envelope and released it to the Mankato area press and legislators. The invisible hand of Ed McMahon and Dave Cowan found us to be more-than-willing allies against a conservative faculty as well as the empire-building machinations of the chancellor.

Dr. Nickerson always used an intermediary to define the issues with students. He would dispatch a patient listener and engage students in a discussion of the possible and impossible. John Hodowonic and Ed McMahan, and later Dave Cowan, filled that role. Judy Mans provided an active ear at the reception desk and was a sure point of access when it was necessary. Nickerson would drop in on the discussion to add his imprimatur once they were defined as achievable. His personal interests were always present in the discussions.

We were all aware that he was trying to build an institution that was relevant to the students. Despite a large institutional budget, the amount of new funds for journalism, urban studies and other programs was limited.

Just as he allowed the faculty to preserve core interests, he allowed the students to maintain core interests. Over my last two years, he permitted the students to redirect the student activity fee from an overwhelming support to male athletics to a variety of other pursuits including the Chair of Ideas, women's athletics and Student Senate. He permitted us to defund the FM radio station, which was funded by activity fees but was viewed as the domain of the Speech Department. In retrospect, I regret the compromise to let the Speech Department keep the FM license but buy out the value of the equipment.

This change made many of the administrative staff like the student union director, bookstore director and athletic director unhappy, but gave the students real control over their activity fees. This independent course eventually led to the establishment of student-paid lobbyists and the student legal aid program.

*Larry Spencer lives in Juneau, Alaska.*

**Don Strasser**
*Emeritus Associate Professor of History*

For me, it began in the summer of 1964 when I first came to Mankato to see the College and find housing. The next morning, the *Free Press* was full of news about the Gulf of Tonkin incident, which was manipulated by the White House to provide President Lyndon Johnson with the justification he sought to turn a limited involvement in Vietnam into an all-out war on the Asian mainland.

When I joined the history faculty that fall, I remember looking up Vietnam on a map of Southeast Asia to see exactly where it was. With hindsight, that seems odd, since President Truman had supported the French retaking of Vietnam, President Eisenhower had taken the battle over from the French, President Kennedy had expanded our involvement, and President Johnson had vowed to carry out Kennedy's Vietnam policy. Why was I looking up Vietnam after almost 20 years of American involvement?

I voted for President Johnson with grave misgivings in November 1964, but the alternative was Barry Goldwater. When Johnson insisted upon the fiction of two Vietnams, I wrote my first letter to a president. South Vietnam was a creation of the United States, and the only legitimacy it had was what my government gave to it. The State Department replied to my letter with the fairy tale of two Vietnams. I was so angry, I tossed their letter in the circular file. Later, I would very much regret not saving it as evidence of the government's deceit.

When the Johnson administration sent a member of the U.S. Agency for International Development to our campus to explain the good things our nation was doing in Vietnam, Professor Abbas Kessel and I peppered him with questions about American refusal to honor the Geneva Accords of 1954. The USAID representative became so rattled, he left the stage of the Old Main small auditorium without attempting to answer.

The accords had called for national elections in Vietnam, which President Eisenhower said privately would be won by Ho Chi Minh by over 80 percent of the vote. Refusing to allow the Vietnamese to democratically unite a war-divided nation under a Communist government, Eisenhower supported the efforts of the puppet government in Saigon to see that national elections were never held. The American people were not told that the battle for the hearts and minds of the Vietnamese people had already been won – by the Viet Minh. From 1954 on, the American government would fight unsuccessfully against Vietnamese nationalism.

In 1965, I was outraged by President Johnson turning a limited war into an all-out one. By 1966, I was posting petitions and other anti-war materials on the faculty bulletin boards in Old Main, where my office was at the time. I remember going into either Kent Alm's or Brendan McDonald's outer office and telling the startled secretary there that I had come to announce what I was doing and not to ask permission for what I considered my right as a faculty member. The administration had no objections, but some students did. They set fire to my posters and wrote "Mickey Mouse" on my petitions. In a few years, MSC would have a larger percentage of its students involved in anti-war protest than any other college or university in the nation.

By 1967, I was writing letters to Sens. Walter Mondale and Eugene McCarthy urging them to support the withdrawal of our troops from Vietnam. I still have their replies. I did not write to Congressman Ancher Nelson, who I regarded as a Republican Party hack. Of course, in 1968, I supported the anti-war candidacy of Eugene McCarthy by going to the DFL caucus, where I found that students, faculty and townspeople for McCarthy were overwhelmingly in the majority. I was elected and served as a county delegate.

By the time of the California primary, I had switched my support to Robert Kennedy. American society was coming apart at the seams, and he appeared our last chance to free ourselves from the quagmire in Vietnam and to heal the wounds of our ravaged cities. Then came his assassination. Then the police riot at the Democratic Convention in Chicago. Then the nomination of Hubert Humphrey, who was seen as so connected to our disastrous policies in Vietnam that he could not be elected and wasn't.

By this time, I was working with other faculty and some students to help to integrate MSC. Two of our few black faculty members, Bob Cobb and George Ayers, thought a young, white history professor was just the right person to head the newly formed College Human Relations Council. That's how I became directly involved with the black students and their many issues. Not only did this lead to my teaching African-American history for the rest of my career, but it enabled me to see the connections between the black struggle for human rights and the burgeoning anti-war movement.

Many white students and faculty were radicalized by the war in Vietnam and the violent white reaction to black protest. They borrowed the tactics of the civil rights movement and actively opposed the war. If the ballot had produced the Nixon presidency, then nonviolent direct action must be used against it.

Students and others against the war did use every peaceful means available to them to register their opposition. They petitioned their congresspersons, they wrote letters, they withheld the war tax from their telephone bills, they supported the Vietnam Veterans Against the War, they attended anti-war rallies and demonstrations, they attended forums and teach-ins, they canvassed the community for peace, they appealed to the MSC Faculty Senate, they had sit-ins, they voiced their concerns to President Nickerson.

The loud music and speakers on the upper campus mall disturbed faculty who were trying to conduct classes, especially in Armstrong Hall. Thus, some faculty opposed the activities of the anti-war students. There were faculty who believed the College should confine itself to academics, period. They resented students cutting their classes to protest the war.

Some of the resentment of conservative faculty manifested itself in an incident in a Faculty Senate meeting, when protesting students entered the room carrying a mock coffin draped with an American flag. One of my colleagues in the History Department jumped up and punched one of the students who was carrying his young son on his shoulders. Such were the tempers of the times.

As noted, the anti-war protest was conducted in a context of other activities and issues. The integration of minority students into a previously almost all-white town and campus, the issues of town and gown, the stirring of the women's rights movement, the growing ecological awareness, the growing pains of a college being transformed into a university, the phasing out of *in loco parentis*, the counterculture movement, the impact of the New Left on faculty and students – all were happening at the same time.

Mankato was a conservative town, but there were liberals in the business community and other segments of the town who were open to what the protesting students had to say. One evening, interested townspeople were invited to a speak-out on the upper campus mall, which was to be followed by a Pete Seeger concert. I was appalled that night when not once but twice young men appearing to be students took the microphone and denounced the townspeople – townspeople of good will. I can only conclude that these young men were agent provocateurs in the pay of the FBI or radicals from some other college. Fortunately, the damage was not irreparable.

Every day brought more news of tragedy in Vietnam and then in our nation as well. There was a sense of great urgency not only in Mankato but across the country to stop the war immediately. There did not seem to be enough time to capture the Democratic Party or to build an independent party of peace. That left only taking to the streets and stopping business as usual.

Of course, what everybody of the Vietnam Era remembers are the demonstrations outside of the Post Office and the marches followed by sit-ins. The Post Office was the most logical of government buildings at which to stage a protest. In fact, a trio of MSC faculty started it all by staging a silent vigil at the Post Office at regular intervals. John Foster and Clarence Perisho took seriously the Quaker call for witnessing for peace. They were soon joined by Abbas Kessel, and eventually I joined them as well. That was the first public protest in Mankato against the war.

Abbas Kessel would go on to become the learned and eloquent voice of the MSC anti-war movement. More than anyone else, it was Kessel who educated us on the tragedy in Vietnam and the treachery and deceit of our own government. There were those who wanted to discredit this bearer of bad news. There were students who learned much from Kessel but, at the same time, found him too somber, too long-winded, and too nonviolent. Kessel spoke out strongly against shutting down the campus, arguing that it would play into Nixon's hands.

In contrast to Kessel, there were two pied pipers of irresponsible radicalism who captured the allegiance of the more radical and frustrated students. One was Barclay Kuhn, who had a one-year terminal contract in the Political Science Department. Kuhn started a small chapter of Students for a Democratic Society. My only encounter with Kuhn was when he and I debated before the Black Student Union over whether a white professor could teach black history. Kuhn tried to argue that I was incompetent because only blacks would intuitively know their own history. I was pleased that none of the black students agreed with him and saw that historical knowledge is acquired knowledge. The nonrenewal of Kuhn's contract for the following year was seen by some students as punishment for his radical views and not simply the expiration of a nonrenewable contract.

The other pied piper was Mitchell Goodman, a nationally known radical poet, who was initially recruited by English professors John Foster and Charlie Waterman at a national conference. The Nickerson administration appointed Goodman as the first person to hold the Chair of Ideas, a position created in response to student demands over the nonrenewable status of Kuhn. Goodman quickly demonstrated that he either did not understand the conservative atmosphere of the Mankato community or that he had contempt for it. He irresponsibly urged students to act out their opposition to the war in ways that were clearly dangerous and illegal. When he began to feel pressure from the Mankato community, he appealed to the Nickerson administration for police protection.

I participated in as many anti-war activities as my heavy teaching schedule and family responsibilities would permit. On some of the marches, I would go home, which was only a few blocks away, get my little daughter and push her in the stroller. She is a political activist to this day.

I am not competely sure why MSC had such a large participation in the protest activities. My conservative colleagues have tried to dismiss it as simply the rites of spring, but those of us who were close to the Larry Spencers and the John Kauls know how serious and informed many of the students were. Of course, there were always the curious and the hangers-on. But, from my vantage point, many of the students had just experienced a revelation about the dark side of American history. You could not explain away the white racism exposed by the civil rights movement or the horrors of war on your television screen every night.

It could be that so many of our students were from working-class families, and, contrary to conventional wisdom, more working-class people opposed the war than upper-class members. In fact, the less formal education you had, the more likely you were to be against the war.

The 1960s saw a rebellion, mainly a youthful rebellion, against the social conformity and political repression of the 1950s. That had to affect our students, and it did. Our students were trying to establish their independence and wanted to be treated as young adults. They rightfully demanded a voice in shaping their own education. Most, if not all, students who served on committees in academic departments took their roles seriously.

The Vietnam War lasted long enough for students to leave the campus, serve in the war and then return to classes with the war still going on. Many of those who served in Vietnam joined the Vietnam Veterans Against the War. Its members did much to destroy the credibility of the government's claims about the war.

The massacre of students at Kent State in the spring of 1970 caused campuses to erupt across the nation. MSC was no different. I did not speak at the rally protesting the gunning down of students in Ohio. But shortly thereafter, at the urging of some black faculty, I spoke out on the upper campus mall against the killings at Jackson State.

With violence and even death occurring on some campuses, why not here at MSC? The answer seems to lie in the wise and concerned leadership of President Nickerson and the cool, calm conduct of Police Chief C.D. Alexander. Both respected the students and their right to protest publicly. Neither tried to prevent the protest, which would have been counterproductive and led to more and more extreme actions. Rather, they tried to channel the protest activities into nonviolent pathways. Therefore, they never became the targets of the anti-war movement as did the presidents and the police at other institutions.

Many students who participated in the campus protest have told me that it changed them forever. They became politically aware and have remained so. I can relate to that very well. To me, it was the best of times and the worst of times. The best was the way so many students and others actively participated in trying to affect public policy. This was truly democracy in action. I became active myself at the time and have remained so. And if you are supposed to become more conservative with age, it has not worked that way with me. If anything, I am more radical and outspoken now than I was then.

*Excerpted from transcripts of a discussion hosted by Jim Nickerson on June 15, 2005.*

Some [students] told me when I was teaching American history that American history was too painful. The past was too painful for them to look at because we were exploring not only the good things, but the bad things. I counseled students. I know John did, who were crying in our presence they were so upset over the war. I know some faculty who did not agree with the protest and our position on the war who said the students are just play-acting. They are just playing at protests.

Well, I would not deny that some of them went out there for a lark and went along with what was going on, but this is not to say that there weren't those who were very knowledgeable and very sincere in their activities and beliefs in regard to the protests. I have seen some analysis of the war protests generally, and one of the things that I have missed that surprised me [is that] they were saying that the higher up you are on the income scale, the more education you had, the more likely you would be for the war rather than against it, that you would support the establishment; that it was the working-class people and working-class students, of which we had an abundance, who did not have a stake in the establishment that could more easily turn against the war and at least question the policies of the war.

And of course, they were the ones who were going to go and fight and possibly die, and this, I think, is at least a partial explanation of the amount of participation that we got. It was the type of students that we had from the backgrounds that they had that they did not have a stake in the American empire, if I can put it that way. That very thing of not having a stake actually works in other ways, too. ...

Here I am about to retire, but here I am an established person. I would not run out and do very much in the way of wild demonstrations for risk of a lifetime of building what I have. And each of us, we are all established here, but I think it would cross my mind as a senior in college about to graduate in business and I am worried about my records or credits and so on or just searching how good or bad I am. I wanted to protect my name. That is part of my established self and that will cross my mind before I swing a ball bat.

Well, on the other hand, they may not have seen themselves as having a stake in the war where they felt threatened by the war, but they have had certain beliefs about this country that they had been carefully taught, and all of us helped to teach them that, and they saw the famous credibility gap of ... LBJ's presidency between what the country said it was doing and what it was actually doing and what the American creed was and our actions in Southeast Asia, and I think this was a great motivation for them. In other words, they were motivated by the same things that motivated protestors all across the country.

What I think may have been somewhat exceptional about them was the background from which they came. These were not rich kids going to elitist institutions, and we know they had their protests, but they did not have the percentage that we had. You cannot document this kind of thing, however, I don't think. I have tried to get some of the University staff to see if they could give me general information on the student body at that time in terms of where they came from, income levels and so forth. It seems to be either impossible or too hard to come up with.

*Don Strasser lives in Mankato, Minnesota.*

## George and Nadine Sugden

*Addressed directly to Jim Nickerson*

George and I received your letter and are sorry to be slow in responding, and also very sorry that we really don't have many personal memories of the Vietnam era in Mankato. We both do vividly recall the march and sit-in protest at the bridge. I particularly won't forget it, because I was very active in Red Cross at that time. The office was in the old Saulpaugh Hotel, close by the bridge, and I happened to be working there when the protest started to take place. Those of us who were there evacuated quickly, looked down the block at the gathering crowd, and left. So, I didn't observe what went on. I was frightened of what might take place.

George was at the bank and watched to see that there were no problems there. He also saw the goings on and just recalls that he was not sympathetic to their cause or method. And he certainly didn't agree when he heard any students, or others, talk about going to Canada to avoid military service.

Our daughter, Janine, worked in the business office of MSC in Old Main. She called us when they had to leave the building – three times – because of bomb threats. She said they just sat on the curb waiting for the all-clear and felt more annoyed than scared by the interruptions.

You and others in the administration were certainly tested by the students' passionate emotions and strident objections to the war. You did such an excellent job of keeping a lid on things that those of us outside of the College community weren't aware of what all was going on – and, worse, what might have gone on.

*George and Nadine Sugden live in Mankato, Minnesota.*

## Linda Cobb Thompson

I was a graduate of Wilson Campus School in 1970 and entered Mankato State College in fall of 1970 as a freshman. My parents, Florence and Robert

Cobb, were professors at the College, and my family lived in Mankato. Nita Nickerson was my yoga teacher and, of course, Dr. James Nickerson was the College president. The Nickersons were very much a part of my world at Mankato State.

The times were turbulent. I remember a sit-in at Old Main to protest the Vietnam War and lack of financial aid among others social issues. The Black Student Union along with other student groups refused to leave the office until we had an audience with Dr. Nickerson. Kent State University shootings and killings had set the stage. Students marched through downtown Mankato and over the Minnesota River bridge. There was a long line of protesters and some of them clashed with the police, causing a riot of tear gassings and arrests.

I remember Dr. Nickerson was always student focused, considering the impact of word events and how they affected and triggered reactions of students. He had the ability to listen, sometimes under great duress and stress, to resolve conflict.

*Linda Cobb Thompson lives in Burnsville, Minnesota.*

### Edgar Twedt
### Professor Emeritus of Educational Foundations

Perhaps it is too much to lean on an overused and misused quote, "It was the best of times; it was the worst of times," but there is a sense in which the latter half of the 1960s and the first half of the 1970s were, indeed, the best and the worst of times for Mankato State College. The College was disrupted, like colleges and universities all over the nation. The town was disrupted. The nation was disrupted. But in the midst of the disruption, there was a sense of moral urgency and moral sensitivity which was perhaps bringing about the words of the popular song, "The Age of Aquarius." The College was in the midst of its own peculiar growing pains, moving from a parochial to a more cosmopolitan institution. It was in the midst of this institutional evolution that the nation was caught in the throes of a highly unpopular war from which there seemed to be no easy means of extricating itself, and over which the nation was deeply divided.

It was the fall of 1971, and I had just joined the administration of President Nickerson as assistant vice president for student services. My only administrative experience was in a small church-related college in Michigan. I was younger then than any of my own children are now, and barely dry behind the ears with a new Ph.D. less than a year old. It was my very good fortune to be able to serve under the supervision of Dr. David Hess, vice president for student services during those early years of the 1970s.

David Hess was probably the intellectual of the administration, and a man of keen insight into the psyche of the students on Mankato's campus. He brought to the campus his considerable administrative experience at West Virginia University, in addition to his work at Michigan State where he served as assistant to the provost and associate director of the Honors College. He was highly respected by all the student leaders at MSC as well as by his staff. In many quiet, and behind the scenes ways, he helped as much as anyone on the campus to keep the lid on. The university owes a great debt to Dr. Hess, and it was his leadership that helped me as I came into a position for which I was, in many ways, ill prepared.

There were many people in the town who took the simplistic attitude that we needed only to clean out the riffraff among the students, send them home, and that all would be well on the campus. It was this misunderstanding of the forces at work in our nation, and on our campus in particular, that would have led to disastrous results had it not been for the insightful leadership of President Nickerson and members of his staff, such as Dr. Hess.

One night, several of us in the administration received phone calls from the president's office. Several students had taken over the administration building, and there was a need for some "baby sitters" to be in some of the buildings on the downtown campus all night long. I remember staying up all night with Ira Johnson in what was then the library on the lower campus. It turned out that it was a very uneventful night, and we all went home very sleepy and tired for a very, very short rest the next morning before returning to our offices for the day.

One of the memorable events was the anti-war march, which started in downtown Mankato at the corner of Main and Second streets. It was a peaceful, yet meaningful march with President Nickerson at the head, and several of us administrators and students walking as well. There were also many students and faculty in the march and it was, for the most part, very peaceful. One of the significant contributing factors to the peacefulness of the march was the fact that it was accompanied by the chief of police and several of his officers. The march was probably the culmination of several peace rallies that had been held at the site of the current fountain in the middle of the upper campus.

Probably the event that is remembered most vividly by all of us who were there was the "taking of the bridge." At that time, the old Main Street Bridge went across the Minnesota River to North Mankato where the street turned into Belgrade Avenue. That old bridge stood at the level of the streets on both sides of the river, and Highway 169 crossed Belgrade Avenue in North Mankato right at the end of the Main Street Bridge. On that memorable day, the students decided to have a sit-in protest on that bridge. Hundreds of students gathered and held their places, covering the entire bridge. But unlike the friendly territory of the city of Mankato where there was a progressive police chief, the students found themselves in very unfriendly territory, and the chief law enforcement officer was the sheriff of Nicollet County. It is an understatement to say that the sheriff was unfriendly to the anti-war movement and to the students and his anger was shown in many ways that day. I remember Vice President for Administrative Affairs Robert Hopper going up to the sheriff and offering to bring in busses so they could make peaceful arrests. The students were very willing to have this happen. But the sheriff was far more intent on knocking heads, under the misguided notion that he could somehow frighten the students away.

I remember his response to Vice President Hopper, although not word for word. He threatened that if Dr. Hopper didn't keep quiet, he'd find himself under arrest. Later Vice President David Hess told me that the sheriff had given him a very similar threat just for making a suggestion. It was clear the sheriff was not interested in a peaceful solution. Of course, many of us from the faculty and administration were there talking with students and trying to make some sense of the situation and trying to see if there was some way to bring the standoff to a peaceful resolution. Some truckers trying to get through on Highway 169 were even threatening to "run them down," and the "them" in this case, of course, was the students who had taken over the bridge.

One of my most vivid memories during the course of our time on the bridge was of Bob Browne coming over to tell me he had just been talking with a police officer from North Mankato who had asked Bob with real concern in his voice, "Bob, have you seen my daughter in this crowd of students?" What a catch-22 for that police officer. And we know it was a concern shared by many parents that day.

During the hours the bridge was occupied, there was a sergeant from the State Patrol, doing what he could behind the scenes. He had no authority to make any decisions, but could advise the sheriff, so he continued quietly to make thoughtful recommendations. As ugly as the situation got that afternoon, I'm convinced that this highway patrol officer did as much as anyone to keep things from becoming a bloody battlefield. I remember one incident where a young man took a serious spill on his bicycle on the bank by the bridge. The highway patrol sergeant came very quickly to the scene and brought his first aid kit to help take care of abrasions suffered in the fall. This was probably only one of many acts of kindness carried out by this true "peacekeeper," while the sheriff continued to threaten and rant and rave.

In the final analysis, it was probably the highway patrol sergeant who convinced the sheriff to agree to a simple request of the students. By this time, the students had been the recipients of tear gas at least twice and even of the police "wading into them" with nightsticks, but to no avail. As soon as the police would move through the front, the crowd would swell around them again. The students' demand was a very simple one. They wanted law enforcement to back off, and they would clear the bridge. I recall that President Nickerson was influential in getting the sheriff to see the wisdom of this request, and I know that the highway patrol sergeant was very influential. In the end, the sheriff pulled back his troops and, within half an hour. the bridge had been cleared voluntarily. It was a day I shall never forget, nor will the many others who were there.

There was, however, something else of considerable importance also going on at this time at Mankato State College. The College was becoming a university, and a university in more than name. Schools were becoming colleges, directors were becoming deans and deans were becoming vice presidents. The leadership of the College was slowly moving away from an in loco parentis institution to a community (universe) of scholars. Although it was left to President Nickerson's successor to bring about the name change, it was clearly President Nickerson who, by his skilled leadership and broad understanding of higher education, already had the university in place long before his successor arrived on the scene. Given the turbulence of the times, this transition would probably not have taken place for another decade had it not been for President Nickerson's presence on this campus at that time.

*Edgar Twedt lives in San Antonio, Texas.*

### Truman Wood, '54

In 1996, I overheard two female students in the office area shared by Political Science and Law Enforcement. "Oh, to have been here during the Vietnam War, that would have been great!" I fought off the temptation to lecture these students about what the war was really like.

That war was the one part of my life that I would edit out if life were like a home movie or video. On the one hand, I was channeling students to the campus pastor, Doug Sampson, who would assist students in filing for the conscientious objector status. On the other hand, I saw students that I knew going off to Vietnam and dying.

The most difficult letter I ever wrote was to the mother of a student I knew well. He had often waited on me at Osco Drug in downtown Mankato, and I had him in class. He went to Vietnam and was soon killed. The mother was a widow, a person I did not know. I needed to tell her how I shared her grief. In the summer of 2000, I went to The Wall in Washington, D.C. My wife, Reta, found that student's name and the directions to locating his name on the memorial. Though many years had passed, I cried as I looked at his name because of the waste of a vital life, a life that could have contributed much to the well-being of this nation.

Trying to teach during the upheaval on the campus was a story in itself. Day after day, a bomb threat would be phoned in, and we would evacuate Morris Hall. At first, we walked well away from the building until the structure had been searched and the danger was over. As time passed, we became more cavalier about it and stood near the building. The front of Morris has a series of large glass windows. George Green, a fellow political science professor, and I stood conversing near those windows, following a bomb threat, and I said, "George, if a bomb does go off, they won't open our caskets, we'll be hamburger."

I was a Republican when the war began, but as the death toll mounted, my politics changed. At one mass gathering on the mall, I read a letter I had written to President Nixon asking him to end the war and bring the troops home. I remember being seated on the pavement by Mankato State College President Nickerson.

I also had flown with several professors to New Jersey with Vice President Kent Alm. We were looking at their supposed creative office designs at a time when we would be adding on to Morris Hall. I roomed with Kent Alm, and he called President Nickerson that night to find out how things were going on campus. Old Main had been occupied by protesting students and the situation was tense. Alm favored police action and the removal of the students by force if necessary. Nickerson wanted to work with the students and diffuse their fury and listen to their demands.

His leadership during the demonstrations, the occupation of Old Main, and the march on Main Street Bridge is a study in courage, restraint, and infinite patience. Three men stand out during this period when there could have been a loss of life perhaps greater than Kent State. One was Jim Nickerson, another was Abbas Kessel, and the third was the Mankato police chief, C.D. Alexander. Subtract any one of the three from the volatile explosive potential and there would have been deadly chaos. Each man, in his own way, was a brake on a runaway vehicle of mob violence.

*Truman Wood lives in Mankato, Minnesota.*

*Ron Yezzi*

I started teaching in the Philosophy Department at then-Mankato State College during the fall term, 1969. By that time, campus opposition to the Vietnam War was already well in progress. Barclay Kuhn, the best-known radical on campus (as I understood), had already lost his position in the Political Science Department.

I showed up at a teach-in in late September or sometime in October. That's when I first heard a fiery speech by Barclay Kuhn. Very impressive (although I do not recall anything he said). There was also a speech by Mark Davidov, a sociologist who had come down from the University of Minnesota. At some point, he made mention of 19th-century British industrial workers. That provoked a challenging, detailed, eloquent response from a little foreign guy. I later learned this was Abbas Kessel.

I came to know, and become friendly with, a lot of younger faculty members through opposition to the war. But of an older generation of faculty who came to be friends, I want to mention Kessel – as well as Jane (not faculty) and John Foster, Margaret and Clarence Perisho and Harold Hartzler. What fantastic people! Kessel, the Fosters and the Perishos were people with whom I was especially comfortable politically. Hartzler and I were worlds apart theologically and ideologically. Still, I so like and admired Harold's willingness, as a fundamentalist Mennonite pacifist, to protest the war even though it meant associating with all these leftist, dirty, unshaven, long-haired hippies.

In my own protesting of the war, I participated in the marches and attended teach-ins and rallies. But I never actually addressed any rallies on the mall or at protest sites in Mankato. I was, however, very active in Mankato Citizens for Peace.

My first year, Barclay Kuhn was active in trying to start a free university, a counter-university, in effect, in a storefront downtown. I did get to meet him and (although I never had much contact with him) they were always friendly encounters. I had become a good friend of Pete Meyersohn in the Sociology Department, who was married to Barclay's sister. This friendship led to some interesting times when Pete had to deal with his wife having gone off with their child to live in a commune with Barclay out West. (Pete also became the owner of a house on Marshall Street where there were some unusual goings-on led by Barclay, according to reports.) I was supposed to teach a class at the free university, although it never actually materialized with real students.

There were numerous events that I recall, although I had no special role in them myself – for example, a performance by Pete Seeger (with the smell of marijuana in the air) to quiet the campus down; Jim Nickerson (rather exasperatingly) suggesting a long march all over Mankato as an outlet to diffuse protest energy; the protest at Front and Main streets that initially had speakers speaking rather jovially about the protest but then delivering harsh harangues to try to keep the protest going, collecting money to send students to join the March on Washington; the chair of the Computer Science Department complaining bitterly at a faculty meeting about students calling him at 3 a.m. and his demanding to know if any faculty there had been present at the meetings where students decided to make these middle-of-the-night phone calls (In a way, I had been at that meeting he was complaining about. But I was justified in self-protectively remaining silent, since I had left at about 9:30 p.m., before the phone-calling decision was made).

There were bomb threats that emptied classes; Mitchell Goodman came as a provocateur; and that led to John Foster's consternation with some of the personal actions of Mitchell Goodman (after he was instrumental in bringing him here for the Chair of Ideas). One of the more interesting events, I suppose, was the early closing of the campus during spring quarter of 1972. Students were supposed to receive whatever grade they had at that point as the final grade for a course, or a permanent incomplete. And some of them were collecting signed statements from instructors signifying that they really were getting a legitimate final grade.

Perhaps the most notable event to me was the night a minister from Chicago gave an incendiary speech. I thought he really was off the wall with his extremism. And at the end, when he had fired everyone up, he said (approximately), "And now, we're all going to march downtown." He got this huge standing ovation. I was in the first or second row; and everybody around me was standing and applauding – including Kessel, the Shrewsburys and a lot of other friends. I may have clapped, but I didn't stand up. I just didn't like what was happening. And rather than join the demonstration, I walked home. That was the night Kessel stopped the student demonstrators from burning down the Post Office.

Mankato Citizens for Peace brought campus and townspeople together to oppose the war. I was active in the group – attending meetings and working on newspaper ads primarily. I must have gotten involved pretty quickly because the first ad went in *The Free Press* during November 1969, and I had a lot to do with the wording there. Meetings were well attended and definitely anti-war. Occasionally, someone might get up to criticize what we were doing and make a plea for patriotism. I seem to recall attorney Cliff Kroon doing this once. And then there was the time a local photo-shop owner turned off the lights to try to show what it must be like for G.I.s fighting in Vietnam.

I remember one forum meant to bring the community together for discussion that evoked a lot of angry comments for and against the war. Dr. Al Sheidel was the moderator who had to deal with a lot of fairly angry people. At one point, since my hand was raised, he called on me (and it seemed that he had a look like he expected me to bring some reasonableness to the discussion), whereupon I proceeded to make some intemperate remarks (perhaps true ones) that did nothing to quiet things down. As a group, we also encouraged people to protest the war by refusing to pay telephone excise tax instituted to help defray costs of the war, thereby forcing the government to take the money directly from our paychecks.

*Ron Yezzi lives in Mankato, Minnesota.*


## Jan Young

*Addressed directly to Jim Nickerson*

I attended Teachers College High (TCH), so I have been associated with the teachers' past presidents for too many years to count. We used to have our junior high prom in what was the old library. We also remember sliding down the fire escape for neighborhood entertainment! That was when we lived on 109 Hanover St. One of our biggest high school victories was when Rock's basketball team beat the much-larger high school across the street.

My 11th-grade students talked quite a lot about all of the existing tension at the College. They also discussed some of information they gained from their parents at home. When things were heating up on the hill on the college campus in Old Main, my students were quite nervous, being aware of impending danger. At about 2:30 in the afternoon, a large gang of college students passed by my classroom. About 25 of my students ran to the window and about 15 decided to walk out of school and join them. I made no effort to stop them. I remember how well you handled both in your office and walking across the bridge to confront the so-called "enemy." Your courage, knowledge, intelligence, and "cool" head resulted in a peaceful ending.

*Jan Young lives in Kasota, Minnesota.*


## Jerome Zuckerman
### Professor Emeritus of English

I would tend to date the years of increased student anti-Vietnam War activity at MSC from about the time of the Tet offensive in early 1968 through about 1971 or 1972. I was never directly involved in any of these activities but rather stood at the periphery, mostly as a detached and sometimes angry observer. Although I was a strong Dove and supporter of Eugene McCarthy, I believed that too often the students were mixing anti-war sentiment with a more generalized anti-establishment, anti-educational point of view, and this mixture fueled my uneasiness. My dilemma was that I was politically liberal but academically conservative.

My memories of these years are vague and generalized. They seem to swirl through my mind like the colored blades of a pinwheel: various colors swirling by very quickly but leaving a strong impression of one color after another. It is there reds and blues and yellows and greens that have lodged in my memory rather than any specific details or statistics or names. And it is these colors that I want to focus on.

Among the memories I recall is coming into Armstrong Hall early one morning and discovering that faculty members were unable to unlock their offices because the door locks had been filled with solder and rendered unusable. I recall the afternoon when students marched to Highway 169 near the Main Street bridge and blocked the movement of any traffic. On one occasion, after I had posted a somewhat provocative cartoon on my office door, I found, penned beside it, a threatening note edged in ominous black. And there were some middle-of-the-night phone calls – at 2:00, 3:00, or 4:00 a.m. – when I was greeted either by silence or by menacing words. Very dramatically, at one time the students disrupted a Faculty Senate meeting marching in masks and carrying a black coffin that symbolized something like the death of education. Disruption seemed to be the order of the day; faculty members could never be certain that their classes wouldn't be disrupted.

The one event that is most vivid in my memory, probably because I was a participant, was the morning the students staged a strike and urged a boycott of all classes. It was the morning when my class in 20th Century British literature was scheduled, and we were due to work on some difficult poems by Yeats. Since this was my favorite class and one of my favorite poets, and since I felt very strongly that the strikers were directing their anger at the wrong targets, I decided that I would defy the strike and meet my class. About six students showed up in our classroom on the second floor of Armstrong Hall, not too far from a stairwell, and we started going through the intricate thought and language of late Yeats. And then the disruption happened: the strikers lobbed a tear-gas canister into the bottom stairwell on the first floor, and the fumes began to swirl upward into the corridor where I was teaching.

I knew that I couldn't continue in the classroom because the smoke would soon seep under the door. And since the classroom was windowless, I knew we would have no source of fresh air. But my office in the outside corridor had a small slit-shaped window like that used for aiming weapons in a medieval fortress, and I knew that I could undo some screws and get fresh air that way. So my six students and I exited our classroom, choked and gasped our way through the smoke-filled hall, the acrid air making our eyes tear and burn, to my cubbyhole of an office. There, for the remainder of the period, seven uneasy people crowded into an unbelievably small space, reading and analyzing the poetry of William Butler Yeats. For me, it was a minor triumph of art over life.

*Jerome Zuckerman lives in Mankato, Minnesota.*